# Pocket International Encyclopedia of Business and Management

## Edited by Malcolm Warner

INTERNATIONAL THOMSON BUSINESS PRESS
I ⓣ P An International Thomson Publishing Company

London • Bonn • Boston • Johannesburg • Madrid • Melbourne • Mexico City • New York • Paris
Singapore • Tokyo • Toronto • Albany, NY • Belmont, CA • Cincinnati, OH • Detroit, MI

**Pocket International Encyclopedia of Business and Management**

*British Library Cataloguing-in-Publication Data*
A catalogue record for this book is available from the British Library

**First edition 1997**

Typeset by Hodgson Williams Associates, Cambridge
Printed in the UK by Clays Ltd, St Ives plc

**ISBN 1-86152113-8**

**International Thomson Business Press**
Berkshire House                20 Park Plaza
168–173 High Holborn           13th Floor
London WC1V 7AA                Boston MA 02116
UK                             USA

**http://www.itbp.com**

# Pocket International Encyclopedia of Business and Management

## Titles from the International Encyclopedia of Business and Management database

*International Encyclopedia of Business and Management*
6 volume set, hardback, 0-415-07399-5
*Concise International Encyclopedia of Business and Management*
1 volume edition, hardback, 1-86152114-6
*Pocket International Encyclopedia of Business and Management*
Paperback, 1-86152113-8

# Contents

# List of entries and contributors

**Accounting**
*Arthur R. Wyatt, University of Illinois at Urbana-Champaign, USA*
**Accounting, creative**
*Peter Walton, University of Geneva, Switzerland*
**Accounting, international**
*Lee H. Radebaugh, Brigham Young University, USA*
**Accounting in Australia**
*Murray Wells, University of Sydney, Australia*
**Accounting in central and eastern Europe**
*Derek Bailey, Thames Valley University, UK*
**Accounting in France**
*Jean-Claude Scheid, Conservatoire National des Arts et Métiers, France*
**Accounting in Germany**
*Wolfgang Ballwieser, Ludwig-Maximilians-Universität, Munich, Germany*
**Accounting harmonization**
*David Cairns, Former Secretary, International Accounting Standards Committee, UK*
**Accounting in Japan**
*Etsuo Sawa, Japanese Institute of Certified Public Accountants, Japan*
**Accounting and organizations**
*Jeremy F. Dent, London School of Economics, UK*
**Accounting in the United Kingdom**
*Peter Walton, University of Geneva, Switzerland*
**Accounting in the United States of America**
*Frederick D. S. Choi, Stern School of Business, New York University, USA*
**Acquisitions and divestments**
*G. Meeks, University of Cambridge, UK*
**Activity-based costing**
*Al Bhimani, Michael Bromwich, London School of Economics, UK*
**Advertising campaigns**
*Colin Gilligan, Sheffield Hallam University, UK*
**Advertising strategy, international**
*Greg Harris, City University Business School, London, UK*
**Agency, markets and hierarchies**
*Anna Grandori, Università Commerciale Luigi Bocconi, Italy*
**Airline management**
*Stephen J. Page, Massey University, Albany, Australia*

**Appraisal methods**
  *Jack Broyles, Warwick Business School, UK*
**Artificial intelligence**
  *Robert Mockler, St John's University, New York, USA*
**Artificial intelligence in manufacturing**
  *Binshan Lin, Louisiana State University, in Shreveport, USA*
**Asset valuation, depreciation and provisions**
  *Dieter Ordelheide, Johann Wolfgang Goethe-Universität, Germany and*
    *the European Institute for Advanced Studies in Management, Brussels*
  *Christian Leuz, Johann Wolfgang Goethe-Universität, Germany*
**Aston Group**
  *Jerald Hage, University of Maryland at College Park, USA*
**Auditing**
  *Paul Saw, Judge Institute of Management Studies, University of*
    *Cambridge, UK*
**Banking**
  *Shelagh Heffernan, City University Business School, London, UK*
**Banking, Islamic**
  *Rodney Wilson, Durham University, UK*
**Banking in Japan**
  *Kazuo Tatewaki, Waseda University, Japan*
**Banking in the United States of America**
  *Taeho Kim, Thunderbird - The American Graduate School of*
    *International Management, USA*
**Banking in western Europe**
  *Philip Molyneux, Institute of European Finance, University of Wales,*
    *Bangor, UK*
**Bata system of management**
  *Milan Zeleny, Fordham University at Lincoln Center, USA*
**Benchmarking**
  *Nick Oliver, Judge Institute of Management Studies, University of*
    *Cambridge, UK*
**Brands**
  *Leslie de Chernatony, The Open University Business School, UK*
**Budgetary control**
  *Michael Lebas, Groupe HEC School of Management, France*
**Business-to-business marketing**
  *Kristian Möller, Helsinki School of Economics and Business*
    *Administration, Finland*
  *David T. Wilson, Pennsylvania State University, USA*
**Business culture, Japanese**
  *Etsuo Abe, Meiji University, Japan*
**Business culture, North American**
  *Jane H. Ives, Bentley College, Boston, USA*
**Business cultures, European**
  *Collin C. Randlesome, Cranfield School of Management, UK*
**Business cycles**
  *Cliff Pratten, University of Cambridge, UK*

**Consolidated accounting**
  *Ken Leo, Curtin University of Technology, Perth, Australia*
**Consumer behaviour**
  *Chris Rice, Nottingham Trent University, UK*
**Coordination and control**
  *Armand Hatchuel, École des Mines de Paris, France*
**Corporate control**
  *William Lazonick, University of Massachusetts at Lowell, USA*
  *Mary O'Sullivan, Harvard University, USA*
**Corporate governance**
  *Jay Lorsch, Samantha K. Graff, Harvard University, USA*
**Corporate pension fund**
  *A. F. Wilson, Watson Wyatt, UK*
**Corporate performance, analysis of**
  *Samuel Eilon, Imperial College, University of London, UK*
**Corporate planning, process of**
  *Ken Peattie, Cardiff Business School, UK*
**Corporate strategic change**
  *Dexter Dunphy, University of New South Wales, Australia*
**Corporatism**
  *Colin Crouch, European University Institute, Florence, Italy*
**Costing**
  *A. R. Appleyard, University of Newcastle, UK*
**Cost–volume–profit relationships**
  *Annick Bourguignon, École Supérieure des Sciences Économiques et*
  *Commerciales, (ESSEC) Cergy-Pontoise, France*
**Country risk analysis**
  *André Astrow, Mina Toksöz, Howard Smith, The Economist Intelligence*
  *Unit, UK*
**Creativity management**
  *Cameron M. Ford, Rutgers University, New Jersey, USA*
  *Dennis A. Gioia, Pennsylvania State University, USA*
**Credit management**
  *Nicholas Wilson, University of Bradford Management Centre, UK*
**Crisis management**
  *Simon Booth, University of Reading, UK*
**Critical path analysis**
  *Milan Zeleny, Fordham University at Lincoln Center, USA*
**Culture**
  *David Cray, Carleton University School of Business, Canada*
**Culture, cross-national**
  *Betty Jane Punnett, University of Windsor, Ontario, Canada*
**Cybernetics**
  *Kevin Warwick, Claire Zepka, University of Reading, UK*
**Decision making**
  *Richard Butler, University of Bradford Management Centre, UK*
**Decision making, habitual domains in**
  *P. L. Yu, University of Kansas, USA*

**Decision making, multiple-criteria**
   *Milan Zeleny, Fordham University at Lincoln Center, USA*
**Decision support systems**
   *Sean B. Eom, Southeast Missouri State University, USA*
**Deconstruction analysis and management**
   *Karen Legge, Lancaster University, UK*
**Design management**
   *Peter Gorb, Morgen Witzel, London Business School, UK*
**Direct marketing**
   *Mary Lou Roberts, University of Massachusetts, Boston, USA*
**Discipline and dismissals**
   *Derek Torrington, University of Manchester Institute of Science and
     Technology (UMIST), UK*
**Diversity**
   *Rosalyn W. Berne, Tandem School, Charlottesville, USA*
**Dividend policy**
   *Ian Davidson, Warwick Business School, UK*
**Downsizing**
   *Kim Cameron, Brigham Young University, USA*
**Dynamic programming and the optimality principle**
   *Tadeusz Trzaskalik, Katowice Academy of Economics, Poland*
**East Asia, economies of**
   *C.H. Kwan, Nomura Research Institute, Tokyo, Japan*
**Economic integration, international**
   *Dennis Swann, Loughborough University of Technology, UK*
**Economic rents**
   *C.G.C. Pitts, Warwick Business School, UK*
**Economics of developing countries**
   *John Cathie, University of Cambridge, UK*
**Economics, institutional**
   *Geoffrey M. Hodgson, Judge Institute of Management Studies,
     University of Cambridge, UK*
**Education and business partnership**
   *David Warwick, Education for Enterprise, UK*
**Efficient market hypothesis**
   *Meziane Lasfer, City University Business School, London, UK*
**Employee development**
   *Martin Hilb, University of St Gallen, Switzerland and University of
     Dallas, USA*
**Employee deviance**
   *Gerald Mars, University of Bradford Management Centre, UK*
**Employee relations, management of**
   *John Purcell, University of Bath, UK*
**Employers' associations**
   *Wyn Grant, University of Warwick, UK*
**Employment and unemployment, ecomomics of**
   *Robert J. Flanagan, Stanford University, USA*

**Industrial Revolution**
*David Mitch, University of Maryland Baltimore County, USA*
**Industrial sabotage**
*John M. Jermier, Walter Nord, University of South Florida, USA*
**Industrial strategy**
*Christos Pitelis, Judge Institute of Management Studies, University of Cambridge, UK*
**Inflation**
*Penelope A. Rowlatt, National Economic Research Associates, London, UK*
**Inflation accounting**
*Geoffrey Whittington, University of Cambridge, UK*
**Information and capital markets**
*Mark Jewell, Lehman Brothers International, UK*
**Information and knowledge industry**
*Fatameh (Mariam) Zahedi, University of Wisconsin-Milwaukee, USA*
**Information revolution**
*Frank Land, London School of Economics and Political Science, UK*
**Information technology**
*Manfred Grauer, University of Siegen, Germany*
**Information technology in developing countries**
*Geoff Walsham, Lancaster University, UK*
**Information technology in marketing**
*John R. Beaumont, Energis Communications Ltd and City University Business School, London, UK*
**Information technology and society**
*Dorothy G. Dologite, Baruch College, New York, USA*
*Julie E. Kendall, Rutgers University, New Jersey, USA*
**Innovation and change**
*Johannes M. Pennings, University of Pennsylvania, USA*
**Innovation management**
*Velimir Srica, University of Zagreb, Croatia*
**Innovation and technological change**
*Andrew Tylecote, Sheffield University Management School, UK*
**Insurance**
*Malcolm Tarling, Association of British Insurers, UK*
**Integer programming**
*Marc J. Schniederjans, University of Nebraska-Lincoln, USA*
**Intellectual property**
*David Llewelyn, Llewelyn Zietman, London, UK*
**Interactive programming**
*Carlos Henggeler Antunes, University of Coimbra, Portugal*
**Interest groups**
*Justin Greenwood, The Robert Gordon University, UK*
**Interest rate risk**
*Richard C. Stapleton, Lancaster University, UK*

**Just-in-time philosophies**
*Robert F. Conti, Bryant College, USA*
**Labour markets**
*Alan Williams, Massey University, New Zealand*
**Labour process**
*Chris Smith, Aston Business School, UK*
**Land economy**
*Derek Nicholls, University of Cambridge, UK*
**Law, commercial**
*Iwan Davies, University of Wales, Swansea, UK*
**Law, contract**
*Lisa J. McIntyre, Washington State University, USA*
**Leadership**
*Frank Heller, The Tavistock Institute, London, UK*
**Linear programming**
*Saul Gass, University of Maryland, USA*
**Logistics**
*Donald J. Bowersox, David J. Closs, Michigan State University, USA*
**Logistics in manufacturing management and operations**
*Kulwant S. Pawar, University of Nottingham, UK*
**Maintenance systems**
*Kathie S. Smith, Consultant, USA*
**Make or buy strategy**
*David Probert , University of Cambridge, UK*
**Management in Africa**
*Tayo Fashoyin, African Regional Labour Administration, Zimbabwe*
**Management in the Arab world**
*David Weir, University of Bradford, UK*
**Management in Australia**
*Russell D. Lansbury, University of Sydney, Australia*
**Management in the Benelux contries**
*Albert L. Mok, 'Maison Thimister' Institute, Belgium*
**Management in Brazil**
*Suzana Braga Rodrigues, Universidade Federal de Minas Gerais, Brazil*
**Management in China**
*Zhong-Ming Wang, Hangzhou University, China*
**Management in developing country environments**
*Tomás O. Kohn, Boston University School of Management, USA*
*James E. Austin, Harvard University, USA*
**Management development**
*Gillian Stamp, Brunel University, UK*
**Management in eastern Europe**
*Krzysztof Oblój, University of Warsaw, Poland*
**Management education, future of**
*Peggy Simcic Brønn, Henley Management College, UK*
*Peter Lorange, International Institute for Management Development*
*(IMD), Switzerland*

**Management in Latin America**
  *Suzana Braga Rodrigues, Universidade Federal de Minas Gerais, Brazil*
**Management in Malaysia**
  *Wendy Smith, Monash University, Australia*
**Management in Mexico**
  *John J. Lawrence, University of Idaho, USA*
**Management in North America**
  *Fred Luthans, University of Nebraska at Lincoln, USA*
  *Richard M. Hodgetts, Florida International University, USA*
**Management in Pacific Asia**
  *S. Gordon Redding, University of Hong Kong Business School, Hong Kong*
**Management in the Philippines**
  *Rodolfo P. Ang, Ellen H. Palanca, Ateneo de Manila University, Philippines*
**Management research, management of**
  *Alain Bultez, Centre for Research on the Economic Efficiency of Retailing (CREER), Belgium*
**Management in Russia**
  *Sheila M. Puffer, Northeastern University, USA*
**Management in Scandinavia**
  *Pat Joynt, Henley School of Management, UK and Norwegian School of Management, Norway*
  *Tor Grenness, Norwegian School of Management, Norway*
**Management science**
  *Samual Eilon, Imperial College, University of London, UK*
**Management in Singapore**
  *Joo-Seng Tan, Nanyang Technological University, Singapore*
**Management in South Africa**
  *Frank M. Horwitz, University of Cape Town, South Africa*
**Management in South Korea**
  *Min Chen, Thunderbird – The American Graduate School of International Management, USA*
**Management in Spain**
  *Miguel Martinez Lucio, University of Leeds, UK*
**Management in Switzerland**
  *Malcolm Warner, University of Cambridge, UK*
**Management in Taiwan**
  *Johanna Böstel, University of London, UK and University of Leeds, UK*
**Management in Thailand**
  *Suntaree Komin, National Institute of Development Administration, Bangkok, Thailand*
**Management in Turkey**
  *Esin Ergin, Istanbul University, Turkey*
**Management in the United Kingdom**
  *Michael Poole, Cardiff Business School, UK*
  *Richard Scase, University of Kent at Canterbury, UK*

**Public sector organizations**
  *Jean-Claude Thoenig, Centre National de la Recherche Scientifique (CNRS), France*
**Purchasing**
  *Lars-Erik Gadde, Chalmers University of Technology, Sweden*
  *Håkan Håkansson, University of Uppsala, Sweden*
**Quantitative methods in marketing**
  *Stephen K. Tagg, University of Strathclyde, UK*
**Queueing systems**
  *Donald Gross, George Washington University, USA*
**Real estate management**
  *Tom Putt, University of Reading, UK*
**Real estate resource management**
  *Virginia Gibson, University of Reading, UK*
**Real options**
  *C. G. C. Pitts, Warwick Business School, UK*
**Recruitment and selection**
  *Sally Riggs Fuller, Vandra L. Huber, University of Washington School of Business, USA*
**Re-engineering**
  *Matthew Jones, Judge Institute of Management Studies, University of Cambridge, UK*
**Relationship marketing**
  *Adrian Payne, Cranfield School of Management, UK*
**Relocation**
  *Helen de Cieri, University of Melbourne, Australia*
  *Sara L. McGaughey, Peter J. Dowling, University of Tasmania, Australia*
**Retail management**
  *Ross Davies, Templeton College, Oxford University, UK*
**Retailing**
  *Peter J. McGoldrick, Manchester School of Management and Manchester Business School (UMIST), UK*
**Sales management**
  *John Lidstone, Freelance lecturer, Hampshire, UK*
**Sales promotion**
  *Ken Peattie, Cardiff Business School, UK*
**Scheduling**
  *Kathie S. Smith, Consultant, USA*
**Securities markets, international**
  *Brian Scott-Quinn, University of Reading, UK*
**Security and information systems**
  *Richard Baskerville, Binghamton University, New York, USA*
**Segmentation**
  *Barrie Gunter, University of Sheffield, UK*
**Services, marketing of**
  *Trevor Watkins, South Bank University, London, UK*

# Introduction

This book is drawn from the six volume International Encyclopedia of Business and Management (IEBM), and contains brief synopses of the longer entries contained in that work. The full IEBM was published in June 1996 and was based on an international collaboration involving over 500 individual authors, advisory editors and subject editors from around the world. The mission statement for the IEBM was 'to create a worldwide work of reference covering all aspects of management that is international both in terms of subject matter and its authorship'. That aim was followed in this pocket guide but here we also had to make the content immediately accessible to readers. Over 400 individually authored entries provide thorough briefings of the issues surrounding a topic so that the reader can quickly gain awareness as well as an understanding.

Each entry provides a short introductory overview to a key area, theory or technique in business and management. There are entries from a wide range of general subject areas: accounting, economics, finance, HRM and industrial/labour relations, international management, manufacturing, information systems, marketing, operations management and research, organization behaviour, comparative management and strategy. In addition, there are entries that cut across such divisions like business and society, environmental management, globalization and multinational corporations. The Pocket IEBM also contains over 50 contributions that detail aspects of management in specific countries or areas; for example, Management in Brazil and Japanese industrial relations.

The Pocket IEBM contains 425 entries arranged in a single alphabetical sequence to enable readers to quickly find the entries they are interested in. The list of entries and their contributors provides a handy outline to the work as a whole. It will be useful for those readers who want to assess the range of information available on certain areas.

I would like to thank all the authors, subject editors, advisory editors, copy-editors and everyone who offered advice and encouragement throughout the development of the IEBM and especially those who helped create this Pocket edition.

*Malcom Warner*
Editor-in-Chief, Cambridge, January 1997

# A

## Accounting

Accounting is a discipline that seeks to provide information about a business organization. Such information is useful to those who are interested in making decisions that may affect the organization or one's relationship with it.

Accounting activities can be broken down into two important types. Firstly, financial accounting, which concerns the whole area of the capture of financial data of a company's transactions. These are reported both within the company and to shareholders, regulators and others outside it. Secondly, managerial accounting, a management tool which includes costing and budgeting.

Accounting as an activity is many centuries old, but the growth of industrial activity in the late nineteenth and early twentieth centuries gave it new prominence as a discipline. Both financial accounting and managerial accounting have now become important managerial decision-making tools. Virtually all large companies, as well as many 'middle market' companies, have accounting expertise available internally. Of greater significance, however, is the use of such expertise within the organization to assist in the management of the business. In many companies, the focus of accounting has moved from those activities needed to meet regulatory reporting requirements to those that are increasingly significant in the management of the company. The accounting process in many companies has evolved into a total information system, with the system supplying data that is not limited to information which is a product of the double-entry accounting system.

In the 1990s there has been a growing awareness that financial reports have lost some of their usefulness for decision-making purposes, and that for many companies historical cost information now has little relevance. There is a growing recognition that quantified information in financial statements tells only part of the story. Accounting is being increasingly required to adapt to the new needs of business.

Today there is considerable diversity in accounting practices around the world, and the rapid change and growth of the world economy means that accounting in turn is undergoing considerable change. Advances in technology, cross-border trade and geopolitical initiatives such as European integration are all having an impact. It is probable that in the near future there will be moves towards the widespread adoption of international accounting standards.

*Arthur R. Wyatt*

## Accounting, creative

Creative accounting is not so much a new phenomenon, but rather a taking to new extremes of what has long been part of the accountant's art. The objectives are generally either to improve reported earnings or to enhance the company's debt/equity ratio. While unadjusted profits often fluctuate from year to year, the market looks for steadily rising earnings, which impact upon both the share price and the market. The debt/equity ratio provides an indication of risk, and is often used by lenders to restrict further borrowing.

Profit enhancement can be achieved by spreading expenses over several years, by changing depreciation, by manipulation of foreign currency loans and by timing of revenues on long-term contracts. Complex capital instruments blur distinctions between debt and equity and provide many opportunities to improve ratios. This can also be done with off-balance-sheet financing.

Mergers and acquisitions bring their own problems – and accounting opportunities. Merger accounting avoids the goodwill problem, but fair value adjustments in acquisition accounting provide ways of influencing future profits and the balance sheet. If all else fails, the company can write off all its bad news in one year, as well as provide against future losses to help cushion future profits.

*Peter Walton*

## Accounting, international

Managers can not make good decisions without the availability of adequate and timely financial information. Although accounting and information systems specialists provide this information, all managers need to understand which data are needed and the problems specialists face in gathering those data from around the world. The accounting and finance functions are very closely related. Each relies on the other in fulfilling its own responsibilities. The financial manager of any company, whether domestic or international, is responsible for procuring and managing the company's financial resources. That manager relies on the accountant to provide the information necessary to manage financial resources.

The actual and potential flow of assets across national boundaries complicates the finance and accounting functions. The multinational corporation (MNC) must learn to cope with differing inflation rates, exchange rate changes, currency controls, expropriation risks, customs duties, levels of sophistication and local requirements.

A company's accounting or controllership function is responsible for collecting and analysing data for internal and external users. Foreign managers and subsidiaries are usually evaluated based on data provided by the controller's office. Reports must be generated for internal consideration, local governmental needs, creditors, employees, shareholders and prospective investors. The controller must be concerned about the impact of many different currencies and inflation rates on the statements as well as being familiar with different countries' accounting systems.

*Lee H. Radebaugh*

## Accounting in Australia

The first professional accounting bodies were established in Australia in the late 1880s. The geographical spread of the Australian colonies led to the establishment of a number of bodies purportedly serving different groups of accountants. Subsequently there were a number of attempts to unify the profession, but these did not meet with success. Despite the continued existence of two major bodies, the accounting profession in Australia is very active and enjoys a strong international reputation. It is unique in the very close relationship that exists between the professional bodies and the universities. Although it has not always been the case, following a series of major corporate collapses, the profession now enjoys a close relationship with government agencies. Australian accounting standards are recognized as part of the corporations law.

*Murray Wells*

## Accounting in central and eastern Europe

The countries of central and eastern Europe – Albania, Bulgaria, Hungary, Poland, Romania and the states formerly incorporated into Czechoslovakia, the USSR and Yugoslavia – are in the course of a socio-economic transformation. As a consequence of repudiating the former socialist regimes in the period 1989–91, an attempt is being made to transform command economies into market economies and to integrate with western Europe. The prospect of economic transformation has made the consideration and implementation of accounting reform inevitable.

In the command economy, accounting was subordinated to the need for centralized direction of economic activities. Its integration into the centralized economic administration was achieved through the implementation of a comprehensive and obligatory standardized accounting system. The purpose of accounting became the routinized accumulation of data for the compilation of periodical accounting reports, or returns, for the central authorities. There was no public disclosure of accounting information.

In the 1990s, the formerly communist-ruled countries of central and eastern Europe began to adopt the accounting practices of the advanced industrial economies through the introduction of new accounting legislation, reform of accounting education and training programmes, and the creation of new accounting institutions. However, the requirements of the central authorities for accounting data tend still to predominate over those of participants (such as creditors and investors) in market activities. Both the nature and rate of accounting reform varies significantly among these countries.

*Derek Bailey*

## Accounting in France

Accounting in France has a number of original features by comparison with accounting in anglophone countries, despite the advance of European and international standardization. Since 1946, standard-setting has been the prerogative not only of professional accountants but also of all those who have an interest in accounts, including businesses, government agencies, trade unions, and banks, and is carried on by the Conseil National de la Comptabilité. Accounting standards are brought together in an accounting chart, the *plan comptable général*, which is used by all businesses and other bodies. Furthermore, public accountants and auditors must belong to one or other of two government sponsored bodies: the Ordre des Experts Comptables (for accountants) and the Compagnie des Commissaires aux Comptes (for auditors).

Financial reporting by listed companies is supervised by the Commission des Opérations de Bourse (COB). The COB is very influential in accounting regulation and has extensive powers. Listed companies must submit their choice of auditor to the commission for approval, and it has access to files of peer reviews carried out on audit firms. Accounting in the public sector is different from that in the private sector in all respects, including principles, methods and people. National accounting, the concern of the Institut National de la Statistique et des Études Économiques (INSEE), has developed its own principles and concepts, which are different from those to be found in the public and private sectors.

Taxation has been and still is a major influence on accounting in France. Since the mid-1970s, however, the financial markets have played a growing role in determining the principles and functions of French accounting.

*Jean-Claude Scheid*

## Accounting in Germany

Due to the Roman law system, German financial accounting is regulated by law in a very detailed manner. The most important part of the accounting law is the *Handelsgesetzbuch* (HGB, commercial code), which contains regulations dependent on the legal form of the business, size and sector. In accounting for all events, even unforeseeable ones, the *Grundsätze ordnungsmäßiger Buchführung* (GoB, principles of regular accounting) must be followed. Although the GoB originate from commercial accounting, they also influence tax accounting, since there is a unified income approach for both commercial and tax purposes. Group accounting is legally (although not in practice) irrelevant for dividends and legally (as well as in practice) irrelevant for taxation.

The financing of German corporations has a number of characteristic features, including a low rate of visible equity financing, a small number of listed corporations, a small number of private shareholders and an ownership structure in which private shareholders play little part. Accordingly, the main objectives of financial accounting in Germany are financial capital maintenance through prudent determination of profit and the generation of information about the net worth and results of a business through either published or unpublished balance sheets. Information is an important aim of financial statements, but the protection of creditors is the dominant concern.

Limited companies are the only entities required to give a true and fair view of financial statements; this is restricted by the GoB, which aim to protect creditors by prudent profit determination. This fits with both the reduction of tax bases in order to defer taxes and the financing environment, where loans by banks or groups are a more important source than equity.

*Wolfgang Ballwieser*

## Accounting harmonization

Current national accounting requirements often differ, with the result that like transactions and events are reported differently in different countries. Such differences can have a significant impact on both the balance sheet and the income statement. This situation is illustrated dramatically by international companies such as SmithKline Beecham and Daimler-Benz, which, for capital market purposes, prepare financial statements based on different requirements and disclose widely different figures for the same transactions and events. These differences make it difficult to distinguish changes in the performance from the effects arising from the use of different accounting requirements.

The aim of accounting harmonization is to make the financial statements of companies comparable with the financial statements of companies in other countries. Accounting harmonization is important because companies want to operate in a business environment in which they can trade, raise capital, list their securities and attract investors in different countries. Investors also want to seek new investment opportunities throughout the world. Accounting harmonization will assist companies and investors and, consequently, the efficient operation of capital markets. Therefore, several major initiatives have been launched to seek harmonization of accounting requirements and the actual reporting practices of companies.

At an international level, the International Accounting Standards Committee (IASC) has developed a set of accounting standards which deal with most of the topics that are important internationally in published financial statements. Compliance with these standards helps to harmonize financial reporting: for example, standards can be used by a national standard setting body as (or as the basis for) national accounting requirements or as a benchmark in developing national requirements, or by a company in its published financial statements in addition to national requirements.

In the European Union (EU), accounting directives provide a legal framework for the annual accounts and consolidated accounts of companies in member states. The directives are generally consistent with, but less detailed and more flexible than, the international accounting standards. The flexibility of the directives has restricted the degree of harmonization which has been achieved; nevertheless, the directives have led to significant improvements in financial reporting in the member states and in those central and eastern European countries which have used them as the basis for their accounting laws.

National bodies are also working together to achieve harmonization through the adoption of common improvements in national accounting requirements. Cooperative efforts include a number of joint projects as well as regular consultations among standard setting bodies, the European Commission and the IASC on issues of common interest.

Efforts to harmonize accounting requirements are further enhanced and are often led by the actions of companies themselves, particularly European multinationals which have adopted accounting practices that exceed national requirements but which meet international expectations. They have done this because they want access to international capital markets. In the 1970s, many continental European multinationals published consolidated accounts long before they were required to do so. In the 1990s, these same companies started to publish financial statements which conform to international accounting standards even when the requirements of the standards exceed appropriate national requirements.

*David Cairns*

## Accounting in Japan

Accounting and auditing in Japan, as in other countries, are a reflection of its history and combine many different strands and influences. As far as large, listed companies are concerned, the infrastructure of financial reporting derives from a complete reorganization of the financial markets in the late 1940s. During the reconstruction of the Japanese economy which followed the Second World War, many Western, and particularly US, ideas were adopted. The stock exchange was reformed and laws introduced similar to the US 1933 Securities Act and 1934 Securities and Exchange Act. The Ministry of Finance also set up a committee, whose successor is the current Business Accounting Deliberation Council (BADC), to specify accounting standards for listed companies.

The regulations for listed companies were created alongside existing accounting rules for limited liability companies which are in the Commercial Code. Listed companies have therefore to prepare two sets of statements. A further constraint upon reporting is the tax statutes which specify some measurement rules for tax purposes. The combination of these three sets of regulations is known as the triangular legal system, and the necessary interplay of the three does not easily permit the rapid evolution of rules. The accounting rules are, however, largely in line with those used in the rest of the world.

Auditing was introduced as part of the post-war reforms, when the Ministry of Finance took on responsibility not only for accounting standards but also auditing standards. This responsibility was passed in 1991 from the BADC to the Japanese Institute of Certified Public Accountants (JICPA). Initially the audit requirement was limited to listed companies, but in 1974 it was extended to large, private companies, and currently some 9,000 companies are subject to independent audit.

Auditors must be members of JICPA, which was also created in the 1940s. Admission to JICPA is by way of a series of professional examinations. There is a second, related profession, that of tax practitioner, of which there are about 6,000. Many certified public accountants are also tax practitioners, but they cannot provide both tax and audit services to the same client. JICPA provides technical advice and support to its members, and issues audit standards. It is also active in the international field.

*Etsuo Sawa*

## Accounting and organizations

Accounting is often presented as a dry, technical subject, so often concerned with precision rather than relevance. However, as it is practised within today's large organizations, accounting is far from dry and technical. Financial calculations are an important ingredient in most organizations' decision-making activities. Finance staff are often intimately involved in the allocation of scarce resources (for example, people and money) among competing projects, operating units and departments.

Pressure for performance is a common feature of corporate life, and often this is manifest through accountability for financial results. Indeed, careers are often made, or broken, according to line managers' performance against plans and budgets. In short, accounting is actively involved in the management process. It is not merely technical in this view, or neutral in its effects. Rather it influences, and is influenced by, behaviour in organizations.

Within organizations, management accounting is distinguished from other activities performed by the finance function. Planning is a central component of management accounting, which seeks to achieve greater coordination and control within organizations. How it does so will differ given the technical systems employed, and in particular the nature of the organization. Different contexts give rise to different organizational arrangements, and consequently to different planning and control systems. Firms using functional, divisional or matrix structures, for example, will have quite different planning and control aims and requirements. There are also international differences in organization and control; these differences are not as yet fully understood, but evidence suggests that practices around the world vary considerably. There are noticeable differences between US, Japanese and European styles of control and, within Europe, between Germany, France and the UK.

At present, accounting and control systems face several challenges. For example, traditional hierarchical control systems do not fit easily with the modern 'delayered', 'empowered', 'process-oriented' organization. There are also questions as to how short-term financial controls can be consistent with the quest for strategic positioning and the creation of core competencies.

*Jeremy F. Dent*

## Accounting in the United Kingdom

The particular features of UK accounting include a gradual development of financial reporting under the impetus of the Industrial Revolution, with Companies Acts prescribing a minimum of rules and the accounting profession developing generally accepted accounting principles (GAAP). European harmonization and the appearance of creative accounting have led to more state regulation since the mid-1980s.

The accounting profession is highly organized, with six representative bodies whose examinations are the key to a serious accounting career, whether in audit, business or the public sector. The UK has a new and active standard setter, the Accounting Standards Board (ASB), which is independent of the profession, together with a body for checking compliance, the Financial Reporting Review Panel. Statutory audit is required for all limited liability companies and the audit industry is dominated by the 'Big Six' Anglo-American audit firms and three or four large national firms. The efficacy and independence of auditors has increasingly been questioned in the wake of financial scandals.

Particular features of accounting principles are those that allow for the revaluation of tangible fixed assets, and goodwill arising on consolidation is usually written off directly against reserves. Deferred tax is provided for, but only to the extent that timing differences are likely to crystallize. Assets obtained under finance leases are capitalized in the lessee's accounts. Taxation has a complicated relationship with reported profits but published financial statements are normally the starting point for tax computation. Systematic differences are that tax law fixes depreciation rates, which are applied independently of the company's accounting policies, interest is accounted for on a cash basis for tax, and no general provisions are allowed as an expense for tax purposes.

Public sector accounting has developed independently of commercial accounting and has a tradition of reporting income and expenditure in relation to sources of funds with no distinction between capital and revenue expenditure. Current pressure is towards systems which recognize assets and provide consolidated financial statements.

Accounting in the UK can be characterized as being heavily influenced by the accounting profession and orientated towards the reporting of large, public companies. Accountants operate in an environment where they control entry to their profession, all limited liability companies are subject to statutory audit, and accountants are the main providers of tax advice. Large accounting firms typically provide significant management consulting activity as well. The regulation of accounting has built up around company law and the reporting needs of companies. There are no accounting regulations for unincorporated business, and public sector accounting has until recently been largely ignored by professional firms and educational institutions.

*Peter Walton*

## Accounting in the United States of America

Accounting and reporting standards in the USA, as elsewhere, are environmentally based. An understanding of these influences is necessary to facilitate financial statement analysis and interpretation when dealing with US-based companies.

While financial statements in the USA are intended to be general purpose, they are heavily influenced by the information needs of private investors, who are the principal providers of external finance in a predominantly free-market economy. Thus financial reports prepared by management seek to provide information that is useful to investors in assessing the amounts, timing and uncertainty of future cash flows that are of interest to them. This contrasts sharply with financial reports that are aimed at complying with statutory reporting requirements of government or fiscal authorities.

Accounting and reporting standards are promulgated largely through the effects of private professional bodies and enforced through public sector actions. The primary objective is to provide a commercial, as opposed to legalistic, framework for accounting prescriptions. To be effective, they must prove acceptable to the major users of accounting information, with variations in the application of accounting standards being revealed primarily through full and fair disclosure. The major standard-setting body at present is the Financial Accounting Standards Board (FASB); other important bodies include the Financial Accounting Foundation (FAF), which appoints members of the FASB, funds their activities and exercises general oversight, and the Financial Accounting Standards Advisory Council (FASAC), which consults the FASB on major issues and organizes working task forces.

The US approach to promulgating accounting standards is a direct consequence of its unique reporting environment. Accounting measurements embodied in US accounting standards differ from those formulated elsewhere for similar reasons. Asset valuation is less conservative and more pragmatic than elsewhere, for example, and the use of discretionary reserves is not permitted, as it is in Germany, Japan, Sweden and Switzerland.

Independent auditors provide a credibility check on management's financial representations by rendering an opinion as to the reliability and fairness of those representations. They are legally liable to third parties. The threat of lawsuits may be viewed as a free-market response to real or perceived audit failures in the USA.

Accounting and financial reporting in the USA are heavily influenced by the information needs of capital suppliers. This contrasts sharply with financial reports that are designed to serve more macro-oriented needs. In the face of international differences in accounting and reporting, demands for increased accounting uniformity are appealing. Statement readers, however, should not be fooled by international standards that paper over reporting differences that are environmentally-based. While accounts which conform to German, US or other codes can be restated to conform to some internationally accepted norm, the resulting measures could mislead rather than inform.

*Frederick D.S. Choi*

## Acquisitions and divestments

In 'Anglo-Saxon' economies with very active stock markets, company expenditure on acquisitions can reach half as much as spending on new

fixed investment. Traditionally this massive expenditure has been justified by pointing to the potential gains from transferring control to more
able managers or ones more committed to shareholders' interests; or to
the gains from scale economies or increased market power. However,
evidence of such gains has been questioned by contributors to the industrial organization, finance and management literatures, and new theories
focusing on managerial objectives and principal-agent problems have
emerged to help explain the disappointing performance of many acquisition programmes and the growing recourse to divestment.

At first sight, the potential gains to shareholders from turning round
companies with flagging performance and for achieving scale economies
or enhanced market power seem to justify the immense commitment of
owners' funds and managers' time to acquisition activity. In practice,
however, the movements of accounting profits and acquirers' share prices
and the large-scale divestment of recent acquisitions raise doubts about
the benefits of takeovers. It has been suggested in some quarters that either
the problems of assessing, integrating and monitoring acquisitions have
been systematically underestimated, or that managers' interests have
tended to prevail over those of shareholders.

*G. Meeks*

## Activity-based costing

From the early 1980s, calls have been made for management accounting
to undergo changes that considerably exceed the transformations witnessed in the field over the last seventy years. Among the many novel cost
management techniques, activity-based costing (ABC) has received by far
the most attention. ABC entails the examination of activities across the
entire chain of value-adding organizational processes underlying causes
(drivers) of cost. It attempts to overcome cost distortions by addressing
cost behaviour parameters, which include non-volume cost drivers reflec-
tive of production complexity and product diversity in addition to volume-
linked drivers of cost. Although one output of ABC calculations is costs
based on resource consumption, the actual process of deriving such costs
offers a number of monitors which may be useful for a variety of
managerial purposes. These include novel performance measures, altered
budgeting techniques and a large amount of decision-making information
tied to the broader concept of activity-based management.

Prior to the 1980s, some accounting commentators articulated certain
of the broad principles which underpin ABC. However, the literature
relating to this accounting approach has developed and illustrated its
potential primarily since the late 1980s. Partly, this may have been linked
to the efforts of the major proponents of ABC and the support of consultants
and other distinguished accounting scholars who promoted the technique

during the late 1980s and 1990s. The routes for extolling ABC's virtues have been varied and the reception it has been given by accounting academics, practitioners and industry has been significant, especially when compared with that given to other new techniques. There is now much evidence to show that major enterprises across the Western world have begun to exploit ABC's offerings. This is being done, by all accounts, in a seemingly irreversible manner. Yet it is also true that many organizations – which for a number of years have acknowledged the necessity of investing in accounting resources that reflect the ideas encompassed by ABC – show little evidence of taking action along these lines. The question remains as to why such a seemingly rational accounting technique has failed to gain total and unreserved allegiance from firms which it would seem likely to benefit.

*Al Bhimani & Michael Bromwich*

## Advertising campaigns

Advertising campaigns are one of the most important methods – often the most important method – of communication used by companies to send messages to current customers and potential customers. Advertising campaigns are a critical part of any marketing strategy, and are often a major item of budget expenditure. Campaigns can vary from small, regionally-targeted programmes of short duration to very large ongoing campaigns which are global in scale and scope.

Advertising campaigns can be used for a variety of purposes, but the basic process of planning and managing a campaign is similar no matter what the end goal of the campaign may be. Advertising managers need to identify their target markets and set their advertising goals, along with any constraints such as budgetary limits, before deciding which media to use and what the message of the campaign will be. Once the campaign is under way, it is important to measure the effects of the campaign and feed these back in order to determine whether or not the campaign was successful.

Companies do not carry out advertising alone. In the vast majority of campaigns the company works in partnership with a specialist advertising agency, which manages many of the key processes of design and media buying. Creating and managing relationships with advertising agencies is therefore critical to the success of advertising campaigns.

*Colin Gilligan*

## Advertising strategy, international

Advertising is an important form of promotion used by companies to communicate with their existing and potential customers. In most instances advertising consists of messages conveyed in paid media such as television, radio, newspapers and magazines, cinemas and posters, but advertising messages can also be transmitted by means such as painting slogans on company vans. Advertising is a key element in the marketing mix and for many companies constitutes a major source of expenditure.

The principal purpose of advertising is to influence consumer behaviour, stimulating consumers towards actions such as product trial, purchase, repeat purchase or retention. As such, when designing an advertising campaign the company must ensure that it understands consumer behaviour and the variables which can affect it. This problem is compounded when marketing internationally, as behaviour varies between cultures and responses to advertising stimuli are also subject to change.

It has recently been argued that global consumer convergence, that is, an increasing similarity in tastes and consumption patterns, compounded with the advent of global media such as satellite television, has made it possible for companies to develop global advertising campaigns which would be more effective at achieving these goals. A number of large multinationals have tried such campaigns, with mixed success. Others have argued that localized campaigns, where advertisements are adapted to local tastes and conditions, are more likely to be successful. The importance of this issue lies in the fact that large companies spend many millions on advertising each year, and failure to target advertising successfully can have a serious effect not only on product or brand performance but on overall company performance itself.

*Greg Harris*

## Agency, markets and hierarchies

The study of agency, markets and hierarchies is concerned with the analysis and comparison of alternative modes of coordination of economic activities. The relatively new branches of economics called information economics and organizational or neo-institutional economics offer major contributions on how to deal with this problem, particularly when integrated with organizational theories of bureaucracy and incentive systems.

A perfect market is said to exist when all actors in the market are able to take decisions based on local information and are able to formulate feasible production or consumption plans. The price of a product is said to embody the information on all other variables relevant to decision-making. However, a number of factors, stemming either from production costs or transaction costs, from information complexity or from insufficient numbers of actors, can lead to market failure. Instead there evolve 'modified markets' the two main types of which are oligopolies and assisted markets.

Hierarchies can be grouped into three classes: informational hierarchies in 'teams', supervisory hierarchies and agency-based hierarchies.

Team-based hierarchies emerge when a group of actors has a common interest; supervisory hierarchies, on the other hand, develop when two groups have conflicting interests and one group exerts control over the other. This type of hierarchy is prone to problems, some of which can be solved by the use of agency-based hierarchy where one party delegates discretionary power to a third party, the agent. As well as the above three forms of coordination, however, there are also others such as group coordination or the setting of rules and norms.

*Anna Grandori*

## Airline management

The airline industry developed as a commercial enterprise during the 1930s as technological advances in aviation enabled companies to develop regular passenger services, cross-subsidized by the provision of freight and air postal services. In the post-war period, modern day air transport emerged as an international business, providing services and products for a diverse group of users including scheduled and non-scheduled (charter) transportation for air travellers and cargo transportation for businesses. The airline industry is truly a global business and by the year 2002 commercial world passenger air transport is expected to generate 3,431.4 billion revenue passenger kilometres (RPKs). The growth in global passenger travel by air has risen consistently in recent years, with the Boeing Commercial Airline Group anticipating an average annual rate of growth in air travel of 5.2 per cent through to the year 2013, led by growth in the Asia Pacific region. This growth is cited by the group as equivalent to adding the capacity of one of the world's largest airlines, with a fleet of more than 600 airplanes, to the system each year. Such a rate of change is not new for the airline industry, since it has a history of dramatic change over a short period of time dating back to the introduction of commercial aviation services in the 1920s and 1930s.

Airline management is particularly complex due to the volatile nature of the airline industry, and to the impact which extraneous political issues can have on the market. One of the principal concerns of airline management is the matching of the supply of services with actual and forecast demand. Issues affecting airline management at present include environmental demands for reduced emissions and noise from jet engines, consumer demands for higher quality service and technological advances in aircraft design.

*Stephen J. Page*

## Appraisal methods

Financial analysis is the means of appraising whether a proposed investment in a commercial activity is likely to be of value from the point of view of the stockholders. Investments in commercial activities are called *capital projects*. They usually involve the purchase of a physical asset, such as a machine or a new factory; a capital project may also involve investment in a less tangible asset, such as a new product or an advertising campaign. An essential characteristic of most capital projects is that cash is paid out now or in the near term in order to increase cash returns subsequently. The value of a project's future incremental cash flows to the company can be estimated; using discounted cash flow methods, it is possible to determine whether a project is worth more to the company than it costs.

*Jack Broyles*

## Artificial intelligence

Artificial intelligence (AI) may be defined as the capability of a device, such as a computer, to perform tasks or functions normally associated with human behaviour. AI has a number of applications in business and industry, ranging from searching databases and credit approval to automatic operations in transportation and manufacturing. The principal AI technologies are engineering systems (expert knowledge-based systems and case-based reasoning systems); perception, understanding and robotics systems (computer vision systems, speech processing systems and robotics systems); fuzzy systems; and neural networks and genetic algorithms. Major areas of application include accounting and auditing, customer service, finance, human resource management, information resource management, marketing, production and operations management, and strategic management.

*Robert Mockler*

## Artificial intelligence in manufacturing

Artificial intelligence (AI) has moved from research laboratories into manufacturing. AI technology as applied to the manufacturing industry has resulted in a substantial number of applications. The past few years have witnessed an increased interest in applied AI in manufacturing. The repertory of AI technologies has evolved and expanded, and applications have been made in the manufacturing domains. Many surveys indicate that AI technologies are slowly but surely moving into manufacturing firms.

The AI technology has been incorporated into computer-aided design software, shop-floor operations software, as well as entering the logistics systems. Many of these applications are stand-alone systems, but others are integrated with more conventional information systems in manufacturing. Most applications are knowledge-based expert systems (ES) or decision support systems (DSS), but there is a growing number of applications of other AI technologies, such as neural networks, knowledge-based planning, fuzzy systems, speech-synthesis systems and voice-recognition systems.

The success of AI in manufacturing can be measured by the growing number of real-world applications, releases of new software products, companies developing and distributing these products, conferences and professional publications. However, thousands of actual applications use the AI technology, often without public acknowledgment, to preserve a competitive advantage.

*Binshan Lin*

## Asset valuation, depreciation and provisions

Economic descriptions of enterprises by accountants are based on asset valuations. The usefulness of any valuation method depends upon the scenario in which the valuation takes place. There are two primary scenarios, a *buy and sale setting* where a single transaction is concerned, and a *going concern setting* where valuation is made on the assumption that the asset is controlled over a period of time.

Economic concepts such as capital, profit, liquidity or the growth of an enterprise are made concrete by accounting measures. Despite their different constructs, all these measures are constructed in a similar way. They are based on stocks or flows of goods that are measured in monetary terms. The concept of an asset embraces in a narrow sense stocks of goods with a positive value only, such as tangible assets, intangible assets or financial assets; however, it is often expanded to include liabilities or negative assets as well. In accounting terms, the fact that an asset has value derives from the fact that it will provide future benefits and/or disadvantages to the economic entity controlling the asset. Valuation allows the aggregation of different benefits and advantages and thereby allows more complex measures for describing the situation of the business.

*Dieter Ordelheide & Christian Leuz*

## Aston Group

The distinctive characteristics of the Aston programme of research in organizational behaviour, which began in Birmingham, England in the 1960s were its completeness (it was an attempt to identify all relevant variables for describing organizations and their context or environment), carefulness of measurement (it used multiple scales and attention to problems of reliability in what is almost the paradigm of psychometric techniques), and its variety of extensions both in terms of the kinds of organizations (business, public sector, colleges, unions, etc.) and of other levels of analysis (roles, groups and climates). Its key figures included

Pugh and Hickson, among others. The major weaknesses were its general lack of theoretical focus and an overreliance upon the use of informants and documents in collecting data on structural variables rather than use interviews. But perhaps the most important lesson to be learned from the Aston programme which is generally not the one mentioned, is the way in which the concepts were developed. All members participated in teams working in a problem-solving mode before quality work circles became popular, and produced research products that were more comprehensive and of generally higher quality than those produced by their contemporaries or even since then.

*Jerald Hage*

## Auditing

In recent years there has been increasing publicity, fuelled incessantly by major financial scandals (such as BCCI, Barings) concerning auditing and the work of auditors. It is a subject with ever-widening horizons, continually developing, in both the scope of what is regarded as the activity of auditing and the nature of the approaches/practices adopted in undertaking that activity. All those who rely on financial statements are affected by the auditor's work, yet the nature, practice and limitations of auditing are not well known outside the auditing profession.

To the layperson, auditing has tended to be an obscure or misunderstood subject. What actually is an audit and how does it differ from accounting? The nature of auditing in terms of its underlying principles leads to questions of why audits should take place at all, who should normally be required to have them and what the basic statutory audit requirements should be. The scope of the audit is highlighted by the various financial statements and accounting records which are subject to an audit. The conduct of audits, auditing standards and the nature of an auditor's report (the only tangible product to outside parties at the end of the audit) are just some of the important issues that need to be addressed.

The comments above apply primarily to the external audit of companies. However, the basic points also apply to the audits of other organizations (such as central government, banks, trade unions) although the scope of the audit then required by the relevant statute or organization may stipulate further audit requirements.

It is important to stress that auditing has its limitations; an auditor's report is only an opinion that provides a reasonable assurance that accounts can be relied upon, not a guarantee of truth. For example, audited financial information is of value only so long as it is reasonably current. Also, it is not the auditor's duty to prevent or detect fraud. Thus, although audited statements are very valuable, they should not be used solely to assess the financial strength of an organization.

*Paul Saw*

# B

## Banking

The term 'banking' can be applied to a large range of financial institutions, from savings and loans organizations to the large money-centre commercial banks in the USA, or from the smallest building society to the big four clearing banks in the UK. Many European countries have large regional/cooperative banks. In Japan, the bank with the largest retail network is Sakura, but its main rival is the Post Office.

The provision of deposit and loan products is what normally distinguishes banks from other types of financial firms. The deposit products pay out money on demand or after some notice. Additionally, banks are in the business of managing liabilities. In the process they lend money, thereby creating bank assets which must also be managed. Thus, one core activity of banks is to act as intermediaries between depositors and borrowers.

The second core activity of banks is to offer liquidity to their customers. Depositors and borrowers have different liquidity preferences. Typically, firms in the business sector want to borrow funds and repay them in line with the expected returns of an investment project, which may not be realized for several years after the investment. By lending funds, savers are agreeing to forgo present consumption in favour of consumption at some date in the future. However, unexpected events may cause either party to change their mind. By pooling a large number of savers and borrowers, banks can meet the liquidity requirements of both parties.

Particularly important, and separate from private banks, are central banks, government institutions responsible for monetary control, prudential control and/or government debt control. There is at time of writing considerable debate over the degree of independence from government that should be given to central banks.

*Shelagh Heffernan*

## Banking, Islamic

The concept of Islamic banking has attracted considerable attention since the 1970s from both non-Muslims and Muslims. Although less than 1 per cent of all world banking transactions are conducted in accordance with the Islamic *shariah* law, the principle of interest-free financing has caught the imagination of many. Most bankers have heard of the Islamic prohibition of *riba* or interest. Knowledge of the alternatives, however, is much less widespread. The principal alternatives are *mudrabah*, in which a bank invests directly in an existing business, and *musharakah*, in which the bank and the business found a new partnership. Both have been used as financing instruments since the time of the Prophet Mohammed, and are well-suited for medium and long-term financing. Islamic banks operate successfully using these instruments both in countries where the entire banking system has been 'Islamicized' (Iran, Pakistan) and where Islamic banks compete with conventional banks, as in most Arab states, Turkey, Malaysia and Indonesia.

*Rodney Wilson*

## Banking in Japan

The Tokyo financial market is now recognized as one of the largest financial centres in the world. It is significant that the world's five largest commercial banks are all Japanese, although Japan's GNP is only the second largest in the world.

Modern banking in Japan is, however, comparatively new. It was only in the mid-nineteenth century that the Japanese government began to establish a modern banking system through the introduction of advanced systems from Western countries. As a result, Japanese banking has much in common with its US and European counterparts. Roughly speaking, Japanese commercial banks are very similar to those of Britain or Europe, while financial markets are almost identical to US markets. In addition, the Japanese government has introduced a number of unique features. In the last decade, Japan has been trying to reform its financial system in order to cope with internationalization.

Financial institutions in Japan are classified into private sector and public sector institutions, and institutions in each category are further divided into depository and non-depository institutions. Private sector depository institutions include commercial banks, foreign banks, long-term credit banks, trust banks and financial institutions for small and medium business, agriculture and fisheries. The commercial banks and long-term credit banks are very active in international operations. Private sector non-depository institutions include firms such as insurance companies, securities firms and finance companies. Public sector institutions include government banks, government finance corporations and the Postal Savings Service. Wide-scale deregulation of the banking system in Japan took place in 1993–4.

*Kazuo Tatewaki*

## Banking in the United States of America

Banking in the USA is a large and complex industry facing rapid changes in both market forces and regulatory environments. In the USA a bank is a financial institution which accepts demand deposits from the public, provides a payment settlement system based on demand deposit accounts and makes commercial loans to business units. However, banks are just one type of financial intermediary; others include other depository institutions, insurance companies, investment companies, pension funds, finance companies and securities companies. Recently, the banks' share of the financial market has been declining. Two major regulatory constraints, interest rate ceilings on deposits and bank capital requirements, are tending to make banks less competitive in asset-based activities. However, commercial banks have increasingly moved into off-balance sheet activities which has helped to halt the decline.

Depending on their classification, banks are regulated through either the Office of the Comptroller of the Currency, the Federal Reserve System or the Federal Deposit Insurance Corporation. Regulators comply with the Basle Accord on capital adequacy and have procedures for taking corrective action and dealing with bank failure. There has been a considerable weight of banking legislation in the USA in the twentieth century, with eleven major statutes devoted to banking regulation from 1913–94.

*Taeho Kim*

## Banking in western Europe

The macroeconomic climate experienced by European banks throughout the 1970s and 1980s has been of a much more volatile nature than that of the 1950s and 1960s. The unpredictability of macroeconomic variables such as interest rates, exchange rates, budget deficits and surpluses has resulted in a much more uncertain environment. The degree of uncertainty and the inability of the banks to plan for cyclical downturns was reflected in the performance of European banks during the recessionary period of the late 1980s and early 1990s.

After interest rates increased in late 1988 and early 1989, Europe went into recession, and the cost to the banking sector became apparent through extensive bad debts. It has been argued that the main impact of this recessionary period on the banking system was that European banking systems became driven more by profitability than by size. By early 1994, European banks were again operating in favourable conditions with low interest and inflation rates. Banking has become characterized by a de-emphasis on lending, and banks have competed aggressively to retain core deposits. The overall impact has been that fee and commission income have become an increasingly important part of bank earnings. The retail banking market has also become increasingly driven by savings products, with mortgages the principal source of loan growth. An increasing proportion of income has been, and will continue to be, obtained from trading activities.

The European financial services sector as a whole has become more efficient as a result of investment in technology, but this has also generated substantial job losses. Bank management has become more focused on cost and profitability rather than purely on market share and capital standards have improved, resulting from the changed (and changing) nature of business. In addition the role of the state in the banking sector has declined and is expected to continue to diminish, particularly in terms of state ownership of banks.

In addition to the above trends, it also important to note that demarcation lines between markets, intermediaries and lines of business have also been rapidly eroding. The blurring of distinction between bank credit and securities, domestic and international paper, and cash and derivatives products has helped to foster the integration of cross-border investment. The implication of the EU's Second Banking Directive in domestic banking legislation has also established universal banking practice for credit institutions within EU countries, rendering the old distinctions between different types of credit institution obsolete.

*Philip Molyneux*

## Bata system of management

The Bata system of management originated from the early ideas of Ford, summarized in his seminal book *Today and Tomorrow*, which were based on worker autonomy, knowledge, just-in-time, waste minimization, quality and customer involvement. These ideas were all but abandoned by Ford when he embraced Taylorism and mass production in the 1930s, but they were picked up and brought to practical fruition in Moravia, in central Europe in the late 1920s and early 1930s by Tomas Bata.

The Bata system is a management system of extrordinary productivity and effectiveness. Its main characteristics include integration instead of division of labour, whole-system orientation, continuous innovation and quality improvement, team self-management, profit-sharing, worker participation, organizational flexibility and an uncompromisingly human-orientated capitalistic enterprise. Bata's first slogan, 'Thinking to the people, labour to the machines', summarizes his views on the roles of human capital and technology. His human resource policies included strong attention to the quality of life for his employees, and the firm provided many amenities and services for its workers.

Bata's system was in many ways ahead of its time. Following the loss of Czech independence in 1939, the Bata system was dismantled first by the Nazis and then by the communists after 1948, who chose instead to adopt mass production practices.

*Milan Zeleny*

## Benchmarking

Although several definitions of benchmarking exist, the term can generally be taken to mean the continuous measuring of products, services or processes against those of competitors or recognized industry leaders. The primary goal is to stimulate performance improvement through recognition of areas where the organization is not performing up to the standards of its competitors. The four main types of benchmarking are benchmarking against internal operations; benchmarking against external operations of direct competitors; benchmarking against the equivalent functional operations of non-competitors; and generic process benchmarking. A number of studies of benchmarking and its efficacy have been conducted. While it seems that benchmarking can lead to significant performance improvements, there is also a phenomenon of 'unconscious managerialism' by which benchmarking is used to lay responsibility for productivity and other business problems squarely on the shoulders of managers, to the neglect of the economic and institutional context.

*Nick Oliver*

## Brands

Branding is one of the most powerful concepts in marketing today, offering marketers at one and the same time a way of communicating product values to consumers and an important product enhancement feature in its own right. So valuable are brands that they have begun to be listed along with the rest of a company's assets on the balance sheet.

Brands are nurtured through well-conceived strategies which involve the integration of many types of resources. Innovative product development, state of the art manufacturing processes, high quality materials and demanding quality control can help produce winning brands that make a statement about what they can do for consumers, while pack design and promotional activity enable brands to make a statement about consumers' personalities and lifestyles.

Brands represent a company or product's intangible values, which reinforce the loyal relationship between producers and consumers. For example, when consumers choose between different brands of cars, they rely not only on the physical characteristics of those cars, but also on the added value they perceive in what each brand communicates about the driver's personality.

Interest in brands has increased significantly since the 1980s, when brands began to be valued for the first time. To some companies these valuations are immense. In 1990 the UK confectionery firm Rowntree, under threat of takeover by Jacobs Suchard and Nestlé, had estimated tangible net assets of around £300 million; in the end, Nestlé won control of the firm by paying £2.5 billion. This price was almost three times Rowntree's stock market value, and twenty-six times its earnings. The 'premium' represented the value that Nestlé and its rivals saw in the potential earnings of strong international brands such as Kit Kat, Polo and After Eight Mints.

Questions have been raised as to whether brands have passed their zenith, yet they continue to play an important role. In April 1993 Phillip Morris cut the price of its best selling cigarette brand by 20 per cent; on that day, since referred to as 'Marlboro Friday', the company's stock market value fell by $13.4 billion. Yet the brand had been continually increasing its price 4 per cent ahead of inflation and had reached the state where, in a declining market, the price was over $2 a pack, compared with the cheapest brands at 70 cents. In an anti-smoking environment and faced with major tax increases, this price reduction appeared as a logical tactical move for survival. Others have pointed to reductions in numbers of lines by Procter & Gamble and Unilever, but these firms thrive through innovation and are continually identifying and targeting new segments; to balance their books, they have wisely addressed scale economies and eliminated marginal brands. Another argument for the decline of brands concerns the declining numbers of people in marketing departments, but this is more likely to stem from the general restructuring and cutting down of size practised by firms in all areas in recent years.

*Leslie de Chernatony*

## Budgetary control

A manager's responsibility is not to forecast the future but to contribute to its creation, and to do so means to be continuously mobilizing all resources in the organization to adapt to and exploit the opportunities that appear. Budgets and budgeting are processes and procedures that aim at contributing to such a mission. A budget is a statement, a declaration of actions intended to be carried out in a coordinated way by the various actors in an organization, whether for profit or not. A budget reflects answers to one key question: how are we going to go from where we are to where we want to be? A budget is one of the ways through which energies are mobilized and channelled for the successful implementation of the business strategic intent.

Budgets and budgeting processes have a variety of purposes, all of which must be pursued simultaneously. First, they offer a forum for coordinated decision making, including identifying and allocating the resources necessary to carry out the organization's mission efficiently and effectively. Second, the promulgation of the budget communicates intent, plans and values, and can then be used to build commitment. Finally, budgets establish benchmarks for performance measures, provide a basis for variance analysis and assist in the management or performance improvement.

Almost all European businesses use some form of budget. Yet many managers are not fully satisfied with their budgeting system. New forms of budgeting are now emerging, and it seems likely that budgeting, like other business tools, will increasingly become subject to processes of continuous adaptation.

*Michel Lebas*


## Business-to-business marketing

Business-to-business marketing encompasses the development and marketing of products and services to business markets. Business markets can include both local and international markets for products and services purchased by businesses, governments and institutions (such as hospitals), for purposes including consumption (production process materials, office supplies or consulting services), use (machinery or office equipment) or resale.

There are important differences between business-to-business marketing and consumer marketing. The customers of business marketers are organizations, not individuals, and their motivations are different from consumers making purchases to satisfy their personal or family needs. The organizational buyer is acting for many others in the organization, and is governed by a set of purchasing policies that define the rules of buying.

One of the key requisites for the management of business-to-business marketing is an understanding of organizational buying behaviour. Another is an understanding of how to build and maintain long term customer-supplier relationships and networks. Finally, as in consumer marketing, the international dimension of business-to-business marketing is becoming increasingly important as new international markets open up and international competition increases.

Business-to-business marketing can be examined using the following key concepts: (1) types and characteristics of business markets, which can be illustrated through types of products, services and customers; (2) competitive and cooperative relationships, and the current evolution away from the former and towards the latter; (3) segmentation and positioning of products in a competitive business market; and (4) the use of relationship marketing to manage a customer portfolio.

*Kristian Möller & David T. Wilson*

## Business culture, Japanese

The business culture of Japan is often viewed as being quite different from that of English-speaking countries. However, there is some similarity with continental countries such as Germany, and there are considerable resemblances to the cultures of Korea, China and southeast Asia, the so-called Confucian cultural area. The major features characterizing Japanese business culture are familism, groupism, long-termism or time continuity, and informal, personal and bottom-up forms of decision-making, as seen in concepts such as *nemawashi* and *ringi*. Fundamental elements of Japanese culture come from the notions of *mura* (village) and *ie* (house), themselves of Confucian origin. This may be seen in regional diversity in Japanese business culture, notably between the Kansai and Kanto regions. In the period following the Second World War, business nationalism was also a key feature of Japanese business culture, but following economic success, that nationalism has begun to weaken.

*Etsuo Abe*

## Business culture, North American

During the last several decades there have been major changes in the environment in which business organizations function. New social and political roles have been defined for business in North America as an increasing amount of attention has been devoted to social and political issues such as equal employment opportunity, product safety and quality, pollution control, and workplace health and safety. These concerns have resulted in a proliferation of new laws and regulations and public policies that restrict or redirect business activities that are seen to affect society in an adverse manner. The long-term effect of these laws and policies are a dramatic change in the 'rules of the game' by which business organizations are expected to operate. Thus the business institution has been reshaped to meet these new responsibilities and is continually changing to respond to new social issues.

North American business organizations in the 1990s are affected by faster communication and knowledge acquisition, growing worldwide population, increasing interdependence and competition on limited resources, diversifying political and religious ideologies, constant transitions of power, global ecological distress, and the changing roles of gender, race, age and culture.

*Jane H. Ives*

## Business cultures, European

Most of the countries of Europe, or at least in western Europe, are mature trading and manufacturing nations. As a result, each nation possesses its own unique business culture which has emerged over decades or even centuries. One way of characterizing business cultures in capitalist societies is by their degree of 'hardness' or 'softness'. The business culture of the UK, for example, is probably the 'hardest' in Europe, dominated as it is by the philosophy of the free market and characterized by fierce competition, short-termism and a capacity to change quickly and radically. Germany, in contrast, can be described as a social market economy, with a large wealth-creating manufacturing base, strong partnerships between capital and labour, and a financial system based on long-term thinking and participation by financial institutions. This culture is well suited to the management of long-term change, but it may be questioned as to whether it is well-adapted to dealing with rapid change and short cycles. Finally, business culture in France is characterized by relatively weak participation by labour but a strong partnership between business and the State. Whether business cultures in Europe will ultimately converge or whether European business will continue to enjoy diversity in unity is a question that has yet to be resolved.

*Collin C. Randlesome*

## Business cycles

Business cycle theory seeks to explain the erratic growth of the output of capitalist economies. Business cycles have three elements. The first is the role of shocks which change aggregate demand or supply. Such shocks include the rapid rise of the price of oil in the 1970s, the application of high interest rates by the UK government in 1991 and 1992 to maintain sterling's exchange rate in the exchange rate mechanism, and rapid unexpected increases in the money supply. The second element is the existence of forces which build on the initial shocks to magnify their effects. For example, investment is determined by expectations about future demand, so a shock which damps down output growth *and* expectations for future growth or increases uncertainty will reduce investment. The third element involves endogenous forces which reverse the movements of output caused by shocks or endogenous changes to explain why booms do not persist and slumps give way to expansion.

*Cliff Pratten*

## Business economics

Business economics is concerned with the analysis of the behaviour of firms in markets and industries and with the determination of costs and prices. It therefore differs from the ways in which economics is most commonly used in business, which are concerned with descriptions and forecasts of behaviour in a macroeconomic environment.

The economics of industry, as the term suggests, has generally focused on the industry as its unit of analysis. Firms within the same industry do not differ from each other, or do so only in essentially trivial ways. The structure-conduct-performance paradigm, which is the dominant empirical tradition, describes how the structure of the industry determines the behaviour of individual firms. Since all firms in the same industry face the same external conditions, all can be expected to perform similarly. Differences in the performance of different firms in the same market – the principal concern of senior managers – are not accounted for.

The field of business strategy, quite distinct from business economics, was developed to account for differences in the performance of firms. More recently, however, business economics has also begun to bridge this gap. These developments include game-theoretic models of small-number interactions, the analysis of principal-agent relationships and activity-based costing systems. The resource-based theory of business strategy, which is concerned with the ability of a firm to add value – to create rents or quasi-rents – brings many of these elements of analysis together.

*John Kay*

### Business ethics

Interest in the ethical quality of business transactions is no doubt as old as the first barter exchange between human beings and their concern that it should take place in conditions of honesty and fairness. Such interest has, of course, continued over the millennia, but in modern times the scope of business ethics has increased and ramified as business itself has expanded and developed to assume global dimensions.

Modern business ethics has three major characteristics: corporate accountability, in which large corporations in particular are held accountable for their actions; social responsibility, in which corporations are perceived to have a responsibility to society at large; and stakeholder theory, which widens the spectrum of groups to whom the corporation is accountable from shareholders and regulators to all those with whom it comes into contact. A stakeholder model can be seen as a series of concentric circles, beginning with the company's responsibility to its own employees and then moving out to embrace customers, competitors and the physical environment in which the company is located. Much research attention has been and is being devoted to business ethics, and it is likely that this will continue to be a subject of importance in the near future.

*Jack Mahoney*

### Business history

The evolution of business history as an academic discipline began at Harvard Business School in the 1920s. This business school environment played an important role in making the case study the main methodological tool of the new subject. It was Harvard-based scholars who set the initial research agendas, first on the role of entrepreneurship and, from the 1950s, on business organizations. Business history also developed outside the USA but the institutional settings and research agendas differed. Japanese scholars, working mainly in faculties of commerce, stressed international comparative methodologies. European business history was closely allied to economic history and for a long time focused on writing company histories. Only recently have these diverse national and institutional influences begun to fully merge to produce a more coherent discipline.

The literature has evolved over time from being largely composed of well-researched company histories to a wider study of the business history. Although company case studies offered a realistic view of business, commissioned company histories made it hard to generalize or to make inter-company comparisons. The work of Alfred Chandler demonstrated how select case studies could be employed to explore major themes in the growth and performance of organizations. This represented a major advance in business history literature and marked its arrival as a mature discipline.

Recent research trends have been towards establishing business history as an integrative force in management studies. The research agenda has widened from entrepreneurship and organization to a considerable number of business-related issues and work is progressing towards building predictive models of business.

*Geoffrey Jones*

## Business information

Information plays an increasingly critical role in international business, both as a resource and as a commodity. The volume of information available to businesses has grown rapidly since the 1970s, and the speed with which this information can be accessed has increased by an order of magnitude with the introduction of new communications technology. However, these increases have not always been accompanied by a corresponding increase in the quality of information.

There are many different types of business information, and a multiplicity of sources of information. A key distinction is that between primary sources of information (information collected by the business through direct research or surveys) and secondary information (information which has already been collected but which needs to be analysed). A corresponding and related difference is that between information which is available publicly and that which is restricted in access.

All business processes depend to some extent on information in order to reduce risk in decision making and strategy formulation. The management of information is now a central management function in most businesses, particularly in larger companies and those that operate internationally. Information management is defined as obtaining timely, accurate and relevant information and communicating it to employees at all levels within the business and thus includes information gathering, interpreting and storage in a logical system. Information management systems, usually based on some form of computer software program, can help to reduce complexity, improve access to information and speed information flows. It must be noted, however, that these systems will be of less value unless the company first sets firm priorities as to the types of information it wishes to collect and the uses to which that information will be put.

*Anne Jenkins & Morgen Witzel*

## Business schools

Since the founding of the first business school during the 1880s, there has been continual controversy concerning the role of the business school and the relative emphasis that should be placed on theoretical as opposed to practical training. Throughout the 1950s, business schools focused too heavily on the rudiments of running a business. Faced with a credibility crisis on research-orientated campuses, there was a significant movement during the 1970s and 1980s to increase the sophistication of business education and research. However, the pendulum swung too far and the 1990s have witnessed a movement back toward the practical needs of the business community.

The philosophy of a broad education with a specialization in business pervades undergraduate programmes in business. Seeking relevance, masters' programmes have adopted a thematic approach that promotes the critical skills cited most frequently by leading executives. These themes include communication, interpersonal and leadership skills, international perspectives, total quality principles, teamwork, business ethics, information systems and familiarity with new technologies. Other significant issues confronting business schools include lifelong learning strategies, achieving diversity across the academic staff and students, enhancing career services in the light of the downsizing of major employers and providing a technological infrastructure capable of maintaining pace with the rapidly changing business environment. The successful business school continues to evolve into an entity that supports a wide variety of activities, ranging from the teaching of practical skills to the conduct of abstract research.

The top business schools share the following characteristics: (1) an internationally recognized research-orientated academic staff that includes experts in all of the core functional areas in business – accounting, finance, management and marketing; (2) highly respected academic programmes at one or more of the levels of undergraduate, master's and doctorate; (3) a set of highly respected specialized, or 'niche', programmes; (4) excellent contacts and interactions with the business community and an extensive lifelong learning programme; (5) excellent funding from external sources; (6) an excellent technological infrastructure with respect to facilities and use of technology throughout the curriculum; (7) an excellent career services operation; and (8) a sound excellent network of supporters and good publicity.

*Andrew J. Policano*

## Business and society

The study of business and society includes all the interfaces between business organizations and the wider community in which they are set. While traditionally it was not considered part of business management to influence the operation of these interfaces, in the modern world managers must be as active in these interfaces as they are within their own firms. Advertising, public relations and market research have an important impact on the public image of the firm, while the firm's activities in its physical environment are widely seen as a measure of its ethical standards. Inside the firm, technological changes can have major impacts on industrial relations and human resource management. Political changes, especially new laws and new taxes, and demographic changes are also important influences on business. All of these contribute to the need on the part of modern managers for general social awareness as well as managerial skills.

*Edmund Marshall*

## Business systems

Business systems are distinctive ways of organizing economic activities that develop interdependently with dominant institutions in market economies. They have three major components: the nature of firms as economic actors; the nature of market relations between firms; and the nature of coordination and control systems within firms. These components vary on sixteen dimensions which together characterize different forms of economic organization. These differences arise from variations in processes of industrialization and in key institutions governing economic activities. Major background institutions which affect the sorts of business systems that become established are the cultural conventions which govern: (1) trust relations between exchange partners; (2) dominant forms of collective identity and loyalty; and (3) norms regulating authority relations. Other critical institutions are state structures and policies, the organization of the financial system and those governing the development and availability of different kinds of skills in labour markets. Changes in business systems occur interdependently with changes in these institutions as well as from the increasing interdependence of, and competition between, market economies.

*Richard Whitley*

# C

## Capital, cost of

The cost of capital is perhaps the single most important strategic variable, providing the principal benchmark for both investment appraisal and performance measurement. The standard measurement of the cost of capital is a weighted average of the costs of debt and equity in which the weights are the respective proportions of intended debt and equity financing; this is known as the weighted average cost of capital (WACC). There are different ways of calculating WACC, however, and it is also possible to adapt the WACC to take account of differing risk levels of projects. It is also important to build in predicted inflation rates, and to do so in a consistent manner; this becomes particularly important and complex when calculating the cost of capital in the appraisal of international projects. Although WACC is a very valuable tool in investment decision making, it is important to realize that each project has its own inherent WACC and not to fall into the trap of using the same WACC for every project.

*Jack Broyles*

## Capital markets, regulation of

Regulation of capital markets is needed to prevent 'market failure' in the form of shocks to the financial system and the exploitation of ill-informed customers, but the scope of regulation may also reflect the interests of firms which benefit from the reduction in competition which regulation may cause.

Regulation brings costs as well as benefits, and it remains to be clearly demonstrated that these costs have been worth bearing in all areas. Undue risk-taking may even be stimulated, as in the case of deposit insurance.

Regulation now incorporates internationally agreed minimum ratios of bank capital to assets (bank deposit liabilities are so far ignored). This is open to various objections, such as the neglect of correlation between the returns on different assets, the use of book values and the international variety of accounting methods. Positions in financial instruments, however, will be regulated on the basis of market values, reflecting liabilities as well as assets. Regulation may therefore become more complex and costly, perhaps diverting business to less regulated types of firm and to new centres.

*Harold Rose*

## Capital structure

The capital structure question is concerned with the factors that determine the optimum balance (if any) of equity and debt used to finance companies. It is one of the key areas in the economics of corporate finance, since it has implications for new security issues, the financing of takeover and buyout activity, and also dividend policy, since retained earnings – the profits retained by a firm after payment of dividends – are a major source of equity funding. The considered view prior to the modern analytical approaches pioneered by Modigliani and Miller in the late 1950s was that a moderate amount of debt finance (in the form of corporate bonds, debentures or loan stock) was beneficial, but that higher levels were not prudent – indeed, high corporate debt levels had been cited as one of the factors causing the great stock market crash of 1929. Their analysis pointed initially to the irrelevancy of the debt–equity split, and in later work to advantages to debt finance as a result of corporate tax effects. Miller subsequently integrated personal taxes into the framework and argued that the tax advantages of borrowing were small. In addition to this 'fundamental' analysis of the problem, there have been numerous other theoretical approaches based on information economics, agency theory, *ad hoc* theories such as the 'pecking order hypothesis' and other ideas. Empirical evidence is weakly supportive of a tax effect but the evidence for the existence of a generalized optimal level of gearing or leverage is weak.

The main conclusion to be drawn from the diverse literature on capital structure and financing decisions is the absence of any universal consensus on optimal financing structure. The four principal theoretical perspectives which emerge are (1) the fundamentalists, who do not agree on any optimal course of action when choosing between debt and equity, (2) agency theory, in which the optimal capital structure is obtained by trading off the agency cost of debt against the benefit of debt, (3) the 'pecking order' theory, whose proponents argue that firms should finance investment through retained earnings as a first choice, then debt and lastly equity, and (4) signalling theory, where information asymmetry is assumed between management and shareholders, thus in theory favouring debt over equity.

*Ian Davidson & Chris Mallin*

## Careers

The historical view of a career has been of a progression up an organization and an occupation which we chose near the beginning of our working lives. Events have overtaken this model. Increased competition, cost competitiveness, information technology and customer focus have all resulted in de-manning and de-layering of organization structures.

Organizations have removed the rungs of the career ladder and instead are concentrating on the optimal use of their 'human resources'.

The study of careers and of the interventions designed to develop them has changed accordingly. The move is away from the determinants of success, where success is defined as position achieved in the corporate hierarchy, towards understanding how individuals construe their careers, how they might better manage them and what is the appropriate relationship between organization and employee. Above all, current research and theory seeks to place careers in the context of individual, organizational and environmental change.

*Peter Herriot*

## Cash flow accounting

Cash flow accounting (CFA) is a formal term which originated in the UK accounting theory literature of the early 1970s. It has become an important part of the language of worldwide accounting practice. CFA describes a system of accounting designed to provide information about the periodic cash inflows and outflows of a reporting entity.

CFA statements are communicated to a variety of internal and external decision makers, and take different forms depending on their specific needs. For example, CFA statements for internal management purposes usually include information on forecast and actual cash flows. However, CFA statements for external use are based solely on historical data required by regulation.

CFA data describe physical movements of cash resources to and from a reporting entity. They are derived from its cash transactions, and accounted for without adjustment for accruals or allocations. CFA avoids many of the measurement problems inherent in conventional accounting. However, CFA data require to be classified for reporting purposes. The main categories of cash flow describe the operating, investing and financing activities of a reporting entity. When articulated in report form, they provide a decision maker with information useful for assessing the liquidity performance of the entity and its management. More specifically, a CFA statement describes the extent to which the entity is dependent on internal and external cash funding, and the uses to which such funding is put by its management.

CFA statements are distinguishable from conventional financial statements, which describe a reporting entity's financial performance in terms of profit and financial position. Conventional statements describe its overall financial performance and, in particular, its profitability. CFA statements focus on the liquidity aspects of that performance. Thus, in practice, CFA statements form part of a total package of financial information. However, in theory, they have been considered as a complete system of financial accounting and reporting.

*Tom Lee*

## Central and eastern Europe, transition of economies of

The economic transition of eastern and central Europe is a multi-phase process of abandoning communist economic institutions and mechanisms and replacing them with market structures and dynamics. This process takes place on both macro (national economy) and micro (firm) levels.

On the macro level, six phases of this process have been identified: the political phase, the early 'marketization' phase, the inflation control phase, the phase of building market institutions, the anti-recession economic policies phase and the growth policy phase. Within this context, the economies of central and eastern Europe are highly diversified; they include institutionally mature economies, economies which are still building institutions, monetarily unstable economies and politically unstable economies.

On the micro level, enterprises can be divided into five types: large, low-value-added state-owned enterprises in heavy industries; enterprises producing higher value-added marketable products; small businesses; large private enterprises; and enterprises with foreign capital participation (joint ventures). These different types of enterprise each face different transition problems in different economies.

*Andrzej K. Kozminski*

## Channel management

Distribution channels are the means by which goods and services pass from producers to consumers as part of the exchange process. Channel management is concerned with the design and selection of distribution channels and the implementation of channel strategy. Design and selection requires the establishment of channel objectives, consideration of customer requirements, costs and marketing mix compatibility, and development of an evaluation framework. Implementation of channel strategy involves motivating channel partners, management of conflict, performance assessment and adaptation of channel design. Channel management is playing an increasingly important role in marketing strategy, and the development and maintenance of efficient relationships among organizations is a critical factor in achieving competitive success. However, channels are often extremely complex; only rarely will a firm be involved in only one distribution channel, and typically several channel structures will need to be managed in order to ensure broad market coverage, appeal to different market segments or achieve deeper penetration of target markets. The complexities of channel management are also increased when firms begin working in international markets.

*Donald J. Bowersox & M. Bixby Cooper*

## Cognition

How do managers perceive the situations and the problems they face? How do they build mental representations of these situations? Indeed, how do they reason about these situations and problems? Understanding how managers – and other actors – reach conclusions about the organizational world in which they work has been, from the start, a key question in management science. A deeper understanding of managers' cognitive processes can give us a better grasp of their decision making, and, more broadly, of organizational behaviour in general.

Recent developments in cognitive sciences provide valuable insight on these matters. Drawn from a very wide range of scientific fields, cognitive science studies highlight cognitive processes at three distinct levels: individuals, groups and more complex sets which combine people, offices, objects, texts and so forth. At the level of the individual, Herbert Simon's idea of bounded rationality has been the cornerstone of management science thinking since it was introduced in 1955 – as well as being probably the most influential contribution since Max Weber's discussion of rationality types. The technique of cognitive mapping has been increasingly adopted as a tool to capture mental processes. On the experimental front, developments in experimental psychology have vigorously challenged many traditional hypotheses. For instance, they have disproved the notion that decisions and actions flow 'naturally' from reasoning and have demonstrated the complexity of the relationship between reason and action.

Such advances have led to fresh approaches to the analysis of collective cognition. Among the many theories being developed, we mostly find questions regarding interactive rationality, organizational learning, organizational memory and collective intelligence.

Finally, extensive work on group cognition has led to one of the most outstanding contributions of the cognitive sciences to management science: the concept of distributed cognition. In this perspective, complex systems created from mixed components such as people, offices, objects, publications, etc. have been identified as the locus of cognitive activity. Memory, intelligence and reason can thus be seen as properties of such systems rather than just limited to individuals.

*Jacques Girin*

## Collective bargaining

Collective bargaining can be defined as the institutionalized process by which workers (usually combined into unions) negotiate with employers with the aim of jointly determining terms and conditions of employment. Collective bargaining is institutionalized because the process in each country and industry is circumscribed by laws, customs and rituals which make the parties' relationships predictable.

Collective bargaining can be justified on the assumption that bargaining between management and individual employees gives management an unfair advantage. To counterbalance this advantage, employees band together to bargain collectively. There are substantial differences in forms of collective bargaining, depending on the nature of representation, bargaining structure and the nature of the agreement. Despite these differences, however, collective bargaining tends to follow a fairly common procedure, during which both parties employ various tactics to put pressure on each other and middlemen or third-party negotiators often play a key role. Bargaining has tended to be dependent on union strength, but with unions on the decline and new forms of workplace participation emerging, it is difficult to see what the future of collective bargaining will be.

*George Strauss*

## Commitment

Commitment to work and commitment to an organization are essentially two different concepts, although they are related to one another. Studies of job satisfaction and job involvement have in the past tended to focus primarily on jobs, ignoring the organizations to which the employees belong. However, recent concerns have been more organization-orientated, with increasing interest in organizational commitment as the secret of raising productivity. More and more employees have been encouraged to commit through an intensive socialization process, which now plays a key role in the formation of an integrated management system, alongside the development of an internal labour market and articulation of a unique company philosophy.

As the interest in commitment has increased, so too has the amount of research. Various discoveries have been made. First, the concept was split into sub-categories, usually dichotomic: a typical distinction is attitudinal commitment versus calculative commitment, with the former playing a larger part in employee commitment. Second, although the determinants used for organizational commitment tended to be wide-ranging (for example, personal and job characteristics, organizational characteristics, labour market conditions and the organizational framework of human resource management), employee internalization, identification, compliance, and the like were found to be closely related to the concept. Third, organizational commitment was found to influence employees' withdrawal behaviours: although it was found in past research not to have any positive impact on organizational performance and labour productivity, it did impact on employees' intentions to search for other jobs.

Japanese management, for example, continues to pay great attention to promoting employees' commitment to their organizations, especially in the case of young newcomers, through orientation, on-the-job training, small group activities and big brother and sister groups.

The concept of organizational commitment has grown in range over the years, becoming increasingly abstract. Organizational commitment was originally intended as a tool with which to manage human resources within a hierarchical organizational structure with a large number of employees. Such organizations are now decreasing in number, with the unit of activities becoming smaller. However, due to its potential for increasing productivity, whatever their form, strategies to encourage commitment will continue to be important in managing human resources in the future.

*Yoko Sano*

## Commodities

Commodities are unprocessed products which account for a diminishing but still sizeable share of world trade. Commodities include very different products, ranging from agricultural and mineral products to crude oil. Commodity markets tend to be unstable due to absolutely low price elasticities of export supply and import demand as well as rather strong fluctuations in world supply and demand. The commodity terms of trade between non-oil commodities and manufactured imports tend to fall in the long run as a consequence of comparatively low income elasticities of commodity demand and relatively high technical progress in commodity production.

International commodity policies such as international price stabilization and compensatory financing schemes, which were designed to affect the level and instability of commodity export earnings in developing countries, have had only very limited success. Given this widespread failure of international market stabilization, it has to be borne in mind that domestic commodity and economic policies can be targeted at the level and instability of commodity earnings, for example by cutting down domestic disincentives against commodity production and by using existing financial markets to stabilize export earnings.

*Roland Herrmann*

## Communication

Effective communication is essential for the management of organizations. Individuals within the organization may be involved in oral, written and visual communication with those above or below them in the organizational hierarchy, laterally with colleagues in other departments and externally. Effective interpersonal skills are required to overcome barriers to communication and to not only communicate with others but to enable them to communicate with you. Cultural factors and organizational structure can both create major barriers to communication, while increased use of electronic communication media provides ways of overcoming these but also poses problems of its own.

*W. David Rees*

## Communication, cross-cultural

In the literature on cross-cultural communication, the terms 'cross-cultural communication', 'intercultural communication' and 'international communication' are frequently used interchangeably. Although 'cross-cultural communication' and 'intercultural communication' can be treated synonymously, an important distinction needs to be made between 'cross-cultural communication' and 'international communication'. 'International communication' takes place across political or national borders while 'cross-cultural communication' takes place across cultures.

*Culture* can be defined as a community's shared values, attitudes, behaviour and acts of communicating which are passed from one generation to the next. *Communication* means a goal-directed and context-bound exchange of meaning between two or more parties. In other words, communication takes place between people for a specific reason in a particular medium and environment. An American meets a Japanese to negotiate a business deal. The context in which the purpose of communication takes place can be either within the same culture or across different cultures. In the example given, the business negotiation takes place across different cultures. Communication is therefore a culture-bound activity. To communicate means expressing the uniqueness of one's cultural heritage, and this includes not only the verbal and non-verbal peculiarities but also the preferred medium and context of communication.

The scope of cross-cultural communication is extremely wide. It is a multidisciplinary field of study with roots in anthropology, sociology, psychology, cognition and linguistics, among other disciplines. In business and management, understanding cross-cultural communication is very important not only in managing people but in marketing between cultures. Growing economic convergence and the increasing globalization of the economy is making cross-cultural communication even more important than before.

*Joo-Seng Tan*

## Competitive strategies, development of

The ability to define and guide the activities that turn the inputs to a business into outputs is the essence of management. At one extreme, these activities are manageable on a day-to-day basis, with managers responding to problems and minor changes in operating conditions; this is operations management. At the other extreme are management decisions that will launch the firm on a trajectory that is expected to continue for a number of years; the long-term character of these decisions is what makes them 'strategic'. In this entry the notion of a firm's distinctive or core competence is used as the anchor to develop an analytical framework – the strategic 'double diamond' – that can provide a useful structure for considering fundamental strategic issues about competition.

Many models have been developed for the content, implementation, evaluation and change of strategy. Any management textbook is likely to have one. A popular format is the 'double diamond' which reflects the interaction between the major elements of strategy formulation and implementation. Its advantage is in the important linkages that are formed between these elements; viewing any single aspect of this model individually is a useful simplifying exercise, though in practice they are necessarily considered in unison.

Strategic management often distinguishes between formulating and implementing strategy. The distinction between the two is not a line that can be clearly drawn, but it is useful for purposes of illustration. In practice, for strategy to become truly institutionalized and successful, it must be a continual process incorporating analysis, action, feedback and adjustment. All four of those elements may occur simultaneously.

For most firms, strategy is a process of reorientation and change, not of first-time development. To be most successful, the process must be continual, incorporating change within the framework of a consistent theme or guiding vision. The process is very unlikely to become continual without a clear commitment from top management to developing feedback mechanisms that can incorporate change into the firm's activities.

*Phil Gorman, Mark Pruett & Howard Thomas*

## Conflict and politics

From Aristotle to contemporary political theory, by way of Machiavelli, Montesquieu, de Tocqueville, Marx and Weber, many social theorists have pointed to the essentially political character of human relations in social systems, of which organizations are an example.

Strikes, plant occupations, boycotts, denunciations in the press, demonstrations, legal action, meetings, negotiations, important decisions, manoeuvring, group strategies, career appointments, influence peddling, work-to-rule action, hidden resistance and open battle provide but few examples of the political life in an organization.

Those who have studied such occurrences have not always made it a priority to explain conflict and politics within such organizations. Indeed, since they were often constrained by a mechanistic and a functional approach to organizations, many analysts hid or denied such problems or simply treated them as social phenomena that needed to be eliminated. Nevertheless, one must appreciate that tension and conflict are central to political life, which is at the heart of the entire social order. The social sciences in general and anthropology, sociology and political science in particular, constantly remind us of this fact.

*Jean-François Chanlat*

## Consolidated accounting

Consolidated financial statements are the financial statements of a group of individual entities combined together by a process of consolidation and presented as the statements of the group as if the group were a single enterprise. The consolidation process involves adjusting and combining the individual financial statements of the entities on a line-by-line basis (that is, by adding together corresponding items of assets, liabilities, equity, revenues and expenses). The consolidated statements are the statements of an *economic entity* rather than those of a single legal entity, the economic entity consisting of the combined net assets of a number of legal entities. The consolidated financial statements generally consist of a consolidated balance sheet and a consolidated profit and loss account (income statement) but may include a consolidated cash flow statement. The main entity in the economic entity is referred to as the *parent entity* or parent undertaking, and the other entities as *subsidiaries* or subsidiary undertakings.

In preparing the consolidated statements, one of the key decisions is determining which entities are to be included in the economic entity. This decision is affected by the objectives of preparing the statements. The consolidation process itself, often undertaken using a worksheet or computer spreadsheet, involves adjusting for investments held by a parent entity in a subsidiary and for transactions between the members of the economic entity. The adjustments for the investment by a parent entity in a subsidiary involve an analysis of the acquisition of shares or other ownership equity by a parent in a subsidiary, which necessitates an analysis of the fair values of the net assets of the subsidiary at the date of acquisition, including any goodwill in the subsidiary. The relative wealth of the parent entity equity holders and equity holders apart from the parent entity, called the minority interest, is also reported.

The preparation of consolidated statements throughout the world is not uniform. Legislation and accounting standards in separate countries produce different rules. The use of variations, such as equity accounting, the pooling of interests, method and proportional consolidation, differs between countries.

*Ken Leo*

## Consumer behaviour

Consumer behaviour as a subject for serious study is relatively new; books on the subject began appearing only in the late 1960s. The subject itself, however, is as old as the commercial world. All of us consume, exchange, buy, influence and are influenced every day of our lives, and our behaviour during these processes is what defines consumer behaviour. Much of the study of this subject to date has focused on consumers as purchasers of goods, but increasingly the underlying principles of consumer behaviour are being studied with a view to their utilization in the marketing of services, charities, political messages and other non-commercial 'products'.

The other principal focus of consumer behaviour studies has been on individuals as consumers, with examination of the factors which influence individual purchasing decisions. However, consumer behaviour can also logically be extended to include industrial and organizational buying and purchasing behaviour.

The main body of knowledge to date has been developed in much the same way as theories of organizational behaviour, from concepts in psychology and sociology; there has also been input from economics and psychiatry. Theories of consumer behaviour and organizational behaviour have many similarities and common elements; the only major difference is the end focus, which is on the consumer rather than the employee.

Consumer behaviour is a vitally important subject: without a proper understanding of it, marketers will be unable to analyse and meet consumer needs. The issues are further complicated by the fact that consumer behaviour itself is unpredictable, dynamic and constantly changing.

*Chris Rice*

## Coordination and control

Coordination is a central concept in business studies that is shared by economists, sociologists and management scientists. Economists distinguish between two types of coordination, the 'invisible hand' in which coordination is an unconscious function of competition and exchange, and conscious coordination guided either by an entrepreneur or a bureaucratic structure. Another view is to define types of coordination by whether they are cognition-based (using the ability to transfer know-how through standards and methods, evaluate expected effects and evaluate professional skills) or relation-based (coordinating through hierarchy, power and leadership and making promises or bargains through a process of mutual adjustment). Most coordination systems use a mixture of both. Although past theory on this subject has created typologies, the need today is for coordination mechanisms that are adapted to dynamic and uncertain contexts and which correspond to design processes or the competitive environment.

*Armand Hatchuel*


## Corporate control

For investment, employment and productivity, advanced industrial econo-mies depend heavily on 'big business', publicly-owned corporations with capitalizations of hundreds of millions of dollars and workforces of tens of thousands of people. A cross-national comparison, the evolution and impact of financial control in the USA, Japan, Germany and the UK over the past century shows that while all four national economies have stock markets that can facilitate the exercise of market control over corpora-tions, yet the relationship between shareholding and corporate control differs markedly across these nations. Within each nation, moreover, the relation between organizational control and market control has changed over time. In terms of the balance between organizational control and market control for each nation, the Japanese and German experiences reflecting the dominance of organizational control, while the US and UK experiences reflecting the dominance of market control. In general, it can be concluded that organizational control is a necessary condition both for innovation and competitive advantage at the level of the enterprise and for sustained economic development at the level of the economy.

*William Lazonick & Mary O'Sullivan*


## Corporate governance

Throughout the developed world, corporate boards play an important role in the governance of publicly owned corporations. In most developed countries, they are intended to oversee the conduct of management on behalf of shareholders and/or other stakeholders. The structures and practices of boards vary across national boundaries, as boards have evolved according to each country's history, culture, laws and economy. None the less, boards in the developed world share many of the same challenges in their efforts to monitor corporate performance. During the 1980s and 1990s there have been calls, particularly in the USA and the UK, for directors to be made more active, independent or accountable, and both countries have seen reforms to corporate governance which have stressed accountability and public scrutiny of board activities. It is possi-ble that in the future there will be a greater degree of convergence of practices in boardrooms around the world, although cultural variables will continue to ensure a certain amount of diversity.

*Jay Lorsch & Samantha K. Graff*


## Corporate pension fund

Most employees can now look forward to a retirement lasting twenty years and some will live for more than thirty years after retiring. Income in retirement comes from various sources, with the basic level generally being met by state provision. In a few countries state provision is still sufficient to cover all the needs of most employees, but in most countries the state provides at best only basic cover. Individuals need to look either to their employers or to private savings to provide sufficient income in retirement.

Companies in many countries have found that to attract and retain a loyal workforce, it has become necessary to offer an attractive occupational pension to supplement state provision. Because of the substantial sums needed (often amounting to several times annual pay by retirement), pension benefits are often the most expensive element of a remuneration package after direct pay itself. A company first needs to satisfy itself why corporate provision should be made for pensions rather than leave the employee wholly to their own devices. Having established this, the next step is to design a package of benefits to meet the requirements of both employee and employer, including not just the quantum of benefit, but also how any investment risks involved should be shared.

In most countries pension funds are given attractive tax concessions to encourage saving for retirement. Often, limits will be put on the amount of provision that could be made in order to limit the extent of that tax advantage, and account would need to be taken of these limits in designing benefit implications. Because pension benefits will be paid many years after the service giving rise to them was completed, by which time the company may no longer exist, it is usual for contributions to corporate pension funds to be paid to an independent fund and invested over the long interim period. Decisions will need to be made about how such assets should be invested, and how the cost is to be met over time, which will depend in part on accounting principles and practices, and in part on the need for security for members, which may involve minimum levels set by legislation.

Despite being simple in concept, corporate pensions are complex in practice, because of the various constraints on them. Proper administration and communication with employees is necessary to ensure their worth is appreciated.

*A.F. Wilson*

## Corporate performance, analysis of

Corporate performance is at the heart of the managerial function of an industrial enterprise. In order for management to make decisions about future actions, it needs to know how the enterprise has performed in the past, whether it has met its objectives and, if not, why not. It also needs to examine ways in which performance can be improved in the future.

Analysis of corporate performance is mainly concerned with the development of a modelling methodology to help in the diagnosis of past performance and thus provide a framework for evaluating the effect of changes in operating parameters as a guide for future planning. The emphasis is on a *methodology*, to be distinguished from a set of recipes that merely prescribe remedies without the necessary analysis of the complex relationships that impinge on the economics of the firm.

*Samuel Eilon*

## Corporate planning, process of

As the size and internal complexity of a business increases, its ability to develop and implement successful strategies in an informal manner typically diminishes. The corporate planning process is a means by which future strategies, and plans for their implementation, can be formally discussed, developed, documented and controlled. Effective formal planning brings a range of benefits to companies. The requirement to produce formal plans encourages managers to gather strategically important information, to analyse it in the search for better strategies and then to think through the implications that favoured strategies will have for the different management functions. These are all tasks which are vital for the future success of a business, but which can be almost indefinitely postponed if companies become too preoccupied with today's 'firefighting' to engage in fire prevention.

A formal planning process helps managers at the centre of a multi-product/market business to develop overall strategies for the company, to encourage the development of synergies between the component businesses and to allocate corporate resources most effectively among them. Corporate planning can also play an important part in controlling a business. It provides a mechanism through which the development of strategies for the components of a business can be influenced and coordinated, and through which progress towards strategic objectives can be measured. The development of formal contingency plans can also ensure that strategies can be abandoned or amended in a controlled manner, which is important for companies faced with an increasingly unpredictable environment.

The introduction of a formal corporate planning process brings no guarantee of better strategies or successful plans. Many corporate planning initiatives have failed to improve company performance because they were poorly designed or poorly implemented. A successful planning process needs to be flexible, user-friendly and designed to suit the structure, culture and level of sophistication of the company. It also needs to support the planning efforts of the managers involved, through the provision of useful information, guidance and relevant planning techniques.

*Ken Peattie*

## Corporate strategic change

Understanding and managing corporate change has become increasingly important in the turbulent environment of the modern world. Systematic theories of corporate change originated with 'scientific management' in the late nineteenth century and have evolved throughout the twentieth century. Major twentieth-century contributions came from human relations and organization development theories of change, which were primarily people-centred. Sociotechnical systems theory in total quality management then provided a necessary balance by stressing the need to take into account change in the technical systems of the organization as well.

The dominant change theory today is the strategic approach, which assumes a marketplace where organizations are acting as purposive competitors, managers are rational decision makers and corporations are passive tools producing the outcomes of planners. There is, however, no one accepted theory of corporate change; all theories are partial, are affected by their sociocultural origins and are in part ideological. The rational strategic model, for instance, has been attacked on the grounds that rationality is always likely to be bounded. It has been argued variously from different perspectives that change should be radical or that it should be incremental, or that change should be driven by leaders or through empowerment. It is apparent that there is a need for global or cross-cultural theories of change that transcend current ethnocentric approaches, and also that there is a need for a valid action research model for collaborative research between institutions and corporations.

*Dexter Dunphy*

## Corporatism

Corporatism describes a form of organizational behaviour in which associations, while representing the particular interests of their members, also discipline them in the interests of some wider collectivity. It has mainly been used to describe systems of industrial relations, although it can be more widely applied to the role of certain kinds of trade association and other industry bodies outside the sphere of labour.

Its significance is that it might enable firms, unions of employees and other participants in a market economy to achieve a high level of cooperation and shared pursuit of collective goods that also serve a wider public interest, despite the fact that they are also in competition with one another. Associations will act in this way only under certain specific and rather precisely balanced situations of organizational design. Within modern social science the concept of corporatism should therefore be used with care and precision. This can be difficult given that it has had a long and strange history. It has mainly been associated with northern Europe, but also with Japan. Some economic branches, in particular agriculture, tend to be corporatist in a wider range of countries. Corporatism enjoyed a peak period of both actual performance and theoretical recognition during the 1970s, since when it has undergone important challenges and changed its form.

*Colin Crouch*

## Costing

A costing system constitutes one of the most important elements of the managerial information system. Its presence enables the organization to meet three objectives. First, it enables the organization to effect managerial control. Without a costing system, organizations would not be able to make managers at all levels accountable for the costs of the resources they consume and identify whether they have been used efficiently and effectively. Second, cost information is an important element of the planning and decision-making process. Businesses develop, produce and market products and services. Identifying which products and services to bring to market would not be possible without a product costing system. Third, most organizations are legally bound to provide reports to external parties. The costing system serves to facilitate this legal requirement.

Poorly constructed costing systems can lead to poor or bad decision making. If the determination of product costs is inadequate, firms may be sourcing inputs inefficiently and producing products that fail to bring them a competitive advantage. Furthermore, the system of responsibility accounting may be rewarding managers for making these poor decisions.

Decentralization of costing, with the establishment of responsibility centres within the organization, can facilitate managerial planning and control. Responsibility centres are often classified into two types, production centres and service centres. Service centres provide services to other centres, and the costs accumulated in these centres are often reallocated to the responsible production or operating centres. Overhead costs can also be allocated in different ways: the two principal ones are absorption costing, where fixed production overheads are considered a product cost, or contribution costing, where overheads are considered a period cost.

The most important costing systems are job costing and process costing. Job costing is literally the costing of each job; this has its drawbacks in that it produces only an estimated product cost, as actual overheads are unknown at the time when the product cost is required. Process costing is used when homogeneous units of output are produced repeatedly through a sequence of processes, but it too produces only an estimated product cost, and neither system takes into account the accumulated costs of other activities such as marketing and distribution. More recently, simpler systems such as backflush costing and operational costing (a hybrid of job and process costing) have come into use.

*A.R. Appleyard*

### Cost–volume–profit relationships

Cost-volume-profit (CVP) analysis provides a model of the relationships between volume sold, costs incurred and profit realized. It relies upon the distinction between variable costs and fixed costs, which is made on the sole basis of volume. There are several forms of this model, including: the basic model, established for single-product firms; an adaptation of this model for companies producing multiple products; several more sophisticated 'probabilistic' models. CVP analysis enables the economic evaluation of short-run decisions. It relies upon simple hypotheses, which necessarily distance the model from reality and thus need validating before relevant usage.

The development of new management forms, especially in the field of industrial organization, makes the validity of these hypotheses more and more open to question. The basic distinction between variable and fixed costs was indeed consistent with a former strategic logic. The emergence of new approaches has given rise to the search for new cost behaviour patterns and new cost analysis methods. Activity-based costing may be viewed as an enlargement and an enrichment of the basic CVP model, which none the less retains a certain conceptual value.

*Annick Bourguignon*

### Country risk analysis

Country risk analysis has been undergoing systematic development since the late 1970s, when it became understood that better tools were needed for understanding the risks of investment in developing countries. The primary emphasis of country risk analysis is on credit risk, but secondary factors such as economic policy and political risk are now routinely covered as well. Financial risk indicators include a number of key ratios such as total external debt to GDP, total debt-service to exports, savings to investment and current account to GDP. Policy risk and political risk factors are less easy to quantify and calculate. The former include fiscal, monetary and export policy, government attitude to foreign investment, consistency of policy and the size and performance of the public sector; the latter aim to assess the ability of the government in power to both manage the economy and meet its external commitments. Although it can only be used as a general guide, country risk can offer companies good advice in determining which markets are worth investing in and which are best left on the sidelines.

*André Astrow, Mina Toksöz & Howard Smith*

## Creativity management

Creative actions are a primary source of organizational learning, development, innovation and, ultimately, competitive advantage. Research on creativity in organizational and professional settings has revealed a number of individual and contextual influences that facilitate creative behaviour. However, this literature is not well organized and has not led to clear practical guidelines for creativity management. Using the diverse findings presented by previous empirical research, it is possible to develop a model of creativity that accounts for the distinctive features of organizational settings. From this model can be derived a number of practical guidelines for effective creative management. Among these are (1) the encouragement of challenges to current ways of thinking, (2) the need to stress that creativity and change will lead to advantage, (3) the development of a culture of trust, credibility and support, (4) the establishment of goals that explicitly contain creative elements, (5) the cultivation of an attitude of focused freedom, and (6) the association of creative efforts with specific evaluative domains and problems. Creativity in the context of organizations has its own unique character, and managing creativity in organizations demands its own brand of creativity.

*Cameron M. Ford & Dennis A. Gioia*

## Credit management

Credit is a term usually used to refer to the transfer of money, goods or services on the promise of repayment at a future date. Thus it represents an amount of money that will be paid at some future date, in return for benefits received earlier. Credit is sometimes used to refer to the financial standing or status of a business or individual, that is, an amount of money for which the business/individual can be trusted. More formally, credit can be defined as the capacity that an individual or organization has for getting economic value on trust, in return for an expected future repayment. Credit is both provided (by the creditor) and taken (by the debtor). Credit is thus a cooperative (trust) relationship between seller and buyer or between creditor and debtor in which both parties stand to benefit in some way.

There are many types of transaction which involve creditors and debtors. It is common to classify different classes of credit as follows. First, trade credit or commercial credit is where businesses deliver goods or services at home or abroad on invoices to be paid later. This represents credit that businesses extend to one another to finance the production and distribution of goods. Second, there is bank credit, which involves long- or short-term financing to individuals or businesses. In the latter case, it finances working capital or the acquisition of plant and equipment. This can be represented by the issuance of bonds or other proofs of indebtedness. A subcategory would be property credit, consisting of mortgages secured on real estate. Finally, there is consumer or personal credit, which comprises advances made to individuals to enable them to purchase goods or services on a deferred payment basis.There is a wide variety of consumer credit products available and financial services companies are always introducing more, but most products can be classified as either revolving credit or fixed-term credit.

*Nicholas Wilson*

## Crisis management

Crisis management deals with disruptive situations that challenge the basic assumptions and operating procedures of organizations. It developed rapidly in the 1980s as enterprises recognized their increased vulnerability to an uncertain and rapidly changing business environment. Research suggests most firms respond to crisis in a spontaneous and *ad hoc* fashion. Analysis of crisis at the level of the enterprise includes at least four basic elements: the dimensions of the crisis; the degree of control; the amount of time available to make decisions; and the number of options available. Firms that adopt a more holistic approach to crisis management adapt their organizational culture to one favourable to dealing with unexpected incidents and change. New structures are created including crisis management teams and planning, monitoring and evaluation cells. A comprehensive approach can provide a competitive advantage for firms as they are more capable of dealing with crisis and can retain the confidence of major stakeholders.

*Simon Booth*

## Critical path analysis

The coordination, management and control of complex systems of thousands of interrelated operations has always presented special challenges. Complex projects typically consist of a number of subprojects, tasks and activities which have to be organized into technologically feasible and managerially desirable sequences and networks, and monitored for progress towards completion. The achieved results must then be evaluated.

Critical path analysis (CPA) is a set of basic tools for project coordination. In a critical path analysis, significant points in time representing the start and end of activities are called events, represented in diagram form by circles or nodes. A network event stands for the completion of all activities leading into it. The longest sequence of activities, the most time-consuming path in the network, is known as the 'critical path', and the activities that comprise this path are the 'critical activities'. Any delay in completing any of the critical activities could delay the entire project. These thus require the greatest amount of managerial attention. Time calculation and cost analysis are thus key factors in critical path analysis, as is the availability of information throughout the organization.

*Milan Zeleny*

## Culture

For a concept so central to organizational behaviour, the meaning of organizational culture continues to be vague, diverse and contradictory. In part this conceptual confusion was imported with the basic analytical framework from anthropology. To some extent, however, the original ambiguity of the term has been exacerbated by the wide range of uses that organizational theorists and practitioners have made out of it.

The vagueness and diversity of the concept have been a hindrance to the development of a theory of culture as it makes comparison and accumulation of results extremely difficult. On the other hand the lack of a paradigmatic definition has meant that theorists have been free to apply the concept of culture and its derivatives to a wide variety of settings.

Exactly when and where the concept of culture entered organization research has been the subject of some debate and conjecture. What is clear is that its early use was nearly coincidental with widespread interest in the way that national culture affected the operation and efficiency of organizations, specifically Japanese organizations. Thus the term 'culture' has always had two major, closely related meanings within organization theory. First, it has stood for the body of values, myths, symbols, stories and artefacts that are held in common by members of an organization. Second, it has represented the value-based commonalities that exist within a nation (or some other large political unit). Despite the early influence of the comparative approach to the study of organization culture and the commonality of methodological tools, the two areas have remained largely separate.

*David Cray*

## Culture, cross-national

National culture is depicted as playing a fundamental role in forming cultural values. In turn, these values interact with the needs, attitudes and norms of individuals and groups and result in behaviours which contribute to organizational effectiveness, or lack thereof. Additional influences are the values derived from the corporate culture and the individual's professional culture; thus individuals and groups within an organization can be expected to share some values, but they can also be expected to differ with respect to others.

The organization's effectiveness will increase to the extent that the factors influencing behaviour are understood by managers. An international firm's performance is likely to be enhanced when systems are in place that are congruent with the various influences that determine behaviours. While it is clearly impossible to understand all of the factors influencing behaviour, national cultures and attendant values appear to be an important starting point.

A focus on national culture has been questioned by some scholars. Their concern is that the idea that nations and cultures may be coterminous is incorrect and, thus, thinking in these terms is misleading. It is certainly the case that nations and cultures are not the same; nevertheless, it seems appropriate from an international organization's viewpoint to consider national cultures, as the following illustrates.

An organization's activities are legally constrained by national requirements, rather than cultural ones. This results in international firms identifying with national boundaries. Human resource considerations encourage firms to take a national perspective. The workforce in a particular location is predominantly a national workforce – labour mobility within a country is often greater than between countries. This means that management systems need to be designed with the national character of the workforce in mind. Governments encourage this through legislation; usually, laws and regulations regarding employees encompass all citizens of a country and do not apply differentially to different cultural groups. In contrast, laws and regulations may differ quite dramatically from country to country. The firm has to function within this system; therefore, it is appropriate to begin its cultural analysis at the national culture level.

*Betty Jane Punnett*

## Cybernetics

The exploration and development of cybernetics holds the key to global development. To merely acknowledge and accept cybernetics is to lose the opportunity of being at the cutting edge of technological development, economic progress and social change. As an emerging field, cybernetics should not be ignored.

Cybernetics is the science of cycles and systems: computer systems, financial systems, ecosystems, biological systems, etc. So-called robot machines exist today, here and now. The majority of people, not only those in the business world, come into contact with them on a daily basis, from turning on a computer, to talking to an answerphone, to being connected through an automatic exchange to another telephone number.

Cybernetics is an all-encompassing science which transcends traditional restrictive boundaries. It is based on the principles of feedback systems and control within these systems. Cause-and-effect theory makes people consider things in straight lines. In reality, things flow in circularity and cycles; from the ebb and flow of the tide to breeding times locked into the cycle of the sun. Cycle speaks to cycle and creates a dynamic system. Cybernetics asks what mechanism is common to all cycles – and the answer is information.

Within the framework created by cybernetics, decision making and control are similar and directly linked to managerial activities. Both activities are initiated and maintained through communication. The balance between the two can be seen in terms of the derivation of 'cybernetics' from the Greek word *kybernetes*, meaning steersman. Encompassing a diversity of technologies, from solar energy, to robotics, to intelligent manufacturing on international production lines, cybernetics is perpetually evolving, constantly shaping the way in which we approach problems, perceive technological advances and consider the technological, economic and social future of the world.

*Kevin Warwick & Claire Zepka*

# D

## Decision making

Decision making has long been seen as a central managerial activity. At the centre of this activity is the problem of choosing a course of action under conditions of uncertainty and ambiguity. A number of different strategies for making a choice are outlined. Underlying these strategies is a dualism between programmed, routine decisions which, given intendedly rational decision makers, would use a computational strategy, and unprogrammed, non-routine decisions which would use an iterative process involving interaction and mutual adjustment between decision makers.

Decision making takes place within an organizational context, setting a timeframe for the definition of problems, solutions and participants. Within this timeframe preceding decisions have already set constraints for choices made in the present which will, in turn, affect succeeding decisions. Concurrent decisions also compete for the attention of decision makers.

Coping with uncertainty forms the nub of decision making. Without uncertainty as to which course of action to take there would be no decision to be made. The dominant paradigm of organizational decision making assumes that decision makers are intendedly rational but that rationality is 'bounded' by lack of knowledge about preferences and any associated instrumentalitites.

Uncertainty involves the interpretation of problems and possible solutions through an interplay between a number of psychological and sociological processes. Psychological approaches to decision making tend to emphasize the inherent biases resulting from information assymetry and framing effects. Sociological approaches tend to be more descriptive and to emphasize the use of power and the interplay between different interests.

Much of the empirical research into organizational decision making has been concerned with finding patterns between variables that attempt to describe the processes found in real-life situations. This research, more by implication than by empirical measurement, has been concerned with discovering appropriate decision patterns for particular situations and types of decision. The general conclusion is that what has been called a 'sporadic' or 'muddling through' process is effective under conditions of high uncertainty while the more orderly 'constricted' process is appropriate for routine, relatively clear-cut decisions. In this respect, the general well-established thesis of the distinction between routine and non-routine decision making is supported.

There is increasing interest in finding linkages between decision-making processes and aspects of the general organizational culture and institutional framework within which an organization exists. According to this approach managerial decision making is seen as being severely constrained both by the cultural limitations upon the way in which problems and solutions are defined and by the external institutional forces acting on an organization, requiring it to demonstrate its worthiness for support through adopting certain structures and procedures.

*Richard Butler*

### Decision making, habitual domains in

Human behaviour is dynamic. Over time, the thinking process changes rapidly in many ways and in a variety of patterns. However, over a period of time, people's experience, learning and memory will gradually be bounded in a certain domain. Conceptually, the collection of one's habitual ways of perceiving, thinking, acting, judging and responding, together with their formation, dynamics and basis in experience and knowledge, become one's habitual domain. Just as a turtle's shell follows the turtle, wherever people go, their habitual domains follow them. Their habitual domains form the boundaries of their thoughts and behaviour and have great influence on their behaviour and decision making.

*P.L. Yu*

### Decision making, multiple-criteria

Multiple-criteria decision making (MCDM) has become one of the fastest-growing fields of enquiry in the operational sciences since the early 1970s. The word 'multiple' identifies the major concern and focus of this area: it is multiple criteria rather than a single criterion that characterize human choice, judgement and decision making.

It has become quite unsatisfactory to view the world in a one-dimensional way, and to use only a single criterion when evaluating or judging it. Humans always compare, trade off, rank and order the objects of their experience with respect to many criteria of choice. Only in very simple, straightforward or routine situations can we assume that a single criterion of choice would be sufficient.

Decision making occurs only when additional dimensions, such as an estimated reliability, a judge's credibility, or the cost of erroneous judgements are brought in. Clearly, no one-dimensional or single-criterion decision problem can ever exist. Other than choosing the tool of measurement, there remains very little to be decided.

Truly singular objectives or criteria occur only under extreme conditions of time pressure, emergency or crisis. Under such conditions, one often concentrates on a single criterion in order to simplify, speed up or control the decision process itself. As soon as the criterion has been determined, the decision has been implicitly made. It only has to be made explicit by the related tasks of measurement and search. However, when facing multiple criteria, even if our measurement is perfect and the search along each of the dimensions is efficient, it still remains necessary to decide. Here, the choice is not implicit in the measurement.

*Milan Zeleny*

## Decision support systems

Decision support systems (DSS) are a subset of computer-based information systems (CBIS). The general term 'computer-based information systems' is a constellation of a variety of information systems such as office automation systems, transaction processing systems, management information systems and management support systems. Management support systems consist of DSS, expert systems and executive information systems. In the early 1970s, scholars in the CBIS area began to recognize the important roles information systems play in supporting managers in their semi-structured or unstructured decision-making activities. It was argued that information systems should exist only to support decisions, and that the focus of the information systems development efforts should be shifted away from structured operational control to unstructured critical decisions in organizations. Decisions are irreversible and have far-reaching consequences for the rest of organizational life. The importance of effective decision making can never be overemphasized. Decision making is, in effect, synonymous with management.

*Sean B. Eom*

## Deconstruction analysis and management

Deconstruction analysis, originally an approach to literary criticism exemplifying postmodernist epistemology, may appear irrelevant to understanding management and organizations. This assumption would be mistaken. Deconstruction analysis can be used to query the certainties of taken-for-granted managerial assumptions and allows for subversive readings of the 'text' of organizational life and allows new interpretations of cause and effect. Deconstruction analysis can, for example, offer useful tools for a critique of human resource management rhetoric, and can uncover hidden meanings and messages in otherwise conventional-sounding texts.

*Karen Legge*

## Design management

Since the 1970s, design has become one of the most widely discussed management resources. It is seen as a key component in achieving quality standards; it is accepted as the mainspring of the innovative processes on which healthy business depends; and it is seen as a critical dimension in adding value to products and thus allowing for higher prices and higher profits.

To many, however, design remains something of a mystery. It has associations with creativity, a concept which many managers have trouble dealing with effectively. In fact these associations are misleading. Design can be regarded as a management process like any other, and its skills and methodology have the power to help managers carry out their tasks more effectively.

Design should properly be viewed as a management function, a process for planning products, business environments and communications. When design is viewed in these terms it can be recognized that many managers already used design skills and methodology as part of their work. These managers have the capability to learn and improve their design skills, and by doing so they can make a more effective contribution to the goals mentioned above.

*Peter Gorb & Morgen Witzel*

## Direct marketing

Modern direct marketing originated in the USA in the late nineteenth century when entrepreneurs such as Aaron Montgomery Ward and Richard Sears began selling goods mainly to rural residents by flyers and catalogues. Merchandise was delivered by train and postal service. Families became loyal customers who eagerly awaited the arrival of the latest catalogue, popularly called a 'wish book'.

Direct marketing remained a small part of the economy in the USA until the 1970s and 1980s when it experienced sudden and dramatic growth. Direct marketing became a convenient method for families where both adults worked and where time for shopping was very limited to obtain unique, quality merchandise. This growth was made possible by improvements in computer technology that permitted cost-effective storage and manipulation of large quantities of data, allowing for greater productivity in processing orders and handling merchandise.

Direct marketing was slower to take root in Europe because of the existence of smaller markets fragmented by language, legal and cultural differences. However, by the 1980s sophisticated direct marketing operations existed throughout western Europe. There is also increasing interest in direct marketing in the rapidly developing economies of Asia and Central and South America, but here its development is being hindered by the same fragmenting factors as well as a lack of efficient postal and telecommunications infrastructures. As the capabilities of the electronic media grow, however, many observers see tremendous opportunity for the growth of direct marketing around the world.

*Mary Lou Roberts*

### Discipline and dismissals

Discipline at work is the regulation of human activity to produce a controlled and effective performance. It ranges from the guard's control of a rabble to the accomplishment of lone individuals producing spectacular performance through self-discipline in the control of their own talents and resources; from the threat or implementation of dismissal to the subtle persuasions of mentoring. Maintaining discipline is one of the central activities that managers have to exercise. Here we consider the sources of managerial authority and what makes it effective. Each organization has a framework of organizational justice within which managers administer rules and procedures and carry out disciplinary interviewing. In extreme cases employees are dismissed, although there are a series of legal rights to protect them against dismissal that is unfair.

Of all management activities, discipline is one of the most culturally constrained, making any international perspective difficult to discern. The burgeoning literature on international human resource management is silent on this topic because of the varied ways in which authority – the basis of discipline – is construed in different countries. The leading study on management and cultural variation is by Hofstede, who takes the concept of power distance as one of the central ways in which culture causes management practices like discipline to vary.

*Derek Torrington*

### Diversity

The twentieth century has seen an accelerated and immense shifting of peoples from different cultures and races across the earth. Whether for political, personal or economic reasons, indigenous peoples have emigrated *en masse* to new homes worldwide. A particular characteristic of the twentieth century is the widely held belief that every human being is equal in human worth, and entitled to equal privileges and opportunities, without regard to race, social status, gender and so on. That belief led necessarily to fundamental shifts in management practices in human resources, and continues to hold profound significance for business management in general.

In the face of rapid demographic diversification, corporation managers are allocating significant resources to recruit, train and retain men and women of diverse races, nationalities and cultures, and to train so called 'majority' employees to accept and work successfully with these employee changes. Managing diversity is one response to the ideological and demographic shifts of the times. In broadest terms, the management of diversity is business's reaction to rapid cultural and sociological shifts. Concern for diversity is a matter of business strategy for successful enterprise in changing world markets. It has both internal and external implications. Internally, managing diversity successfully provides a climate where employees feel themselves to be valuable to the organization with their particular human qualities. Externally, it means that organizations are flexible and astute in changing world markets. In order to be successful, however, the management of diverse human resources must be calculated not only as a business strategy for profits, but must be rooted in the moral commitment to appreciate the inherent value of a diverse workforce.

*Rosalyn W. Berne*

## Dividend policy

A difficult decision for directors of both public and private limited companies is to determine the appropriate level of dividend to be paid to shareholders, and to decide whether or not to offer non-cash alternatives such as scrip dividends. From the perspective of the theorist, rationalization of the corporate dividend decision (or in its obverse form, the corporate savings function), provides one of the severest difficulties for the development of a unified theory of finance. The 'irrelevance' theory, although logically consistent within its idealized framework, does not explain observed dividend behaviour. As a consequence, a number of partial theories such as those based on 'signalling' and 'agency' models have been developed, but empirical testing of these generally gives disappointing results. However, empirical models of the partial adjustment type work quite well in capturing the time series variation of dividends at both the aggregate and individual company level. Unfortunately, since these models are essentially *ad hoc*, they do not give any real advice to directors to enable them to arrive at a theoretically justifiable assessment of the appropriate dividend level to set.

Arguments based on these models could lead, in a given instance, to one level of dividend being preferred to all others. Such a result might come about because of value effects relating directly to the investors' personal circumstances (for example, personal tax); or from the dividend level being interpreted as a signal of the directors' future intentions or degree of confidence of earnings growth. The existence of some share price reaction on dividend announcement prompts an analysis of the evidence for both shareholder clienteles and possible interaction of firms' dividend policies with key activities such as internal investment.

*Ian Davidson*

## Downsizing

Organizational downsizing refers to a set of voluntary activities undertaken by management to reduce costs. It is usually, though not exclusively, accomplished by reducing the size of the workforce, encompassing a range of activities including personnel layoffs, hiring freezes and consolidations and mergers of organizational units. Downsizing is focused on improving the efficiency of an organization, and can happen either as a defensive response to organizational decline or as a proactive strategy to enhance organizational performance. Wittingly or unwittingly, downsizing affects work processes; for example, when the workforce contracts, fewer employees are left to do the same amount of work and this has an impact on how the work gets done.

Downsizing is a pervasive activity that has been undertaken by a majority of organizations in the industrialized world since the 1970s. The long-term impact on organizational performance and individual wellbeing, however, has been largely negative. Research has demonstrated that the way downsizing is implemented is more important than the fact that it is implemented. Of the three approaches available to downsize, systemic strategies (including organizational renewal) are significantly more effective than workforce reduction or organizational redesign strategies. Organizations whose performance improves as a result of downsizing have managed the process as a renewal, revitalization and culture change effort, not just as a strategy to reduce expenses or organization size.

*Kim Cameron*

## Dynamic programming and the optimality principle

Dynamic programming is an approach to problem solving that permits the division of one large mathematical model that may be very difficult to solve into a number of smaller problems that are usually much easier to solve. The dynamic programming approach allows us to break up a large problem in such a fashion that once all the smaller problems have been solved, we are left with an optimal solution to the large problem. It relies on the optimality principle, formulated by Bellman in the 1950s. This rule facilitates the identification of optimal policies by means of decomposition instead of the brute method of total enumeration.

Dynamic programming is a general approach to problem solving. There is no universal algorithm which can be applied to all problems. Although there are some common characteristics which all dynamic programming problems share, each application must be formulated afresh and almost all these problems need individual specification.

The adjective 'dynamic' indicates that we are interested in processes in which time plays a significant role. However, it is possible to reinterpret many static processes as dynamic processes into which time can be artificially introduced.

Dynamic programming problems can be classified as deterministic or stochastic, discrete or continuous, bounded or unbounded, single criterion or multi-criteria. The most frequent business and management applications of dynamic programming deal with inventory replenishment, production scheduling, equipment replacement and allocation of resources.

*Tadeusz Trzaskalik*

# E

## East Asia, economies of

The economies of east Asia have established a remarkable record of high and sustained growth. In addition to the immense economy of Japan, they consist of South Korea, Taiwan, Hong Kong and Singapore (known together as Asia's Newly Industrializing Economies, or the Asian NIEs), Indonesia, Malaysia, the Philippines and Thailand (which, together with Singapore, are founding members of the Association of Southeast Asian Nations, or ASEAN), and China.

The pattern of economic development in post-war east Asia has been likened to a flock of wild geese flying in formation. The development process began in Japan, rippling out to the Asian NIEs and later to the ASEAN economies and China. Traditionally these economies have depended heavily on the USA for trade and investment but the trend towards intra-regional economic interdependence has accelerated since the Plaza Accord in 1985. The end of the Cold War has also helped promote the integration of the socialist countries (China, Vietnam, Laos, Burma, Mongolia, North Korea and Far East Russia) into the regional economy. While strengthening ties among the east Asian economies has until now been achieved mainly through the initiative of the private sector, multilateral economic cooperation at the government level is also gaining momentum. The emergence of east Asia as a powerful economic growth pole poses both challenges and opportunities for the global economy.

*C.H. Kwan*

## Economic integration, international

Regional economic integration can be viewed in terms of a hierarchy of arrangements which extend from the preferential tariff agreement to the free trade area, the customs union, the common market and, in the extreme case, the economic union. The latter is now frequently described as economic and monetary union.

Various economic benefits are said to arise from the removal of internal tariff and quota barriers to trade in goods between the partner economies, although some protection from import competition from third countries will remain. Further integration benefits arise from the removal of protective devices generally referred to as non-tariff barriers. Higher beneficial forms of integration would depend on the removal of internal obstacles to trade between the partners in services. A common market involves an attack on mainly government-inspired regulations which impede the free cross-frontier flow of services of production, that is, labour, professional persons, capital and business enterprise.

The highest form of economic integration is economic and monetary union. This involves not just the removal of inter-state barriers to the free movement of goods and services but also extends the integration process to monetary and fiscal matters. At a minimum such additional macroeconomic arrangements involve a system of fixed exchange rates between participating national currencies: at a maximum they imply the introduction of a single unified currency and national fiscal systems. Such an extension of integration carries with it additional economic benefits as well as a further erosion of national economic sovereignty. The decision-making structures associated with the specific economic integration policies now in place in various parts of the world economy vary widely from highly-centralized and administratively well-supported systems to those which exhibit considerable decentralization and minimal bureaucracy. Theorists of integration speculate that economic integration can spill over into political integration; the European Union is a classic case of the latter process at work.

*Dennis Swann*

## Economic rents

The aim of business may be variously expressed as making a profit, adding value, or getting more out of the business than is put in. An economic rent, or rent for short, is a measure of success in doing this. Relentless competitive pressure from other businesses, and from both customers and suppliers, all make it difficult to achieve rents; constant striving is necessary to maintain them. The situation is like that of a bird of prey incessantly defending a territory against others of its species who are also fighting to find sufficient food to survive. Easy pickings in the business world, as in the natural world, quickly attract others, and as a result rarely last long.

It is therefore difficult to give operational rules on how to achieve economic rents. As soon as an easily followed rule that enables firms to earn rents is set down, existing businesses will adopt the rule or new businesses will move in, driving prices down to the level at which the rents are eliminated. Alternatively, suppliers to a business earning rents may try to usurp the rents by increasing their prices. So at best, only general indications of the character of economic rents and of ways to seek out opportunities to earn them can be given; it is to be expected that the easier they are to obtain, the more short-lived the rents will be.

*C.G.C. Pitts*

## Economics of developing countries

The economics of developing countries are concerned with those major theories and policies that may bring economic growth and prosperity to poor countries in the world economy. Since the emergence of the idea of developing countries, in the period since 1945, the means to achieve economic growth has been subject to changing fashions in economic theory and policy practice. The experience of economic development in the world economy has been mixed, with sub-Saharan Africa having had a poor economic growth performance since the 1960s, while southeast Asia has recorded high and sustained rates of economic growth. The multilateral economic institutions, namely the International Monetary Fund, the World Bank and the General Agreement on Tariffs and Trade (GATT), have promoted policies to encourage free trade in the world economy, while the Food and Agricultural Organization, the United Nations Conference on Trade and Development and the European Union have promoted policies to intervene in markets, either by the nation state or by agreements among nation states, to achieve particular economic and social objectives in addition to economic growth.

Free trade has not been universally considered as the best policy for primary commodity producing countries, largely because of the decline in the terms of trade and the perceived bias of the trading system in favour of the rich and industrialized countries. Policies to promote industrialization through import substitution and state intervention through economic planning, in most developing economies resulted in inward-looking strategies which did not provide the basis for lasting and sustained economic growth. The combination of import protection of industry and state intervention in the economy often resulted in unsustainable inflation and the collapse of economic growth.

Economic aid, or the transfer of resources from rich to poor countries, while contributing to the social and economic welfare of some developing countries, has not universally proved to be as effective a means of promoting growth and development when compared with trade. Agricultural growth, while having increased in both the developed and the developing countries, has not meant that hunger and malnutrition has been eradicated in the world. The growth of the world population, particularly among poor countries, taken together with increasing environmental degradation, poverty and food insecurity, suggest that the economics of developing countries will continue to cause concern that economic growth, stability and prosperity eludes so many of the poor countries in the world.

*John Cathie*

## Economics, institutional

The study of economics includes three schools of thought: first, the mainstream or 'neo-classical' school; second, the 'new' institutionalism of North, Schotter, Williamson and others; and third, the 'old' institutionalism founded in the USA by Veblen, Commons and Mitchell.

Neo-classical economics is defined as an approach to the analysis of socioeconomic phenomena that embodies the assumption of maximizing behaviour by economic agents, has a predilection for equilibrium analysis and excludes chronic information problems. Although many of the 'new' institutional economists adopt neo-classical assumptions, 'new' institutionalism is regarded typically as embracing a broader range of economic theorists. This raises the issue of the appropriate definition of the 'new' institutional economics. The 'new' institutionalists are united by their common acceptance of the individual as given, taking his or her preferences as exogenous.

The 'old' institutional economics involves a radical break from both neo-classical and 'new' institutional economics, although there are some concerns and themes that are common to the latter. The fundamental assumptions of the 'old' institutional economics are quite different. For instance, 'old' institutionalists do not start from the assumption that the given, atomistic individual and equilibrium theorizing is replaced by the evolutionary analogy. Accordingly, this 'institutional' economics is much more than the study of economic institutions: it is an alternative approach to the analysis of economic phenomena in general. Despite its being eclipsed in recent years by the rising 'new' institutionalism, the Veblen–Commons–Mitchell tradition has more to offer to business and management studies.

*Geoffrey M. Hodgson*

## Education and business partnerships

The interdependence of business and education is recognized the world over as having been a key factor in the development of school policies at institutional, regional and national levels. Yet it is only since the Second World War that its significance for the business community has come to be fully recognized and partnerships have begun to emerge. Social, vocational, economic and behavioural advantages of both an immediate and long-term nature lie behind all such activities, which operate at a variety of levels and take many forms.

Although there are a number of variances in national and international practice, most partnerships involve activities in one of three venues: in the classroom, with company personnel visiting schools to participate in activities; in the workplace, with pupils undertaking visits to company sites to learn directly; or elsewhere in the community, for example when groups of pupils briefed jointly by company personnel and educationalists go out to conduct field surveys on traffic or shopping activities.

Benefits can be seen for all three parties. Schools benefit by having their curricula enhanced and updated, and pupils gain in terms of greater relevance in their education and general all-round development. Benefits to companies include a better understanding of the educational background of potential employees, improved corporate image and opportunities for staff development.

*David Warwick*

## Efficient market hypothesis

The efficient market hypothesis (EMH) holds that capital market prices fully and correctly reflect the knowledge and expectations of all investors. This implies that any publicly available information set, say $\phi$, is compounded into share prices in such a speed that there are no trading opportunities for investors to generate economic profits by trading on the basis of $\phi$. Under this hypothesis, it is futile to seek undervalued securities or to forecast market movements.

EMH assumes that securities markets are characterized by a large number of profit driven independent individuals where new information regarding securities arrives in a random manner. Under this setting, investors react to new information immediately. They buy and sell the security until they feel the market price reflects correctly the new information. In this market, the process of determining prices is a 'fair game' where there is no way of using the information available at a point in time to earn abnormal return. In such a market share prices are right and reflect all publicly available information regarding the value of the company.

The efficient market hypothesis has, historically, been subdivided into three categories, each dealing with a different type of information. The first is the weak form market efficiency hypothesis where security prices reflect all security market information including all past prices, volumes, etc. This hypothesis holds that current prices cannot be predicted from past price patterns. The second is the semi-strong form of market efficiency where current share prices fully reflect not only historical information but also all publicly available information relevant to the company's securities. The third is the strong form of market efficiency where market prices fully reflect all public and private information that is known to all market participants about the company.

*Meziane Lasfer*

## Employee development

The primary objective of employee development is that all employees should have purpose, satisfaction and freedom to act. It should also foster the capability of employees to find a balance between learning, working and leisure time. Employee development can take place at three levels: at the level of the individual, at the level of the group or team and across the organization.

The traditional definition of employee development is still career development, but the flattening of organizational structures and change in corporate values opens up the possibility of other development strategies, such as job rotation, outplacement and job enrichment activities. Employee development also needs to take account of changes in the employee's own career cycle, from initial entry to the organization through promotion, 'levelling off' and pre-retirement.

Employee development is still an underdeveloped area in terms of both research and practice. Although there is no shortage of textbooks which prescribe best practice, there is still lacking a credible analytical framework which can be used by either students or practitioners. In the practitioner sphere, employee development tends to lack strategic orientation; in particular it is often not properly integrated with systems for selection, appraisal and reward of employees, neither are there systems for the objective evaluation of the success of development activities.

*Martin Hilb*

## Employee deviance

Deviance, as a term, comes from criminology, but in practice covers a wider range of behaviours than crime, which only refers to actions that break the law. When used in management, it normally covers illicit workplace behaviours, not all of which are illegal. Employee deviance focuses on pilferage and cheating by employees at all levels, with benefits taken from employers, customers and clients, or both. It is frequently extended to thefts of time, tax evasion/avoidance, payroll and expenses padding, restrictive 'customs and practice' and sabotage; in short, all behaviours formally disapproved of by managements that involve illicit movement of resources to employees and to managers. Called 'fiddling' in the UK, 'skimming' and 'scamming' in the USA, self-report studies have consistently shown its widespread extent, while recorded examples of employee deviance have a long history from Pharaonic Egypt through Classical Greece to the present.

Psychological explanations for deviance attempt to identify propensities associated with particular personality types. This 'rotten apple in the barrel' approach, whereby one deviant personality allegedly contaminates others, has led to extensive commercial screening programmes, especially in the USA. Situational explanations that examine how the social context of the workplace contributes to deviance and often creates it have, however, been more fruitful both for understanding and control.

Many attempts to check deviance have been, and will continue to be, problematic since deviance satisfies undeclared and covert interests, often including those of management, and because new variants and opportunities are continually offered by changing markets, forms of organization and technology. Endeavours to change work systems that ignore deviance or aim to eradicate it without understanding its social context and functions are likely to involve serious and often unanticipated effects.

*Gerald Mars*

## Employee relations, management of

The term 'employee relations' has been used for many years as an alternative to other, better-established descriptive terms such as 'personnel management', 'industrial relations' and now 'human resource management'. Each of these is used to describe a particular feature of the world of work and employment, but each overlaps with the others across ill-defined margins. The result is both confusing and misleading, especially when, as in recent years, the meanings of the terms begin to change. 'Employee relations', used as a descriptive label, has the potential to unify this confusing picture, and may well become widely adopted as 'human resource management' falls out of favour.

The variety of managerial styles to employee relations can be related to a variety of internal and external conditions in the business, economic and legislative environment. Choices about the way individuals are managed can be related to business strategies and underlying requirements for the type of employees recruited, defined in terms of skills, qualifications and experience. In general terms, the more emphasis the company puts on added-value, product differentiation strategies, the more likely it is that high-commitment work practices will be required. In contrast, cost minimization and lowest-cost price strategies will generally be linked to simple work processes where it is easy to recruit cheap labour. Each of these requires its own approach to employee relations.

*John Purcell*

## Employers' associations

Employers' associations represent the interests of business to government and engage in collective bargaining with trade unions. Associations in some countries, such as Germany, undertake a much wider range of functions than associations in other countries, for example the UK. In countries with associations that display a high level of organizational development, tasks are undertaken that would otherwise be the responsibility of public agencies and a more comprehensive range of services is provided to members.

Associations are influenced by the political systems in which they operate and three broad patterns of government–business relations can be identified: company state; associative state; and party state.

There has been an increasing emphasis in recent years on the need for employers' associations to organize at the European Union level. This is achieved both through European federations of national federations and direct membership associations.

Even in countries where it has been relatively centralized, collective bargaining is increasingly undertaken by individual firms. Large firms have also developed their own government relations divisions to represent their interests to government. Although these developments undermine the role of employers' associations they remain the main mechanism for defining and representing business interests.

*Wyn Grant*

### Employment and unemployment, economics of

The historical evolution of employment follows the evolution of spending patterns that accompanies economic growth. At early stages of growth employment is concentrated in agriculture and raw materials. Later, employment grows in the production sector and finally in the public and private services. At any particular time, a country's employment structure tends to reflect its stage of growth and its particular comparative advantages in international trade. Short-run changes in employment and unemployment are influenced by the fact that in modern industrial economies there are both fixed and variable costs associated with hiring labour. When fixed labour costs are important, employers are more likely to adjust hours of work before they change the number of employees in response to changes in output. Changes in employment and unemployment thus lag behind changes in output. Fixed labour costs associated with turnover and training tend to rise with the skill of a worker. As a result, employers are more reluctant to lay off skilled than unskilled workers, and the unemployment of unskilled workers is more responsive to cyclical changes than the unemployment of skilled workers.

Economic analysts identify four general types of unemployment. Deficient demand unemployment can be reduced by fiscal and monetary policies that increase the demand for labour. Frictional, structural and seasonal unemployment, which exist even when business conditions are good, depend more on relative wage adjustments, labour mobility and other aspects of the functioning of labour markets. There are significant international differences in unemployment, and since the 1970s unemployment in Europe has increased relative to unemployment in North America and Japan. Much of this change appears to reflect an increase in the structural and frictional components of unemployment in European labour markets.

Frictional and structural unemployment can be reduced by avoiding policies that raise the incidence and duration of unemployment and by pursuing policies that reduce them. The structure of unemployment insurance provides an example of the former. Unemployment durations will generally be lower when unemployment benefits are low relative to prior earnings and when benefit eligibility periods are relatively short. Policies that may reduce unemployment include retraining programmes, wage subsidies, and subsidies for worker relocation. Most industrialized countries have pursued such policies in the post-war period, but the results have been mixed.

*Robert J. Flanagan*

## Energy economics

Energy in any context matters. Since the Industrial Revolution, it has been a key input into the economic process as an input into the transformation of factors of production into goods and services, and as an input into the macroeconomic system governing a country's ability to grow, trade or provide employment. Individual welfare is intimately linked with the availability of energy, whether for the provision of heat, light or work. In international terms, energy also matters. Energy, predominantly oil, is the largest single item in global trade whether measured in volume or value terms. Changes in the price of energy, notably since 1973, have had a profound effect on the international economy. Energy has been the cause of wars and the cause of winning or losing wars.

Energy also matters in terms of the way societies work. The energy sector has characteristics which make it more likely to be imperfectly competitive. The production and consumption of energy create significant externalities such as environmental pollution. This means that leaving the production and distribution of energy to unrestrained market forces may be sub-optimal. Governments might be expected to play a greater role in the energy sector compared to other sectors of the economy.

Economics is about choice. Unlimited wants and scarce resources force choice. Economics studies the optimal means, however defined, by which choices can and should be made. What should be produced, how and for whom. This very basic notion provides the framework within which the issues which collectively constitute the study of 'energy economics' can be studied.

At first, energy economics was limited to the study of specific energy industries. Energy, notably oil, was in plentiful supply at falling real prices and interest was limited. All this changed with the quadrupling of oil prices in 1973, the first oil shock. Energy economics for the next ten years rapidly grew as a subject revolving around issues of impending scarcity and the macroeconomic consequences of higher prices. During the 1980s, perceptions of scarcity became less pressing. Instead, issues of ownership of energy utilities, regulation, competition and the role of energy policy came to the fore. During the 1990s, the environmental impact of energy production and use complemented these concerns.

*Paul Stevens*

## Entrepreneurial strategies

Entrepreneurial strategies are innovative links between the company and its environment, as shaped by demographic patterns, social trends, government policy and emerging technology. New and/or different links between the firm and its environment are usually the product of an inclination to test – and sometimes ignore – conventional wisdom about how things are done, as well as an entrepreneurial mindset that empowers the execution of untried ideas.

At the core of entrepreneurial strategies is the assumption of risk by the entrepreneur, defined for this purpose as the person or persons who have the prerogative to take action. Such a prerogative derives from ownership, either literally in the case of a shareholder-manager whose stockholdings confer a control position, or symbolically in the case of a manager or group of managers whose emotional investment and delegated authority enable them to place the firm's resources at risk.

Entrepreneurial strategies are not a twentieth-century phenomenon. When Marco Polo established trade routes to the Far East, he was demonstrating the risk taking behaviour we associate with entrepreneurship. The match he found between his skills and the environmental opportunity (demand for goods by consumers previously separated by geography and culture) is a perfect illustration of an entrepreneurial strategy. The example of Marco Polo is particularly apt to the contemporary understanding of entrepreneurship, with its increasingly global scope. Entrepreneurs today face an explosion of opportunities deriving from the proliferation of potential links between their companies and the ever more internationalized environment.

Innovation is the driver of entrepreneurial strategies, and the innovation can take a number of different forms. Such strategies may be innovative in terms of the product or service offered, the marketing or distribution approach taken and/or the organizational structure established.

*Richard L. Osborne*

## Entrepreneurship

The word entrepreneur is derived from the French *entreprendre*, meaning to undertake. The entrepreneur is one who undertakes to organize, manage and assume the risks of a business. In recent years entrepreneurs have been doing so many things that it is necessary to broaden this definition. Today, an entrepreneur is an innovator or developer who recognizes and seizes opportunities, converts those opportunities into workable/marketable ideas, adds value through time, effort, money or skills, assumes the risks of the competitive marketplace to implement these ideas, and realizes the rewards from these efforts.

The entrepreneur is the aggressive catalyst for change in the world of business, and is the independent thinker who dares to be different in a background of common events. The literature of entrepreneurship research reveals some similarities, as well as a great many differences, in the characteristics of entrepreneurs. Chief among these characteristics are personal initiative, the ability to consolidate resources, autonomy, risk taking, competitiveness, goal-orientated behaviour, opportunistic behaviour, reality-based actions and the ability to learn from mistakes. It should be recognized that if some characteristics are taken to their extreme then entrepreneurs exhibit a 'dark side' which could result in destructive behaviours.

While no single definition or complete profile of an entrepreneur exists, research is providing an increasingly sharper focus on the subject. A brief review of the history of entrepreneurship illustrates this. In addition, entrepreneurship has now extended into major corporations where innovative activity is revitalizing organizations. Known as *intrapreneurship*, this entrepreneurial strategy inside established companies has become a major force for growth and development of organizations.

The entire world is currently in the midst of a new wave of business and economic development, and entrepreneurship is its catalyst. Yet the social and economic forces of entrepreneurial activity existed long before the 1990s. In fact, it has been the entrepreneurial spirit that has driven many of mankind's achievements.

*Donald F. Kuratko*

## Environmental management

The global economy is a major planetary sub-system serving to provide the products and infrastructure whereby humankind secures the goods and services it needs for survival and improved quality of life. Throughout the Industrial Revolution the economy has operated on the assumption that unlimited economic growth is both desirable and possible forever. However, the planet is experiencing a number of environmental problems which can be tied directly to unchecked economic activity, including upper atmospheric ozone depletion, soil erosion, water and air pollution, species loss and deforestation. Problems such as these are providing signs that the economic sub-system is out of balance with the natural environment, which is the source of energy and resources for the economy and the receptacle for its wastes.

Rectifying this imbalance requires that strategic managers in business organizations fully incorporate concerns for the natural environment into the decisions they make. This is only feasible within a framework which allows strategic managers to make decisions which are both economically successful and environmentally sensitive. The concept of sustainability provides such a framework. Sustainability is based on the idea that humankind can perpetuate an economic system that provides the goods, services and creative work necessary for human fulfilment within the biophysical limits of the Earth. However, economic activity must be predicated on the assumption that it must coincide with the planet's carrying capacity, its evolutionary energy transformation, resource creation and waste processing cycles.

Applying sustainability in organizations means implementing sustainability strategies which provide economically beneficial ways for organizations to effectively incorporate environmental responsibility into their decisions. Sustainability strategies designed to reduce costs and/or generate revenues by reducing waste, pollution and resource usage are becoming pervasive in industrial organizations, and these strategies are providing the means for beginning the crucial restoration of ecosystem–economic system balance.

*W. Edward Stead & Jean Garner Stead*

### Environmental reporting

Environmental reporting is a recent response by companies who are under increasing pressure to provide information about their environmental impact. Though small in number, the companies producing environmental reports are influential industry leaders.

In the absence of a legal standard, environmental reports exhibit a great diversity. The best include performance data from an environmental management system, quantitative targets and financial information. With no agreed single format for environmental reporting, a number of guidelines have been issued. They recommend the contents and style of report for the various audiences that exist, and encourage companies to be more open about their environmental policies, practices and performance.

*Chris Hope*

### Environmental and resource economics

The concern of economists with natural resources and the environment is as old as economics itself, but the forms and nature of that concern have shifted with perceived problems and priorities. In the eighteenth and nineteenth centuries, Malthus and Ricardo worried about the relationship between growing populations and a land base of diminishing marginal fertility. Mill noted the negative effects on human welfare of a deteriorating natural environment. Jevons wrote of British industry's imminent demise due to the depletion of its coal.

In the 1930s the foundations of the modern discipline of environment and resource economics were laid by Pigou and Hotelling, whose organizing concepts were, respectively, the externality (welfare effects which escape the price mechanism) and the concept of optimal depletion (use of the resource such that the present value of profits or consumption from it are maximized).

In the 1960s and 1970s sharp differences of opinion emerged, to some extent within economics but more between economists and others, regarding the extent to which the environment could accommodate the ever-increasing human demands on it before it imposed limits to economic growth. The differences remain largely unresolved. Economists tend to stress the ability of technology to discover and develop new resources as old ones become depleted, as well as the role of economic growth in both stimulating technological innovation and providing resources to improve environmental quality. Those less sanguine about technological progress point out that economic growth of itself tends to increase demands on the environment, which is still deteriorating despite decades of both economic growth and increasingly stringent environmental policy.

Most recently, following the report of the Brundtland Commission and the 1992 United Nations Conference on Environment and Development, environmental sustainability and sustainable development have become the organizing concepts in the ongoing attempt to secure global environmental integrity with increasing global prosperity. It is still very much an open question whether these two objectives can in practice be simultaneously achieved.

*Paul Ekins*

## Equal employment opportunities

Equal employment opportunities refers to a desirable situation in the labour market and work organizations, where access to employment opportunities and rewards is based on individual merit and ability rather than a personal characteristic which is not job-related. The provision of equal employment opportunities is regarded in many countries as a desirable situation. International conventions and recommendations establish standards for equal employment opportunities and have encouraged the enactment of legislation and the implementation of policies which seek to remove discrimination in employment. Affirmative action is one of the means used to create equal employment opportunities.

Equal employment opportunities have consequences for the formulation and implementation of all human resource management policies. In particular, promotion and training criteria need to be designed so that they are unbiased regarding personal characteristics such as gender or race, are clearly understood and documented and can be effectively implemented by selectors. There are also implications for recruitment, which may need to adapt practices to ensure that a pool of applicants with a variety of personal characteristics is attracted. The implementation of policies may also have to overcome resistance within the organisation. This resistance may be based on a disbelief in the need for change, or a desire on the part of those who benefit from existing employment arrangements to protect their position.

*Robin J. Kramar*

## Evolutionary theories of the firm

Biological analogies for firm growth can be found in the work of Marshall and Veblen, who first became prominent in the decades following the Second World War. The work of Nelson and Winter is perhaps the most important development of this theory. They proposed an evolutionary model based on three key concepts borrowed from the natural sciences: selection, which operates on firms' internal routines; mutation, which has its organizational counterpart in the concept of 'search', encompassing changes in routines; and the 'the struggle for existence' which has clear parallels in market competition. Nelson and Winter make it clear that there is not an exact correspondence between organizations and biology, but that evolutionary theory is an important metaphor. Evolutionary theory continues to be challenged from the older, contractarian perspective, notably by writers such as Williamson.

*Geoffrey M. Hodgson*

## Exchange rate economics

The current exchange rate regime, subscribed to by the leading industrial countries, is one of quasi-flexible exchange rates and has existed since 1973. The present regime did not come into being as a result of a careful consideration of the supposed advantages of flexible rates, but rather as a result of dissatisfaction with the previous Bretton Woods regime of fixed but adjustable exchange rates, which, in turn, was a reaction to the experience of flexible exchange rates in the inter-war period. No sooner had the present regime been inaugurated than there was widespread discussion of the problems with the regime, particularly the relatively high volatility of exchange rates, and proposals for alternative regimes, based on greater fixity of exchange rates, have been widely canvassed. The evolution of exchange rate regimes would appear to be a classic example of history repeating itself.

The problems facing governments are first, how to set an exchange rate regime, and second, how to determine exchange rates themselves. The standard base-line view of exchange rate determination is purchasing power parity (PPP), which asserts that exchange rate is determined by the ratio of a domestic price level to an equivalent foreign price level. An alternative is the balance of payments approach, which asserts that the exchange rate moves to ensure the sum of the current and capital accounts of the balance of payments is zero. More recently attention has focused on the asset market model, which interprets the exchange rate as the relative price of two assets (monies), instead of traded goods or balance of payments.

Recent experience with flexible exchange rates has been unsatisfactory because of the excessive volatility exchange rates exhibit when they are market determined. There is now some pressure towards a return to more fixed exchange rate structures. However, the success of these structures may well depend on which of the three methods above will be used to fix exchange rates.

*Ronald MacDonald*

## Exchange rate management

International financial management would be no different from domestic financial management were it not for the fact that at the international level problems are introduced by two factors: the presence of different *countries* and the presence of different *currencies*. This is an important distinction, because the domain over which countries are defined (political divisions) is different from the domain over which currencies are defined (currency areas, or areas within which exchange rates are fixed). For example, different countries may use a common currency; Panama and the USA both use the US dollar, and on a larger scale one of the ultimate aims of the European community is to introduce a common currency for all of Europe. Similarly, it is possible to deal in different currencies within a given country; term deposits denominated in various currencies are commonplace in the major international financial centres.

A consequence of the existence of countries and currencies is the need for international financial managers to assess and manage political and exchange rate *exposure* and *risk*. Exposure represents the amount at risk while risk relates to the dispersion of possible outcomes. Exposure and risk are therefore conceptually and even dimensionally different. However, at the same time as countries and currencies create special problems they also create special opportunities, including higher returns and/or better diversification than is possible in any one country or currency. If exposures and risks are to be properly managed, then it is necessary that they be correctly measured. While measurement is in principle straightforward, there are major problems in practice.

The key concepts are the balance of payments (the record of transactions between domestic residents and residents of foreign countries over a period of time) and the exchange rate; important issues include the relationship between exchange rate policy and monetary policy, and the link between the balance of payments and the exchange rate. The most prominent models of exchange rate determination are the neo-classical or monetarist model and the Keynsian model, which distinguishes between internal and external equilibrium and makes calculations assuming prices are fixed in the short run. More recent models emphasize the role of international capital movements. Current issues in international finance include the role of the International Monetary Fund and the World Bank, the development of the European Monetary System and whether the efficient markets hypothesis can be applied to exchange rates.

*Maurice Levi*

## Executive information systems

Executive Information Systems (EISs) are essentially an attempt to harness some of the power and benefits of information technology (IT) to help support the activities and meet the requirements of senior management in organizations. The relevance of IT at the operational level is now unchallenged, except perhaps in the smallest of organizations, but the relevance of IT to support senior managerial levels and their specific activities is still in some doubt. The development of EISs is challenging this doubt in the context of improving technology, the increasingly competitive business environment and the vast amount of computerized information now being generated by organizations. The organizations and executives that best utilize the technology, it is argued, will give themselves a significant competitive advantage, and EISs are a key element of best utilization. EISs are designed to provide timely information relevant to the activities of senior executives. To achieve this they must be easy to use and provide a variety of information views including summaries, trends, exceptions and 'what if?' modelling. The data provided may be both quantitative and qualitative, external as well as internal. The architecture and design of the EIS is a critical factor for success, and the users (in this case senior executives) need to participate in the design process to ensure that the EIS effectively addresses their requirements.

*Guy Fitzgerald*

## Executive training

The new forms of organization which have emerged in the 1990s mean that managers need to develop a fundamentally different array of skills and competences in order to function in this new environment. Managerial competences are now needed at all levels of the organization. New approaches to training are needed, possibly using both in-house learning and formal external training programmes. As executive competences are redefined and corporate attitudes to learning change, training suppliers are having to respond with a new mix of learning approaches.

Current efforts are focusing on identifying the executive competences and capabilities needed in today's organization, and then on 'bridging the capability gap' through a variety of training methods. Much attention is being paid to opportunities for learning through the job, although clearly this needs to be much more systematic and effective than it is at present in many Western firms (in contrast to Japan, where on-the-job learning is widespread and effective). Formal programmes and courses, either in-house or delivered externally, also need to adapt to new competence needs. Current trends are pointing towards an increase in self-managed learning, with managers providing vision, support and training specialists, while still developing core competences in traditional ways, becoming more deeply involved as agents of change.

*John Blakey*

## Expert systems

Expert systems may be described in simple terms as an art that uses science. Expert systems skills include computer science, cognitive psychology, behavioural sciences and domain sensitivity. The product of expert systems is knowledge-based systems which emulate human intelligence. These include expert systems, hypermedia systems, CASE (computer-aided/-assisted software engineering), intelligent tutoring systems and hybrid systems.

Expert systems are the most important branch of applied knowledge engineering. They are based on theoretical concepts of artificial intelligence, machine problem-solving and emulation of the declarative and procedural knowledge of human experts. They are developed by knowledge engineers and transformed into a computer system composed of a knowledge base, a control program and an interface for explanation and communication with a user. Such systems, which emulate human experts, are of great assistance to managers and workers in all areas of business and public administration.

*Velimir Srica*

## Exporting

The adoption of an international strategy may be a response to industry change in regulation, market demand, product and process technology, suppliers, competition, or the firm's growth objectives. Exporting is one strategic option for international market development, distinct from locating marketing, distribution or manufacturing operations or subsidiaries in foreign markets or entering into alliances and partnerships. It may be used as a lower risk entry strategy to test a new market or to develop experience of international trade.

Exporting is taken here to mean the sale of goods/services across national boundaries to an independent organization. Exporting may be either direct or indirect. Direct exports are those goods sold to an independent organization outside the domestic market. Indirect exports are those goods sold to an intermediary based in the domestic market for onward sale in international markets. These two exporting routes have very different levels of commitment and risk for the company.

Associated with the decision to use exporting as the chosen method of foreign market entry are the major decisions of market selection, where markets need not necessarily be countries but customers or regions with appropriate characteristics (sophisticated consumers with high disposable income might suggest a target of major cities), channel selection, and the development of an international marketing plan.

The strategic circumstances of the company will influence the objectives to be achieved through exporting and the way in which these objectives will be achieved - including decisions about how many markets to enter, the degree of product development, the time horizon for seeing returns, channel choice and methods of selling - and affect company capability.

*Anne Jenkins*

# F

## Finance, international

International finance, or 'open country macroeconomics', is concerned with a country's international transactions in goods and assets. Several inter-related variables are involved, including balance of payments, exchange rates, real income and consumption over time and short- and long-term interest rates.

The balance of payments (the record of transactions between domestic residents and residents of foreign countries over a given period of time) consists of three elements: the current account, the capital account and official financing items including foreign borrowing by government and drawings on or additions to official reserves. The relationship between balance of payments and other variables is complex. Governments often attempt to manage this relationship through tools such as fixed or targeted exchange rates or manipulating interest rates. Since the collapse of the Bretton Woods agreement on fixed exchange rates in the early 1970s, many countries have been concerned about the negative effect of volatile exchange rates on their economies. In the European Union, the planned establishment of a currency union between EU members is designed to counteract such influences.

*Shelagh Heffernan*

## Financial accounting

The beginnings of accounting, which precede even the first use of figures, date from before the time of recorded history. The first attempts at modern corporate accounting, however, are usually traced to the late Middle Ages. Double-entry accounting, now used throughout the world, is not a fixed set of techniques, but rather a system that is continually being perfected and adapted to the needs of firms and their economic environments. Some authors, such as the German economist Werner Sombart, would see it as a major factor in the development of capitalism. Without question, double-entry book-keeping is still the primary information system available to firms.

Today, it is possible to define accounting as a system of producing and communicating information about the firm. This system can be divided into two main sub-systems. The first provides information used within a firm itself for internal management. For this reason, it is called management accounting. The second sub-system provides information for external use by a firm's economic and social partners. It is called general accounting, or, more frequently, financial accounting.

Information is provided by financial accountants through a series of documents, including the balance sheet, the income statement, the statement of retained earnings and the cash flow statement. The formats of these tend to be regulated and standardized, depending on the regulatory regime in the country in question. These basic documents have limitations, in that they cannot provide complete information about the firm. Accordingly, new types of reports are now beginning to be used, such as methods of accounting for inflation, employee reports and social accounts, reporting on the organization's social programmes.

*Bernard Colasse*

## Financial management, international

International financial management is not a separate set of issues from domestic or traditional financial management, but does involve a number of risks and complexities not confronted domestically. International financial management means that all the standard financial activities and decisions within a firm (capital budgeting, capital structure, raising long-term capital, working capital and cash flow management, etc.) will be complicated by the differences in markets, laws and especially currencies of conducting business internationally. This management requires many different activities from those of traditional domestic financial management practices. An added distinction in this area of management is that between a firm which only imports and exports, an *international* firm, and a firm which not only conducts direct import/export business but also possesses foreign affiliate and subsidiary operations, a *multinational* firm (sometimes referred to as multi-domestic and transnational).

International financial management requires knowledge of a number of different markets and institutions. These include currency markets, along with a knowledge of exchange rate determination and terminology; international money and capital markets; and international debt and equity markets. International financial management activities in turn include international capital budgeting, managing international capital structure, working capital management and performance evaluation and control.

*Michael H. Moffett & Bernard Yeung*

## Financial markets, international

In economics, a market is defined as a set of arrangements whereby buyers and sellers contract to exchange goods or services. An international financial market works on exactly the same principles. Financial instruments and services, which range from currencies and private banking services to futures for pork bellies, are traded. A market clearing price is established when demand is just equal to supply. The most important types of international financial markets are the international money markets, international bond markets, international stock markets and derivatives markets. The major global financial centres are London, New York and Tokyo, but there are also important offshore centres such as Switzerland and Hong Kong.

Issues for the future include the coordination of international financial regulation, along the lines of the Basle agreements on capital adequacy, the increasing domination of global markets by large financial conglomerates, and the extent to which rapid financial innovation could undermine the existing system. New technology, which is increasing the speed with which information can be transmitted, may reduce the need for discrete centres such as London and New York, although in fact technology tends rather to increase centralization, which could lead to still more concentration.

*Shelagh Heffernan*

## Financial planning

The consensus view, that of the rational model, of financial planning in mainstream finance is that it is a process that starts with goals, compares these to anticipated achievement to identify any gap, analyses alternatives and monitors progress towards the goals. The basic goal is shareholder wealth maximization. This model, however, is not the only one, and it has been criticized on a number of grounds. An extreme alternative is the 'disjointed incrementalism' model, which is based on making only marginal changes to existing policies as problems arise. Other models attempt to combine the strengths of these two models. Procedures and calculations have a role in supporting planners' more intuitive and political skills. Computer models may also be of some help, although they have their shortcomings.

*Robert H. Berry*

## Financial reporting, social theories of

Accountability can be defined as the requirement for one party (an agent) to give an 'account' to another (a principal). The principal requires, or is entitled to require, that the agent acts in particular ways and accounts for his actions, thereby providing evidence of the discharge of his duties. Where the relationship is one of financial accountability then the agent will provide financial accounts. However, accountability relations need not always be financial in form; different societies at different times support different forms of corporate and personal accountability. Perhaps the most commonly understood relation of accountability is established by explicit legal contract between two parties. In this case, financial accounting may provide a basis for monitoring compliance with the contract. Alternatively, ideas about accountability may be informed by moral and political frameworks. For example, if society is concerned with accountability for the welfare of future generations then this might require a form of accounting very different from the financial reporting practices which exist currently. The general point is that an accountability structure describes social relations and expresses social values and choices which are either presumed to exist or presumed to be desirable. Social theories of financial accounting are concerned with two aspects of this structure: the identity of principals and agents and the nature of the information flows between them.

*Michael Power*

## Financial statement analysis

Financial statement analysis (FSA) is a general term used to describe the activity of interpreting and using, as opposed to preparing, financial statements, primarily accounting data. It therefore extends from professional financial analysts employed at great expense by financial institutions for their skill at 'reading between the lines' of company balance sheets to employees and potential employees who simply want to know things such as how well the firm is doing and who owns it. The traditional tools of FSA are financial ratios, including profitability, activity, the management of working capital, growth, liquidity, the balance sheet, capital structure and investment data. Traditionally, financial analysts have used historical ratios combined with experience and judgement; recently, the development of powerful statistical techniques and databases has resulted in the application of statistical mechanical methods which can be used to make forecasts and predictions.

*Paul Barnes*

## Firms and networks, growth of

The firm is as an economic organization in a market economy, acquiring tangible and intangible productive assets for the purpose of producing goods and services for the market at prices that yield a profit. Innovation is an important part of its activity. This concept of the firm is the concept used in business and managerial economics and in such works of economic history as the superb analyses of Chandler, where he relates the strategy and performance of firms to their structure and where the 'visible hand' of firms becomes as important as the 'invisible hand' of the market.

This approach to the firm differs from the definition of the firm in the theoretical branch of microeconomics which is often called the 'neoclassical', or 'marginalist', theory of the firm, where it is defined almost exclusively with reference to the determination of price and output of a given commodity under given and unchanging conditions. In that theory, the firm is not an organization but an abstract entity; its equilibrium output (size) is determined by the intersection of cost and demand curves under carefully specified competitive circumstances. The theory does not deal with the operations of the firm as such, for it is designed to deal primarily with the logical implications of profit-maximizing behaviour for prices and output, for which it has proved indispensable in the analysis of market systems. Nevertheless, it is already being seriously challenged by a more institutional and sociological approach.

However, even in the neo-classical theory of the firm, the concept of disequilibrium points to considerations that promote expansion of output and which also apply when the firm is defined differently. For example, indivisibilities of plant and equipment which make economies of scale available where plant can be used more fully show up in falling costs and greater equilibrium output. But this concept can only be applied to a given product or an unchanged collection of products because it is impossible to establish the cost curve of a firm if the composition of output to which the costs refer continually changes. Joint costs arising from indivisibilities of output are also important – as, for example, in the production of wool and mutton at the same time. For the same reason, however, they cannot be used in the neo-classical theory of the firm to explain diversification of output.

If the firm is treated as an organization, its growth can in some respects be looked at in terms of the nature and development of organizations. An organization has boundaries, but in the case of firms the effective boundaries are often fuzzy and ill-defined. In a general way, however, the firm can in principle be distinguished from its environment, and its boundaries for all practical purposes reflect the extent to which its administration governs its activities. It is the administrative, bureaucratic, hierarchical or managerial characteristics of decision making with respect to transactions within the firm that distinguish these transactions from those made between independent participants in the market. Unlike market transactions, the activities within the firm are linked to each other within an administrative and managerial framework, although the characteristics of both administration and management vary widely among firms.

*Edith Penrose*

## Flexibility, workplace

In the study of employment, work and organization, the issue of flexibility in the workplace has come to represent a key focus for discussion. Analyses of changes taking place at several levels, from work practices, production strategies and employee relations arrangements to broader industrial and labour market structures, and even the organizing and control principles of capitalism itself, have drawn on the notion of flexibility to summarize both a series of developments and a key managerial objective behind those developments.

The notion of flexibility denotes pliability, adaptability and a responsiveness to change. In principle, flexibility relates equally to the structure and processes of organizations. To date, however, most attention has been concentrated on aspects of workforce flexibility (and at the macro level, labour market flexibility). In turn this reflects a greater attention paid to flexibility on both sides of the Atlantic by industrial relations and labour market specialists than by those with an organizational behaviour perspective. In practice, however, many of the changes introduced to extend workforce flexibility go hand in hand with other changes designed to bring about greater organizational responsiveness, such as decentralization and the utilization of more adaptive technologies.

Several factors are widely associated with giving added significance to organizational flexibility – in particular, greater market uncertainty and changes in technology and production processes. In considering the future of flexibility, it is evident that various difficulties and unanswered questions remain. If management is serious about goals such as building greater employee commitment and sustaining high quality output, it must look at reciprocity over flexibility. In the past the flexibility agenda has tended to be defined by management, but in the longer term flexibility is only likely to be sustained if management takes account of employee interests as well as its own objectives.

*Paul Blyton*

## Forecasting in marketing

Every act of preparing for the future implies some forecasting of impending conditions. In the context of business management, forecasts can be used to support long-term strategic decisions, operational decisions or short-term tactical decisions. Management requires forecasting information when making a wide range of decisions. The sales forecast is particularly important, as it is the foundation upon which all company plans are built in terms of markets and revenue.

Management would be a simple matter if business was not in a continual state of change, the pace of which has quickened in recent years. The result of this constant change, however, is that business tasks are becoming more complex and business decisions are being more long-term in nature. It is becoming increasingly important and necessary for businesses to predict their future prospects in terms of sales, costs and profits. The value of future sales is crucial as it affects costs and profits, so the prediction of future sales is the logical starting point for all business planning. Thus, the company's customers and their likely purchasing behaviour during the period to come are the starting point for business planning, and this idea lies at the very heart of all marketing activity.

As well as helping to plan expansion into new markets and new product lines, forecasting can also be viewed as the act of giving advance warning in time for beneficial action to be taken. In order to predict the future it is usual to examine the past in order to observe trends over periods of time, and to establish the degree of probability with which these trends are likely to repeat themselves in the future. Future predictions are therefore inherently wrong as they are based upon probability; it is up to management to decide upon the degree of imprecision that can be tolerated when planning for the future. One general rule which can be applied to forecasting is that more accurate forecasts will be more expensive than less accurate ones because they employ more sophisticated analyses in their computation.

Forecasting techniques can be either subjective or objective. Subjective techniques are generally based upon qualitative opinion or intuition; objective techniques are normally quantitatively based and use mathematical analysis in their computation. Objective techniques are in turn divided into trend projections of previous sales, and causal methods which attempt to assess the relationship between two or more variables.

The availability of appropriate data is of central importance to the development of a forecasting system. Depending upon the degree of accuracy required, most forecasting techniques require a considerable amount of data to be collected and analysed. This data must then be judged in terms of its usefulness and validity in the forecasting process. Selection of the most suitable forecasting technique will in turn depend on the availability of existing data and the company's ability to access this data.

*Geoffrey Lancaster*

## Forecasting and statistical methods

Forecasting and statistical modelling encompass a rich field of research tools specifically designed for longitudinal analysis. These tools are an essential part in the toolkit of the modern business economist. The success or failure of the business person is intimately connected to his or her ability to predict the long-term changes in the business environment and their implications for decision making, as well as the short-term fluctuations in the critical success factors of the economy in general and of the firm in particular. The importance of formal techniques as an aid in business forecasting is evident, but should not be over-emphasized. Statistical methodology properly combined with human judgement is expected to yield the best outcome in particular forecasting problems.

Time-series modelling is widely used in many managerial decision problems relating to financial management, quality control, marketing, investment analysis and other areas. A time series is a sequence of observations on a variable of interest, recorded at equally spaced points in time. In certain situations this variable is called a 'response' or 'endogenous' process. Occasionally, the response variable is linked to one or more signal (exogenous) variables. Knowing this linkage may be useful in forecasting the response variable. A variety of models, including ARIMA models, regression analysis, state–space models, Bayesian methods and frequency-domain tools, can be developed.

*Ralf Östermark*

### Foreign exchange risk, management of
Since the demise of the Bretton Woods system of quasi-fixed exchange rates in 1973, the international monetary system has experienced an ever-increasing degree of exchange rate volatility coupled with periods of prolonged over- or under-shooting in currency values. This metamorphosis of the foreign exchange market has spurred the creation of new hedging instruments/techniques, whose proliferation – although welcomed by players in the currency market – has confounded many a would-be treasurer as to the appropriate instrument to be used in resolving their elusive foreign exchange risk management conundrum. When exchange rate volatility is coupled with the ever-growing integration of the world economy, it is easy to understand why foreign exchange risk management is increasingly woven into global strategic management.

The three basic concepts of foreign exchange risk exposure are transaction exposure, translation exposure and economic exposure. Transaction risks are incurred when contracts provide for deferred payment in a currency not that of the receiver's own country. Translation risk occurs when multinational companies translate earnings from foreign holdings into their own domestic or reference currency. Economic risk represents the effect exchange rate movements may have on the value of the firm itself. There are a variety of techniques for hedging each type of risk.

One of the critical issues in this field is the inability of current techniques to generate reliable forecasts of foreign exchange movements. It is imperative, therefore, that managers in international operations are able to manage foreign exchange risk.

*Laurent L. Jacque*

### Foreign market entry strategies
Entering foreign markets presents several strategic choices to the manager. Let us suppose the objective is to deliver a product or service to customers in a new market abroad. The first choice is whether to produce

inside that country, or whether to produce the good or service in the company's existing plants and ship the item to the new market. The first decision, then, is between local production and exports. Several economic and strategy criteria affect this choice. To export the item to a foreign market means additional costs of freight, customs duties, insurance, special packing and other taxes which may be avoided if the item were to be produced in the country itself. On the other hand, setting up production in the foreign nation involves additional capital investment, and might make for higher production costs compared to the company's existing facilities (especially when we take exports from the latter on a variable cost basis). The manager also has to consider the risks and organizational issues associated with a new foreign investment, such as political instability, currency fluctuations and training a new management and staff to fit in with the company's existing procedures, hierarchy and operating specifications.

Licensing the company's expertise, patents or brands to another firm in the foreign market, and to have this firm produce the good or service for customers there, is another option. The licensee company receives training and the rights to intellectual property, and in turn pays fees and royalties to the company as licensor. This is sometimes a 'hands-off' approach to international expansion, involving less control over the foreign operation than an equity investment. Since it is the licensee company that makes the investment and assumes the risk of developing the market in their country, the royalties and technical fees they are willing to pay the licensor are often inferior to the dividends and growth in equity value the company could have earned if it had made the foreign investment by itself.

Each option involves different levels of investment, expected return, control, risk, duration, competitive threat, tax and strategy implications. There is no single optimal choice. The decision depends on the product and market in question, on the company's financial and managerial resources, its risk averseness and overall global strategy. First, the 'classic' foreign market entry choices of exporting, licensing and foreign direct investment as strategy alternatives are presented, and how a firm may choose a particular mode in developing a particular country market is shown. Reality, however, is often far more complicated. For one thing, tax, risk and strategy often call for combining some of the options rather than treating them as substitutes for each other. Second, globalization trends call for treating a foreign market not as a compartmentalized operation, but as one that is integrated with the rest of the global firm's activities. When the actual actions of mature global companies are examined, foreign affiliates (equity investment) which have received technology or intellectual property from the parent (under licence) are often found, while at the same time their inputs are supplied by an affiliate in another nation (intra-firm exports).

However, direct investment, licensing and exports are not necessarily substitutes; they can also be complementary strategies. Firms beginning their international expansion are more likely to view these options as substitutes, but mature globalizing firms can often be found using all options simultaneously.

*Farok J. Contractor*

## Forward and futures contracts

A forward contract is a firm agreement between two counterparties to exchange an asset at some future date for an agreed price. It enables the counterparties to lock into a certain price today for a transaction that will occur in the future. The contract specifies *inter alia* the type and amount of asset to be exchanged, the price at which the exchange will take place (the 'delivery price') and the date of the exchange (the 'delivery date').

A futures contract is also an agreement that enables two counterparties to fix the price at which an asset will be exchanged at a certain time in the future. However, futures contracts are standardized with respect to the specification and amount of the asset to be exchanged and require the exchange to occur on one of a limited number of maturity dates each year (often four). This contract standardization enables futures contracts to be traded on regulated exchanges that provide a clearing house mechanism to ensure that contracts will be honoured.

Forward and futures contracts are of major importance in the management of financial and commodity price risk exposure for companies and financial institutions. They offer low-cost and convenient ways of setting up highly-geared positions for speculators seeking bets on movements in financial assets and commodity prices. Institutional investors can use such contracts to alter the allocation of their funds between major classes of assets very rapidly and at low cost. The pricing of forward contracts is based on simple arbitrage relationships. When using futures to hedge risk exposures, great care should be taken to eliminate or reduce mismatches between key characteristics of the futures contract and the risk being hedged.

*Peter F. Pope & Pradeep K. Yadav*

## Futurology

Futurologists study current trends in order to anticipate future developments. A variety of actors and institutions are interested in predicting the future. Futurology is widely practised by corporations, forecasters, government institutions, think tanks and universities. In the recent period futurologists have been interested in exploring a range of issues, including the impact of information technology, the effect of demographic trends such as the 'greying' (ageing) of industrial societies or the long-term consequences of pollution on the environment.

Since the future has not yet happened, futurology must to some extent rely on the imagination. This endows futurology with a speculative or subjective dimension. Since the Second World War, many sophisticated methods of analysis have been developed to assist the task of exploring the future. However, such techniques help to temper the futurist imagination but do not overcome its speculative elements.

Ideas about the future are strongly influenced by social interaction in the present. Those working in the broad field of futurology are products of their time. During the confident decades of the post-war boom, futurologists were convinced that they could make accurate forecasts of the future. Today, the claims of mainstream futurology are far more modest. A lack of certainty about contemporary society has also diminished confidence in the view that it is possible to influence the future. Consequently, the contributions of futurology are far less normative and policy oriented than in the past.

*Frank Füredi*

## Fuzzy expert systems

Fuzzy expert systems are designed and developed for management with: expressive power of knowledge representation embedded in linguistic variables and their linguistic values in natural language expressions; and generalized methods of inference based on fuzzy logic which is a generalization of multi-valued logic. Fuzzy expert-system models for management are either: approximately good in comparison with their classical counterparts, for example, for the cases of production and spare parts planning, or much better than their counterparts, for example for the cases of job shop scheduling and consumer preference prediction and market share analysis. Such models are classified as second generation systems from the perspective of both the expert and management systems.

*I.B. Türkşen*

# G

## Game theory and gaming

Game theory is a mathematical modelling system that analyses situations in which the optimal action for a decision maker depends on the choices and responses made by other decision makers. The essence of game theory is multilateral decision making. Informally considering the impact that other decision makers may have on a decision is referred to as gaming the situation.

The same competitive and interactive elements of athletics and other games are also present in many economic interactions. It is in this respect that interactions among economic agents can be viewed as games. Most economic games, however, differ from the typical athletic or parlour games in one important respect. In the typical athletic or parlour game, the objective is to simply beat the opponent. In economic games, the players often have both competing and common interests. For example, consider an oligopolistic pricing situation. The oligopolists have competing interests in terms of market share, but a common interest in maintaining a high price.

Clearly in such gaming situations, before players make decisions or take actions, it is important to consider how other players are likely to respond. Informally considering the ramifications of actions and decisions is referred to as gaming the situation. Game theory provides, however, a systematic mathematical treatment of gaming situations. It can be used to systematically analyse situations in which the optimal action for a decision maker depends on the choices made by other decision makers. As a mathematical modelling system, game theory enables economists and social scientists to analyse human interactions, and, as with modelling in general, to focus attention on specific aspects of an encounter, leading to the eventual identification of driving forces.

*Dorothy E. Klotz*

## General Agreement on Tariffs and Trade (GATT)

The General Agreement on Tariffs and Trade (GATT) was an international organization established in 1948 and headquartered in Geneva, Switzerland, to oversee the conduct of international trade. Most nations of the world became members.

The GATT sponsored eight multilateral trade negotiations that sharply reduced tariff restrictions on the flow of international trade in manufactured goods, stimulating a very rapid increase in world trade and output. However, as tariffs were negotiated down, non-tariff trade obstruction multiplied, especially after the mid-1970s. Furthermore, trade in agricultural products and services were not covered by the GATT and its dispute settlement mechanism proved to be cumbersome and time consuming.

It was to address the shortcomings of GATT rules and operation that the eighth multilateral trade negotiations (the Uruguay Round) was started in 1986. This was completed in December 1993. One outcome of the Uruguay Round was the establishment of the World Trade Organization (WTO) to replace the GATT as of 1 January 1995.

*Dominick Salvatore*

## General management

Although industry and commerce are among the oldest of human activities, it is only comparatively recently that business management became recognized as a discipline in its own right. The first scientific management principles were laid down in the early twentieth century with a view to rendering production more efficient and cost-effective; following these came similar attempts to lay down general principles for other activities such as marketing, personnel/human resource management, finance, distribution and the other fundamental activities which all businesses undertake.

From the 1950s onwards, influential thinkers began to argue that there was too much specialization in management disciplines, and that what was needed was a new breed of general manager, capable of managing all corporate functions. This image of the general manager is now broadly accepted by both companies and business schools.

The challenges facing general management are, however, very great and steadily increasing. The information revolution has led to increasing information flows which both enhance and complicate the managerial task; similarly, globalization means that managers are having to work more and more across borders in unfamiliar cultures. The scale, scope and speed of the general management task is increasing steadily.

*Malcolm Warner & Morgen Witzel*

## Global strategic alliances

International alliances are cooperative arrangements formed by organizations from two or more countries. An international alliance is considered strategic when it involves the allocation of the resources that the general manager of the firm deems important to the organization's future success.

An international alliance may be established as a greenfield operation, or may be the result of several companies deciding to combine existing resources. The purpose of most international strategic alliances is to allow partners to pool resources and coordinate their efforts to achieve results that neither could obtain acting alone.

In recent years international strategic alliances have become increasingly popular. They have moved from being a way to enter foreign markets of peripheral interest, or of gaining some returns from peripheral technologies, to become a part of the mainstream of corporate activity. Major firms from all over the world are using global strategic alliances as a key element of their corporate strategies. Even firms such as IBM that have traditionally operated independently around the world are increasingly turning to alliances.

*Paul W. Beamish & Peter J. Killing*

## Global strategic planning

Strategic planning in today's dynamic global environment is the most difficult, complex task managers face. In many industries the dynamic nature of the global environment creates a constant pull towards domination by global business units and a simultaneous opposing push towards domination by domestic units. Business units displaying a wide variety of configurations and resource deployment characteristics exist and even thrive in this turbulent environment. In many industries, domestic, multimarket and global participants all thrive; however, the determinants of success do not remain constant.

The cornerstone of business success is the achievement of competitive advantage within a market or sector. In this respect the marketplace is local rather than global, and competition takes place between business units within industries rather than at the level of firms; it is important therefore to focus on industry structure rather than firm structure. The four key determinants of industry structure are industry characteristics, consumer behaviour, competitor behaviour and the political and regulatory environment within which business units operate.

A simple conceptual scheme, the Four Cs model (customers, competitors, climate, capabilities), can be used to formulate strategic plans in the light of industry structure. Analysis of customers and competitors identifies the potential of a particular strategy; analysis of industry climate and the business unit's capabilities identifies the business unit's ability to realize the potential of a given strategy.

*Lawrence H. Wortzel & Heidi Vernon-Wortzel*

## Globalization

Globalization is the process of increasing integration in world civilization. The transformation of its definition reveals the extent to which globalization has proceeded in the last decades. In the 1970s, globalization was seen in terms of the increasing interdependence among states. In today's economy, interdependence among nations is of less central interest, as powerful global actors (for example, multinational corporations and financial institutions) have created a world in which borders are less consequential.

The extent of globalization can be captured through a number of descriptive indicators: parity in prices – prices and interest rates should converge with globalization; effect on behaviours – nation states, firms, and other actors consider their actions and others' actions in one state as influencing their interests in another; world culture – the sharing of cultural values across countries; ideological – the convergence in beliefs about what constitutes a desirable polity. Each of these indicators hides the distinction between *interdependence* and *integration*. Financial markets may converge to price parity, as long as investors can move money from one country to the other. They need not be integrated in the form of a world market for equities. Governments and firms may respond to the actions of their counterparts in other countries, and yet the political and economic significance of borders may be preserved. National cultures and ideologies can respond to foreign ideas in a reactionary way. Austrian churches are topped by onion-shaped cupolas and the French croissant is derived from the Islamic crescent. Yet both of these cultural artefacts are symbolic of the clash between competing and interdependent cultures, not their integration.

The transition from interdependence to integration is seen in the many regional economic groupings that have been spawned over the last forty years. The period immediately after the Second World War saw the creation of international institutions to manage interdependence, although under the tutelage of a few powerful countries. The success of these institutions has varied, but the ones created in the economic sphere have unquestionably increased in membership and importance. The IMF has grown considerably in size. The World Bank Group has expanded into project financing in developing countries. In the area of trade, the failed attempt to create an international institution in the 1940s has been rectified through the establishment of the World Trade Organization in 1995.

Unnoticed in the discussion over interdependence were the forces that have led to a growing integration in the world economy. At the regional level, the results of integration are the most obvious. The European Union is clearly the most prominent example of interdependent states seeking to resolve conflict and to enjoy the benefits of a wider market through economic and political integration. Yet their example is reflected in the less ambitious efforts of other countries. The North American Free Trade Agreement (NAFTA) is a case of low-level integration in so far as the elimination of tariffs and some harmonization of environmental and labour laws are involved. But the world trend is towards more integration, albeit at the regional level, with agreements in Latin America (for example, Mercosur) and in east Asia (for example, Asean), and increasing *de facto* integration in southern Africa occurring only since the mid-1980s.

Interdependence and integration are not unilateral trends in world history. There are counterbalancing factors, particularly those unleashed through the actions of threatened groups or governments. Because globalization influences power and social standing among groups, it is a process that lies at the heart of social change and political policy in all countries. Extreme examples are the responses of countries (for example, Iran) undergoing rapid change which incur a reversal in their openness to the world economy. The debate is not only economic, but ideological and religious. Less extreme examples are no doubt the more modal cases, such as the decision of France in the early 1980s to impose constraints on capital movements.

It is misleading to believe that globalization is determined simply by the development of new technologies in communication and transportation. Since groups and governments can influence the extent and pace of globalization, world integration and interdependence are not simply exogenous and given factors in the course of history. They are both the cause and effect of social and political change. Globalization constrains governments and other actors, such as firms, in their capability to carry out domestic policies. But since governments and firms are also powerful actors, they can influence the process of globalization. Decisions to deregulate or to lower tariffs influence the degree of commerce. In this regard, globalization is both an endogenous and exogenous factor determined in its pace and development by the actions of governments, firms, and other social actors, but influencing also in its turn the behaviour of these same actors.

From the perspective of economics, integration appears as inevitable because of the gains to eliminating institutional imperfections in the movement of goods, services and capital. There is in other words a powerful dynamic unleashed through the creation of positive feedback to integration. Larger markets should increase a more efficient allocation of world resources. Yet, not only is this dynamic sensitive to the process by which integration occurs (for example, by regions or by world agreement), it also results in the dislocation of workers and important social groups and institutions. Even if one were to accept that integration improves world welfare in some global assessment of the costs and benefits, the distributional consequences are substantial, as are the effects on the relative power of nation-states.

*Bruce Kogut & Michelle Gittelman*

## Globalization and corporate nationality

The discourse of globalization draws much of its strength from the imagery of 'global' or 'stateless' corporations which are said to have transcended national boundaries and made the very concept of the nation-state obsolete. In order to examine, in a scientific manner, whether and to what extent these corporate entities (formerly labelled as 'international', 'multinational' and 'transnational' firms) are truly stateless and global, it is necessary to construct and apply a number of objective and verifiable criteria. Six key criteria of corporate nationality versus stateless globalism are: geographical spread and scope of operations, ownership, control, people, legal nationality and tax domicile.

Applying the six criteria together leads to the conclusion that there is no such thing as truly transnational, global or stateless firms, in the sense which the terms intend to convey, of entities that have transcended nation-states. Apart from the few 'bi-national' companies (that is, those having two home nations), there are only national firms with international (that is, foreign) operations.

This apparently simple conclusion has a number of important implications. For the public debate on the impact of globalization and on 'who is Us?', it is just as important to know what is *not* the case as it is to be able to make specific assertions or predictions. For healthy firms and healthy nations, the home nation (or even localities within the home nation) is seen to be the primary source of the firm's international competitive advantage, and the firm and its home nation need each other to maintain dynamism and competitiveness. For the research agenda in international business, 'national firms with international operations' are obviously a less homogeneous category than is implied by terms such as multinational, transnational or global firms, and nationality or national character may be as important, if not more important, a determining characteristic and distinguishing hallmark of firms operating abroad as 'multinationality' or 'globalism'; this will affect the theory of multinational enterprise as well as the search for universal recipes of 'international management' and 'global strategy'.

*Yao-Su Hu*

## Globalization and society

The study of globalization in the social sciences revolves primarily around two main classes of phenomena which have become increasingly significant in the last few decades. These are the spread of transnational corporations (TNCs) through processes such as the globalization of capital and production and the new international division of labour, and the global scope of the modern mass media.

There are at least four sources of 'globalization' research in the contemporary social sciences, and they can be loosely identified as the world-systems approach; the global culture approach; the global society approach; and the global system approach. The first is characterized by 'international' and the fourth by 'transnational' conceptions of globalization, while the second and third use both conceptions.

The world-system approach is based on the distinction between core capitalist, semi-peripheral and peripheral countries in terms of their changing roles in the international division of labour. The global culture approach focuses on the problems that a homogenizing mass media-based culture poses for national identities, while the global society approach focuses more on problems of global governance and security. The global system approach is based on the concept of transnational practices operating in the economic, political and culture-ideology spheres of the global capitalist system. There are also three important cross-cutting issues: global environmental change; gender and globalization; and global cities.

*Leslie Sklair*

## Government, industry and the public sector

There is a range of possibilities for the involvement of government in the affairs of industry – from total hands-off unregulated capitalism to the exact reverse, where the state owns all economic activities and the government controls them through a central planning system. Experience shows that neither extreme works well.

A total hands-off system will most likely lead to the growth of monopolies and restrictive practices in industry, to extensive environmental pollution, to unsafe and unhealthy working practices, to crime, and to personal suffering. Competition alone will not allocate resources efficiently and effectively and will not, therefore, maximize the welfare of a nation (although some people will benefit greatly). On the other hand, if the state owns and controls everything, diversity of personal preference is restricted and the opportunities for personal initiative and product and process development are stifled.

In the 1990s, almost all countries are converging towards a middle ground. The international trend is privatization, both as contracting out and in the form of ownership transfer to the private sector. It would be wrong, however, to expect all countries to end up with identical economies. History, culture, politics, location and opportunity will lead to a diversity of economic structures and market models. The problem for each country is to find a balance that will satisfy its needs and aspirations.

The key issues, therefore, concern the form, extent and consequences of privatization, the residual role of the state and the ultimate balance between state and private provision. Where state enterprises continue to exist – and almost every country retains a few – there is the problem of securing efficient and effective relationships between them and their governments.

*John Heath*

## Groups and teams

Many organizations are involved with the introduction of teamwork. A team can be considered as a number of people (a group) organized around a set of objectives. Teamwork can be regarded as a remedy for the dysfunctions of bureaucratic structures which are still dominant in organizations. Today, bureaucracies must operate in a far more complex and uncertain environment than ever before. They threaten to be destroyed by the burden of activities created by themselves to control and coordinate the segmented organization.

In order to survive they must invest in new control strategies. Two of these strategies imply the introduction of team concepts in the design of the organization. One strategy involves the introduction of 'lateral linkages'. These are groups that horizontally cut across the existing boundaries of functions. A special form of this is the management team. The creation of self-contained units is the second team-based strategy. With this alternative the functions are integrated around a certain order flow; complete little firms are created within the walls of a bigger firm. The autonomous production team is an important example of this.

The creation of a teamwork organization is to be approached from a double perspective. The team is both the result of organization design choices and of a development process by which the team members learn from their experiences. Organization design and organization development are to be viewed as two sides of the same coin. The introduction of teamwork in organizations is a matter of careful design. The team is an organization in itself, but at the same time is part of a larger system. Tasks must be allocated between and within teams. Systems must be introduced to control the work process. A number of important structural criteria apply to both the lateral and the production teams: a complete task to be carried out independently; a good link with other groups in the organization; sufficient instruments to steer the group's own process; and a good internal organization.

*Friso den Hertog & Thera Tolner*

## Guru concept

From the turn of the century onwards management gurus have played a central role in the manufacture, transmission and application of management knowledge. To explain their influence, one has to understand both the nature of managerial work and the needs that it creates among occupants of managerial positions. Those management ideas which meet those needs are likely to be the most popular. Moreover, the nature of management itself also predisposes the profession to look to management gurus for guidance since, at one and the same time, these gurus develop, represent and also act as conduits for the application of their ideas into organizations.

During the twentieth century at least six bodies of management theory and knowledge have emerged, and each has had its associated gurus. These include bureaucracy (Weber), scientific management (Taylor), classical management (Fayol), human relations (Mayo), neo-human relations (McGregor) and guru theory (Peters, Moss Kanter and Iacocca). These individuals have become popularly associated with the ideas they have expounded. Much therefore depends on the personal qualities of these individuals. Managers, as people who prefer verbal communication and rely on personal judgement and intuition, tend to decide on the value of a management idea not through an in-depth evaluation of its content, but through an assessment of the on-stage performance of the management guru who is propounding the idea. The nature of management in capitalist societies all around the world will ensure that the guru concept will continue to play a vital role in future management thought and action.

*Andrzej Huczynski*

# H

## Hawthorne experiments

The Hawthorne studies (1924–33), initially undertaken to investigate the relationship between workplace conditions and worker productivity at Western Electric's Hawthorne Works, near Chicago, introduced a wide range of topics to the field of management study. Investigators found no strong relationship between workplace conditions and productivity but reached several conclusions: individual work behaviour is driven by a complex set of factors; work groups develop norms which mediate between the needs of the individual and institution; employees should not be considered appendages of machinery; awareness of employee sentiments and participation can reduce resistance to change; the workplace is an interlocking social system, not simply a production system; social structure is maintained through symbols of prestige and power. These findings opened the door to the study of client-centred therapy, small group behaviour, organization theory and research methodology.

*Jeffrey A. Sonnenfeld and Jennifer M. Myatt*

## Health management

Health systems throughout the world are subject to common pressures of cost containment, increasing technological sophistication and a growing elderly population. The approaches to tackling these issues vary in terms of the state of development within each country and the political direction set by governments attempting to tackle the issues. Some countries, such as the USA, use a mix of private and public health care systems, while others, notably the UK, rely almost exclusively on public health care delivery. In both private and public sector, there has been since the mid-1980s a degree of consensus as to the value of allowing market forces to control the cost pressures on health services. This approach has taken many forms and varies primarily in terms of the extent of the market place and the degree of constraint or regulation imposed. The level of success has also been variable, but it does seem that the market-led approach may persist. This means that health management will need to become more entrepreneurial and flexible, more customer oriented and more performance oriented, and finally more accountable to both patients and taxpayers.

*Peter Spurgeon*

## Hotel management

The modern hotel industry had its beginnings in the early European grand hotels of the mid-nineteenth century and is now a major global international industry, increasingly dominated by a small number of multinational organizations. Hotel managers face many similar problems to other service industry managers: of understanding guest expectations, of matching resources to guests, of controlling employee behaviour, of balancing the need to please the guest against the need to make profits and of handling a multi-activity operation. The use of staff within hotels is particularly problematic both because hotels are labour intensive organizations and because hotel employees are part of the hotel product. Hotels have traditionally been seen as providers of low skill and low paid jobs to a transient workforce, but recruitment problems and a competitive environment where good quality staff may give an edge in the marketplace have prompted some interest in different staffing practices.

Hotels have been seen as a rather specialized type of business. Hotel managers have been developed through separate educational programmes and have tended to follow careers exclusively within the hotel industry. A premium has been placed on the development of technical knowledge rather than general management skills and management style tends to emphasize day-to-day operational activities. There are some signs, however, that the hotel industry is becoming more open to ideas from other industries.

*Yvonne Guerrier*


## Human capital

The idea that expenditure on such things as education, on-the-job training and health care can be thought of as an investment in an individual's future ability to generate income is not a new one. An early statement of the concept of human capital was made by Adam Smith in 1776, and while human capital theory has been developed and expanded over the last two centuries, a number of its basic concepts can still be found in *The Wealth of Nations*. First, expenditure on the productivity-enhancing skills of people has similarities with investment in physical capital which can be expected to generate income in the future. Second, expenditure on education, on-the-job training, health care or migration to areas with greater employment opportunities, can all be thought of as investments which are normally rewarded in the future by higher income. Third, differing levels of investment in human capital can explain productivity differences between individuals and therefore differences in their rates of pay. Fourth, it is in the individual's interests to invest in human capital when the net benefits exceed the net benefits of investing in an alternative asset.

It is not only private individuals who make decisions to invest in human capital but also in most countries, the state undertakes considerable investment in this area, for example in education and health. One rationale for this intervention is that benefits from investment in human capital accrue not only to the individuals directly involved but to society at large; for example, a more educated and informed community should make better political decisions and raising public health standards reduces the incidence of disease to everyone.

*Anne Daly*

## Human-centred manufacturing systems, design of

The conditions for the industrial production of technical goods change constantly. Dynamic technical development, the permanently changing market and changing values, together with the relationship of individuals to their work, have a significant influence on the organization and the planning of workplaces. The substantial economic, technical and human factors are not isolated and have to be considered within the context of mutual dependencies.

The move towards human-centred manufacturing systems has been given impetus by the recognition that conventional manufacturing structures have largely reached their productive limits. A change of paradigm to an anthropocentric labour organization is seen as one option. Focusing on the individual takes place in five dimensions: the reduction of time-pressure, job rotation, job enlargement, job enrichment and semi-autonomous teamwork. New concepts of integrated and decentralized organization are also required, and the entire production process needs to be planned and reorganized in the form of production cells. The resulting activities of employees will be characterized by mainly independent control of working and cooperation, linked with planning and control functions, and the renunciation of a rigid division of work, thereby extending the room for manoeuvre of individual employees.

*Hans-Jörg Bullinger & Martin Schmauder*

## Human relations

Broadly speaking, the two major strands in modern management are recognized to be *scientific management*, based on the logic of economic man and efficiency, and *human relations*, based on that of the social individual and sentiment. The human relations movement, as an academic discipline, grew out of scientific management in the 1930s especially via the contribution of Follett. Both sides aimed at achieving high productivity, but scientific management sought to adapt worker to task whereas human relations veered towards adjusting task to worker. Since its academic accreditation, the human relations movement has developed through various schools: mainly group dynamics and industrial relations, to organizational humanism, through to individualism and systemic interdependence. The evolving trend is towards the growth of mutually accountable, self-managing teams (against hierarchical relationships) working in the flexible organization which sees itself an integral part of the overall ecosystem.

*Pauline Graham*

## Human resource flows

Employers can staff vacancies from a wide array of sources. External labour markets may be tapped for new organizational members when there is a need for expertise that is cost-prohibitive to develop internally; for an infusion of new perspectives that might improve business processes; for compliance with equal employment opportunity mandates; or for additional manpower to redress shortages in semi-skilled and unskilled labour. How far afield a firm must go to satisfy its demand for qualified persons varies greatly across countries and over time. The skill mix within a given nation can be quite dynamic, affected by demographic shifts (for example, altered labour force participation rates among key population subgroups), migration flows (for example, brain drains from emigration, skill booms from in-migration), government policies for human-capital formation (for example, magnitude and targeting of expenditures on education, vocational training initiatives) and large-scale technology transfers. Even when skills are abundant in the indigenous population, strong norms about the acceptability of certain types of work may create artificial shortages that necessitate importing labour. For example, menial or dangerous jobs in the manufacturing, construction and service sectors of industrialized economies are often filled by individuals from less developed countries. All of these factors must be considered when establishing the appropriate geographic scope for external searches.

Alternatively, employers may seek full exploitation of their internal labour markets when vacancies arise within business units. There are numerous advantages in doing so for domestic firms, such as providing incentives for employee retention, extending the returns on company-specific skills or knowledge, or simply decreasing recruitment and selection costs. However, this strategy assumes that the firm has sufficient human resource slack to be stockpiling skills for creative deployment internally. Major downsizing trends in western economies have made it more difficult to rely heavily on such sourcing in recent decades. It is increasingly the case that firms are shrinking to a smaller permanent core of key employees and drawing upon a large flexible pool of contingent workers from the outside as demand dictates. Multinational enterprises (MNEs) appear to be in a better position in this regard, having bigger internal labour markets that transcend the skill constraints associated with any single national labour force. Yet they seldom utilize the wide range of talents available within their far-flung operations.

By the 1980s, human resource management practitioners had also intensified efforts to have human resource supply and demand analyses incorporated into business strategy formulation. Thus, firms that repeatedly experience human resource flow imbalances may not be taking full advantage of the planning technologies at their disposal.

*Gary Florkowski*

## Human resource management

Managing human resources effectively has become vital to organizations of the twenty-first century. The heightened levels of global competitiveness has alerted all firms to the fact that all their resources must be utilized better than ever before. Human resource management has received much attention recently because of the recognition that much more could be gained from a better handling of the field. Consequently academics have begun to devote more attention to the topic.

Academics and human resource management professionals together have identified several human resource activities that are critical for organizational survival. Survival is enhanced because of the ability of effective human resource management to attract, retain, motivate and retrain employees. These goals have become particularly important in the 1990s because of the rapidly changing environmental forces such as global competition. For human resources to be effective, however, requires that not only do the several human resource activities need to be performed effectively, but also that the human resource departments in organizations need to play several roles and that those in these departments need to have a broader and deeper range of competencies than previously required.

*Randall S. Schuler*

## Human resource management, international

The successful operation of a multinational firm is contingent upon the availability of technology, technological know-how, capital and human resources. Without a highly developed pool of human resources (including managerial and technical talent), technology, technological know-how and capital cannot be effectively and efficiently allocated or transferred from corporate headquarters to the scattered subsidiaries. Developing and managing this managerial and technical talent is the function of international human resource management.

International human resource management has five main dimensions: first, the selection and recruitment of qualified individuals capable of furthering organizational goals; second, the training and development of personnel at all levels to maximize organizational performance; third, the assessment of employee performance to ensure that organizational goals are met; fourth, the retention of competent corporate personnel who can continue to facilitate the attainment of organizational goals; and fifth, the management of the interface between labour and management to ensure smooth organizational functioning.

Each of the five salient aspects of international human resource management noted above can affect organizational functioning. In the future, international human resource management will take on even greater significance in the overall strategic planning and management of multinational firms, for several reasons: the globalization of the world economy; the globalization of the workforce; and regional economic integration.

*Rosalie L. Tung*

## Human resource management in Europe

Human resource management as a concept was developed and popularized in the USA and has been extensively criticized in Europe. A key question is whether the concept in its US guise is applicable in Europe. Evidence suggests that the essentially unlimited managerial autonomy assumed in most US theories of this subject is not found in Europe. Consequently, there is a need to develop a new perspective, a 'European' model of human resource management. This model must take into account the internal and external limitations on management in Europe, and provide a vision which can link human resource management to economic success.

Important to this new analysis is the recognition of differences in managerial culture between the USA and Europe, and accordingly that variations in human resource management practice are possible. Part of the problem lies in the fact that there is a relative lack of hard data on relative practices in the USA; there is a danger in comparing empirical evidence from European studies with normative statements of what should be emanating from the USA. Much of US literature on this subject can be read as a prescriptive indictment of what is not happening, rather than a description of what exists. A final point is that the core elements abstracted from the US texts are precisely that: abstractions. No conception of human resource management in the USA or among its adherents in Europe mirrors this version exactly, and many have other perspectives. As noted above, the concept of managerial autonomy underpins nearly all the leading texts, and this has consequences for management in Europe.

*Chris Brewster*

## Incentives

Incentives have grown in popularity across a wide spectrum of employing organizations worldwide, particularly since the mid-1980s. The motivating effect of 'extra income' has enjoyed growing interest even in times of recession. Incentive payment schemes represent an attempt to influence the behaviour, and therefore work performance, of employees through the provision of a monetary or non-monetary reward which is extra to basic remuneration. This reward is assumed to bring forward a level of contribution to the company which is greater than that normally forthcoming in return for basic pay. Such payments, or bonuses, can be made for extra effort on the shop floor, shouldering extra responsibility in the office, selling more than quota in the sales division or achieving increased profits in the boardroom. In one form or another, therefore, incentive schemes can be applied to all categories of work.

Incentive schemes have proved more popular in the UK than in any other industrial nation. By way of contrast, in the USA remuneration policies and practices have tended to concentrate on remuneration as a whole. Pay is thus for the job and any performance or contribution expected of employees is not generally linked to some unique element such as an incentive payment. In the UK incentives have been linked to individual or group performance criteria. In the USA pay has been linked to business strategy as an integral part of human resource management, not as some separate motivating incentive-based strategy. In Europe incentives are less popular than in the UK, with more emphasis given to structure and equity. Interestingly, the newer Third World industries, which use incentive payments extensively, parallel British industry conditions of the early twentieth century when shop-floor incentives grew apace. In some industries incentives represent a considerable proportion of the task of managing remuneration. For the individual on incentive the payment can represent a significant element of earnings. For the trade unions incentives are a subject for negotiation. For management the incentive scheme is deemed to offer some hope of a reduction in unit costs of production or in more general terms an improvement in corporate well-being. Unfortunately, translating an incentive effect into some measure of improvement in corporate performance has proved difficult and it is a paradox that reward for employee performance is very rarely linked to the strategic approach to company objective achievement.

*Ian Smith*

## Industrial conflict

Conflict is widely seen as one of the central principles of organizational life. Interpretations of its origin, nature and effects vary substantially, however. In particular, beginning in the 1980s, accounts associated with human resource management and Japanese management often argued that conflict was being eliminated, or at least being made into a minor feature of organizations. This developing orthodoxy contrasts with an earlier one, that conflict was inevitable and even desirable: the issue was not its elimination but its management.

The continuing centrality of conflict is indicated by, first, the conceptual argument that conflict is a central principle of any organization in which workers labour under the authority of management. Second, levels of overt dispute in the Western world have not declined by as much as is sometimes thought, and such declines have been balanced by increases in overt conflict in the Third World. Last, studies in organizations where conflict may appear to have been eliminated, notably Japanese firms and 'high-tech' companies, show high levels of work pressure and a tendency for conflict and tensions to be internalized within employees, rather than being expressed as open disputes between management and worker. Claims that conflict can be eliminated misunderstand how organizations work. It is not a question of its elimination, but of the changing ways in which it is organized and expressed.

*Paul K. Edwards*

## Industrial democracy

The term 'industrial democracy' refers to the structures and institutional mechanisms that give workers or their representatives the opportunity to influence organizational decision making in their places of employment. Programmes vary in the amount of involvement they allow workers in the decision-making process and the degree of influence workers have over decision outcomes. There has been some debate over whether mere worker involvement, or participation, in decision making was a sufficient condition for industrial democracy, or whether joint decision making, or power sharing, between workers and management was necessary before one could speak of democracy in the workplace. There is, in practice, a large range of programmes and institutions that enable labour's voice to be heard in a formal way within the enterprise. These differ in the scope of decisions they include, the amount of power workers can exercise *vis-à-vis* management, and the organizational level at which the decisions are made. Some are purposefully designed to give workers a very modest role in decision making while others are intended to give the workforce a substantial amount of power in organizational governance.

Industrial democracy, or worker participation in management as it is usually called in the USA, can be direct or indirect (through representatives), and prescribed by law, established through contracts or granted by the employer. It is convenient to place the different models or forms of participation in two categories based on their origins - legal statutes and employer grants. Legally based or prescribed structures such as worker representation on corporate boards of directors, works councils or trade union representation (collective bargaining) are formal systems with written rules and regulations that provide uniform guidelines for involving workers in decision making in all organizations that come under the jurisdiction of the law or contract. Employer-granted or employer-initiated participation usually does not specify employees' legal rights to be involved in decision making. To the extent that formal written agreements exist in granted programmes, they are specific to a given enterprise. Examples of granted participation are shop floor employee involvement programmes, labour-management committees, like those found in productivity gainsharing plans, and autonomous work teams.

*Tove Helland Hammer*

## Industrial economics

Industrial economics (IE), also known as industrial organization (IO) and industrial economics and organization (IEO) represents an integration of a number of different strands within economics, including institutional economics and international economics, with other disciplines such as strategic management and organization studies. The origins of industrial economics lie in the debate between competition and monopoly in the nineteenth century. Neo-classical models of IE were based on the structure-conduct-performance paradigm, with a largely unidirectional causal link leading from structure through conduct to performance. Alternative perspectives include the Marxist, post-Keynsian, Chicago and Austrian school perspectives.

These theories often assumed that firms operate in a closed economy; however, it is all too apparent that firms are increasingly operating in open, indeed global, economies, and that such an environment has a considerable effect on IEO. Internationalization and the transnational corporation require new models and new directions. Examples of new developments include transaction costs, markets and hierarchies theory, new international trade theory and new theories of industrial strategy.

*Christos Pitelis*

## Industrial and labour relations

Industrial (or labour) relations encompasses the study of the employment relationship. Ultimately the rationale for the discipline is the continued significance of work for the maintenance and advance of human societies. This necessitates the existence of a vitally consequential labour or employee group, which is involved in a fundamental economic, social and political relationship with employers and management. Moreover, the outcomes of this relationship are so crucial to the long-term survival, let alone continued prosperity of any given country, that it inevitably includes the state or government as well.

In more detail, industrial relations scholars tend to assume that in every industrial and industrializing country, there are three main 'actors' or parties with partly common and partly divergent interests: employers and managers, employees and labour (and often trade unions), and the state. A degree of conflict between these groups is regarded as inevitable, but there are typically mechanisms to ensure that it is channelled or accommodated, notably: (1) individual resolution (supported by freedom of contract and by the lack of any substantial restrictions to the operation of the labour market); (2) unilateral determination (by employers, managers, the state, trade unions or workers); and (3) plural modes of regulation (typically under collective bargaining and in which differences are 'expressed, articulated and defended' through independent associations of employers and working people and in which joint determination and responsibility for the terms and conditions of employment has been instituted).

It is further assumed that interests may be shared or conflicting in both so-called production and distribution spheres (the first encompasses the actual work process, the second economic rewards which accrue from employment). On the one hand, then, a series of creative or productive activities are defined by the functions of all organizations. But while their performance may be free of conflict (for example, when managerial decision making is legitimated), equally there are often fundamental struggles along the so-called 'frontier of control', between working people who seek 'freedom on the job' and managers and supervisors who endeavour to plan the overall organization and conduct of work. On the other hand, the allocation of rewards from work may also occasion consensus or conflict. The former depends on fairness or justice governing the principles of distribution. However, in its absence, antagonism is likely and is reflected in familiar disputes over pay and income.

*Michael Poole*

## Industrial relations in developing countries

Industrial relations in developing countries have been products of both endogenous and exogenous factors. In several countries, predominantly former colonial dependencies, the sudden creation of the original and formal cradle of industrial relations – wage-employment – had been externally induced. Subsequently, these initial structures gradually grew in the designated countries and remained intact for varying periods beyond political independence and through the 1970s. But, for reasons also internally and externally accounted, the industrial relations institutions in these countries have undergone further regimes of transformation and regeneration – sometimes chaotic and disruptive of macrolevel development – through the 1980s and 1990s.

The major elements of industrial relations in developing countries have been: the colonial impact; nationalism, post-colonial states and crises of development; an overbearing role of government, coupled with political problems and instability; the impact of structural adjustment programmes; the democratic challenge; and the emergent demands of social partnership.

The patterns of industrial relations in developing countries are still largely disparate, but with a few coherent features gradually emerging. The continuity of these in the very long term, and the probable additional benefits of social well-being and political peace in these nations, should strengthen the overall framework of relationships.

*Segun Matanmi*

## Industrial relations in Europe

Since the 1970s industrial relations in Europe have undergone much change, the majority of which has come from beyond the boundaries of Europe. The emergence of a global economy dominated by large multinational companies, structural transformations in the economies of western Europe from manufacturing to services, developments in new technology, an increase in white-collar employment at the expense of manual jobs and a continuing rise in unemployment have all had a major effect on industrial relations in all European countries.

The major impact on European industrial relations has been: increased decentralization in collective bargaining; a decline in trade union membership and influence; the emergence of new forms of management, including human resource management; new forms of participation and work organization; and the growing importance of European Union employment initiatives. Because of the wide diversity in industrial relations systems across different European countries, the changes have affected countries in Europe in different ways and there is little evidence to suggest that a European-wide industrial relations model is developing.

*Colin Gill*

## Industrial relations in Japan

Industrial relations in Japan is one example of cooperative employer-employee relations in an industrialized country. These relations are based on the following mechanisms: enterprise union, works council, and spring labour offensive. The essential elements of the enterprise union and works council also apply to some Japanese companies operating abroad under different styles of industrial relations.

Good employer–employee relations are beneficial for several reasons. They contributed to the competitiveness of Japanese companies in the 1980s and to the high nominal wage level of Japanese workers when compared with other developed countries. Enterprise unions can stimulate joint efforts between employers and employees to increase productivity and thus maintain employment levels. Works councils can promote the exchange of opinions concerning management policies as well as discussion of the working condition of the company. These two mechanisms provide conditions for information sharing between employees and their employer which further develops the feeling of joint commitment. Meanwhile, the establishment of the Japan Trade Union Congress in 1989 indicates a new direction taken by Japanese enterprise unionism.

One drawback of such a system, however, is that it may promote the overcommitment of Japanese employees to their company. In addition, ideological differences among workers supporting different political parties disturbs uniform political action to improve the social system for the working class as a whole.

*Koji Okubayashi*

## Industrial relations in the United States of America

Both the relative power of the US economy and the global influence of its managerial and industrial relations models justify the effort necessary to understand it, despite the difficulties posed by its exceptionalism and complexity. The US influence on the global economy derives from the early development of professional management techniques in the USA, its guidance and financing of the post-Second World War recovery, and the size and worldwide scope of US multinational corporations.

The pressures of international competition have opened a Pandora's box of troubles for the US industrial relations system, among others. The move from oligopolistic markets to competitive ones has created the need for many industries in the USA to create new ways to organize work and cut costs. It may be that the necessary level of quality of some goods, such as automobiles and electronic equipment, cannot be attained without developing cooperative mechanisms that are inconsistent with the US adversarial model. However, it is unclear whether more cooperative work methods can endure under US capitalism, where the 'fast buck' is held in reverence, the pressures of predatory takeover artists keep management constantly squeezing for more profits, managers hold opposition to employee collective action as a part of their philosophy, and hierarchical habits are deeply ingrained. The trust that is the foundation stone of labour–management cooperation is difficult to build in such an environment.

Meanwhile, the traditional collective bargaining structure in the USA has fared rather well. It has devised means to cut labour costs. Unions have generally not opposed the adoption of new technology, and have bargained for innovations in cooperation, profit sharing, health care costs and holidays. Child care may be the next frontier. Similarly, in the unionized sector, the grievance and arbitration procedures continue to guarantee workers protection. In the non-union sector, many employers are adopting progressive and positive employment policies. There remains a concern about the overall strength of the US labour movement, which like those in many other countries, has declined in recent years.

*Hoyt N. Wheeler*

## Industrial Revolution

An industrial revolution can be defined most generally as a fundamental set of changes associated with a markedly rising share of the manufacturing sector in economic activity. The term is often used to refer to changes in Britain during the last half of the eighteenth century and the first half of the nineteenth century, the British economy being commonly regarded as the first to undergo a rise in its manufacturing sector of sufficient magnitude to produce fundamental economic and social change.

Aspects of economic change in Britain during its Industrial Revolution that have been considered revolutionary include an increased number of economically important technological innovations, a marked rise in per capita output in the presence of rising population levels, the rise of the factory and a shift towards social and economic relationships based on impersonal exchange. The concept of industrial revolution has been generalized beyond the British case to encompass all situations in which the rising share of the manufacturing sector in economic activity has been associated with fundamental economic and social change.

*David Mitch*

## Industrial sabotage

Sabotage or the threat of sabotage is a central determinant of the balance of power in contemporary organizations. Throughout the history of industry and commerce, it has been used as a weapon by those with less formal power and has been practised and refined as an art of resistance. It has been discussed widely, but has been the subject of only a few comprehensive and sustained studies. Loose definitions of the concept predominate. It is defined here as deliberate action or inaction that is intended to damage, destroy or disrupt some aspect of the workplace environment, including the property, product, processes or reputation of the organization.

In contrast to the image of the 'mad saboteur', careful review of existing research leads to the conclusion that most acts of sabotage are highly symbolic, are restrained and selective, are the product of collective or even conspiratorial efforts, and are performed with technical sophistication. They tend to be deliberate and calculated rather than impulsive and careless.

Some level of workplace sabotage corresponds to the class-based organization of society and its associated distribution of advantages and disadvantages. This is compounded in effect due to issues of gender, race and ethnicity and other social barriers that exist. However, these macro conditions for sabotage do not fully explain its occurrence. It is also necessary to consider micro factors that manifest themselves in organizational and occupational settings, such as lack of control and exposure to systematic injustices. Simple desires for fun are sometimes considered as motives for destructive behaviour but such acts are not properly defined as sabotage.

The contemporary and future importance of sabotage are hard to deny. It is therefore time for theorists of organizational behaviour and management to make a sustained effort to understand it.

*John M. Jermier & Walter Nord*

## Industrial strategy

Western industrial policies since the Second World War have tended to be *ad hoc*, short-term and reactive, with a focus on free market, free trade and ideology. The prime exemplars of this type of strategy have been the USA and the UK, where the free market and non-intervention have been strongest. France is known as an example of a more strongly interventionist strategy, while German industrial strategy, while much more low-key, also includes a role for government.

Despite national differences, the Western approach with its free-market focus and relatively static comparative advantage contrasts sharply with the Eastern approach of Japan and the newly industrialized countries, which has been based on a close state involvement in industry, attempting to shape market forces with an eye to creating dynamic comparative advantages. However, while these industrial strategies have been very successful in the East, it seems unlikely for a number of reasons that they could be transferred successfully to the West.

Another option for the West is the development of narrowly self-interested industrial strategies, based on the lessons from new theory and international experience. However, this Machiavellian scenario may be neither desirable or possible. A third alterative is to depart from short-termism and develop an industrial strategy for the West which would emphasize global welfare in a dynamic fashion over the long term.

*Christos Pitelis*

## Inflation

The rate of inflation is generally taken to mean the prevailing annual increase of the average level of prices of consumer goods and services in the economy. It is generally agreed that a high or volatile inflation rate is a major economic ill. The problems that arise when inflation is high, or volatile and unpredictable, include distortions of income distribution, bias in investment decisions and inefficient allocation of resources. The control of inflation is therefore an issue of primary concern for policy.

A number of different markets are involved in determining the rate of inflation, including the market in goods and services, the labour market, the foreign exchange market and world markets for primary commodities and for finished goods. The process by which prices are set is somewhat different in each market. To understand fully the nature of the inflation spiral, it is necessary to understand the processes determining price setting in each. The current price level and the going rate of inflation will both be taken into account when prices are set: this is called the 'no money illusion'. The resulting pressures in the economy lead to rapid rises in world prices of primary commodities, overheating in domestic consumer markets and various imperfections in domestic labour markets.

Policies for preventing high inflation include restructuring an inflation-ary labour market, preventing bottlenecks occurring, avoiding damage to productive capacity and avoiding inflation rates significantly higher than those of trading partners. There is some potential for offsetting temporary inflationary pressures through manipulation of the exchange rate.

The choice of policy options for the cure of inflation is limited. Macroeconomic policies can have a substantial impact on the rate of inflation, but only in certain circumstances will these lead to a persisting reduction in inflation. Government intervention in the operation of the labour market can also influence the rate of inflation.

*Penelope A. Rowlatt*

## Inflation accounting

Inflation implies a decline in the purchasing power of money. This may distort the information given by accounts that use money as their unit of measurement. Changes in prices of particular commodities may not move exactly in line with one another. Thus, there is a choice between adjusting items in the accounts for specific price changes or for changes in the general price level. It is therefore better to use the broader term, *price change accounting*, rather than the narrower term, inflation accounting, the latter implying only general price level adjustment.

The accountant's traditional method of accounting, historical cost accounting (HCA), makes no allowances for general inflation or for changes in the prices of assets that have not been sold. Current purchasing power accounting (CPPA) is a means of adjusting HCA accounts for inflation by using general price level indices. The idea of general index-based CPPA systems owes its origins particularly to the hyperinflation in Germany in the 1920s. The English-speaking world also advocated CPPA as a response to the inflation of the early 1970s, but it was adopted only in Latin America, where its practice continues as a response to hyperinflation.

Real terms accounting (RTA) is a means of combining revaluations of specific assets at current prices (reflecting specific price changes) with general index adjustments (reflecting the impact of inflation). Current value accounting (CVA) revalues assets at current prices, but makes no general index adjustment. It is therefore a method of price change accounting but not of inflation accounting (since it does not have regard to changes in the general price level).

Replacement cost accounting (RCA) revalues assets at current replacement cost (a form of current valuation) but also uses a replacement cost index to adjust the owners' capital of the business in calculating whether a profit has been made. This means that appreciation in the value of the firm's operating assets is not recognized as a gain (as it would be in CVA), because the firm needs its assets to maintain its operations and therefore is made no better off if their market value increases, since it has no intention to sell them. RCA is not strictly an inflation accounting method, but a system of price change accounting.

The choice between methods of price change accounting is a difficult one. In particular, there is a trade-off between relevance and reliability. Current values, although unreliable, are often regarded as relevant to economic decisions and assessments, whereas historical costs are more reliable (having a basis in verifiable transactions) but are less useful as indicators of the economic condition of a business in times of rapid price changes. The choice of accounting method may also benefit one party with an interest in the firm at the expense of another. General price level adjustments are particularly useful in aiding comparisons across series of years, although it is important that the adjustments be applied consistently. The management accounts of companies, which are used internally for decision making and control, may also be affected by price changes. Appropriate adjustments need to be made in order to avoid decisions being based on misleading information. The possibility of taxes or tax reliefs based on price change adjustments has played an important role in determining the adoption in practice of such adjustments.

*Geoffrey Whittington*

## Information and capital markets

Capital markets are concerned with the origination, marketing and trading of wholesale financial products. Investment banks and merchant banks exist to bring together organizations wishing to raise capital – governments, corporations and supranationals like the World Bank – with investing institutions like pension or mutual funds and insurance companies. The products of the markets can be split broadly into debt and equity, but the divisions between the two are becoming blurred as more complex instruments are created to meet particular needs.

Companies come to the market to raise funds with a variety of objectives which affect the type of service they require and the associated information demand. Typical reasons might be to raise money as cheaply as possible for expansion or takeovers, to re-finance existing debt more cheaply as economic circumstances change, or to raise their profile with investors in other parts of the world. British companies with substantial US interests, for example, recognize the advantages of having a New York Stock Exchange listing and US investors for its ability to raise funds.

In the UK and USA particularly, growth in capital markets has been fuelled by the movement of retail funds out of retail bank deposit accounts into investments such as pension funds, mutual or unit trust funds. These institutional investors need to place clients' money where it will gain an acceptable return, and where maturities and liquidities will enable them to meet expected future obligations.

Investment banks need to be aware of all these factors and be able to deliver the information that helps the client and the investor meet their needs. This information comes from sources specific to the capital markets which are used for these purposes, and largely excludes the real-time data feeds used to sell and trade stocks and bonds.

*Mark Jewell*

## Information and knowledge industry

The information and knowledge industry supplies the pieces necessary for building information and knowledge-based systems, and feeds data, information and knowledge to these systems and their customers. This industry has experienced rapid growth since the 1950s, moving from a very specialized arena, only affordable by large companies and well-endowed government departments, into the mass global market of business, public and personal systems. This growth is expected to be sustained and even accelerated in the future, with the prediction that the information and knowledge industry will expand into other fields of consumer-based services such as entertainment, shopping, education, recreation, travel, property and banking.

*Fatemeh (Mariam) Zahedi*

## Information revolution

The agricultural revolution, followed by the industrial revolution, made possible the growth in economic and material wealth in the industrialized nations. A third revolution – the information revolution – made possible by technological advances in communication and computing technology is providing the means for what has been called the 'information age'. Although information played a part in the earlier revolutions as well, the current revolution is being largely driven by increasing demand for information and the transformation in technology.

The new technologies have made access to international communications networks an everyday occurrence. The development of the Internet is the latest example of the impact of a new technology. The result is a far-reaching and complex social change, with significant implications for business around the world.

*Frank Land*

## Information technology

Information technology (IT) covers any form of technology, that is any equipment or technique used by a company, institution or any other organization which handles information. The handling of information has an ancient history, going back to the invention of the printing machine and even further, for example to the devising of the abacus. The term 'information technology' was probably coined in the late 1970s to refer to this nexus of computer-based technology for handling information. It incorporates the whole of the computing and telecommunication technologies and major parts of consumer electronics and broadcasting. Spearheaded by the computer, the past few decades since the mid-1960s have been characterized by major developments in IT. Since the late 1970s, cheap microelectronics have permitted the diffusion of this technology into almost all aspects of daily life and have, furthermore, almost inextricably cross-fertilized and intermingled their multiple application branches, which include industry, commerce, administration, education, medicine, scientific and professional work, and domestic work.

Nations with advanced IT industries have realized that developing competence in IT is important, expensive and difficult; large-scale IT systems are gaining economic feasibility and various national research and education programs for stimulating development have been founded. Three fundamental capabilities that are usually perceived as being essential are:

VLSI (very large-scale integration) circuit design, production facilities and a common infrastructure for the storage and transmission of digital information (including digitized voice and image data in addition to conventional data and text). Major research problems include improved distributed systems and software technology, advanced programming techniques, knowledge-based systems and improved human–computer interfaces.

*Manfred Grauer*

## Information technology in developing countries

Information technology (IT) is an important area of concern for the developing countries of the world. National IT policy varies from being a central part of the government's development strategy, as in Singapore, to the dependent state of many of the poorer developing countries, where they have little control over their IT acquisition. The effective use of IT in organizations requires the sensitive handling of human issues in addition to technical matters. Approaches taken from the industrialized countries may not transfer effectively to the different environments of the developing countries. Human resource development underpins all aspects of IT policy and organizational implementation; education and training is necessary for the general public, policy makers, technology users and IT professionals. Who benefits from IT in the developing countries is not determined by the technology, but is related to human choices concerning technology use.

*Geoff Walsham*

## Information technology in marketing

Information and communications technologies, if managed effectively, can support marketing in two fundamental ways, by providing information for marketing decision making and the infrastructure or channel to deliver services in new ways.

Marketing is not simply about products and services. The focus of attention must be on consumers (or potential consumers) and how their needs can be satisfied in the context of the overall market. Moreover, the mass consumption which characterized the decades following the Second World War is being replaced by growing concerns for service and quality with the development of a mosaic of desired individual consumption patterns. The consumer rules in the sense that he or she should start and finish the marketing process; it is, however, obviously important for long-term consumer satisfaction that an organization undertakes its business in a profitable manner.

Information technology (IT) is the infrastructural platform used to acquire, store, process, distribute and retrieve data of different kinds, numbers, text, images and voice. It will become increasingly a competitive necessity for marketing (although not a source of sustainable competitive advantage). Indeed, with good information being vital for effective marketing, marketing management becomes primarily an information-processing activity. The traditional four Ps of the marketing mix, Price, Promotion, Place and Product, can be extended by a fifth, (data) Processing, that comprises data collection, data collation, data analysis and data presentation.

*John R. Beaumont*

## Information technology and society

There is scarcely a segment of any developed society that has not been touched by some form of computer-based information technology (IT). 'Information technology' is a term that reflects the convergence of several streams of technical developments, including microelectronics, telecommunications and software engineering. It dramatically increases a person's ability to record, store, analyse and transmit information in ways that permit flexibility, accuracy, immediacy, geographic independence, volume and complexity.

From the perspective of business and management, the impact of IT on society can be seen in three principal areas: the social changes generated by IT, which are evident in the individual's work environment, privacy concerns and other quality of life issues; the applications of IT for improving delivery of social services, education and a variety of other services that evolve in modern and developing societies; and the emerging trends in IT, specifically in telecommunications, microprocessors and software, that are destined to accelerate social change globally.

*Dorothy G. Dologite & Julie E. Kendall*

## Innovation and change

Change and innovation are two terms that have become central elements in business and management. Organizations undergo strategic transformations or changes in structure, technology and human resources, where the change is more or less autonomous or deliberate, top-down or bottom-up, and either induced internally or by external conditions. In the former case, it is currently common to refer to restructuring, reorganization or retrenchment. Organizational change can be reviewed at the strategic level and at the design or implementation level. At least five implementation areas (or design 'levers') can be distinguished: structure, control, reward, selection and socialization and culture to effect strategic change.

Innovation is a subsidiary concept because any innovation implies change. The concept of innovation has often been broken down into:

diffusion of new idea, product or process; adoption by individual organization; and level of innovativeness through readiness or ability to experiment.

The phenomenon of innovation can be applied to various levels of analysis, for example, the new idea itself, the process of adoption and the organization whose innovativeness fosters a certain innovative conduciveness. Organizational change can be exogenous or endogenous, but presents fewer problems in relating to the unit of analysis.

Organizational change is not traditionally linked with innovation and much of the literature on the two themes is disjointed. Yet there is currently a *rapprochement* among these strands, because organizations seek to maintain their survival by transforming themselves into learning, self-designing and renewing institutions, thereby forming a platform for innovation and subsequent change. Conversely, there is a growing recognition that innovation requires the organization to have the capacity to absorb external information, as well as an ability to tolerate changes in structure, human resources, and so on. The most innovative organizations are those which have the internal proclivity for change.

*Johannes M. Pennings*

## Innovation management

Innovation is the effort to create purposeful, focused change in an enterprise's economic or social potential. Innovation is also the successful application of ideas and processes to solve current problems and create new opportunities. It requires knowledge, creative thinking, ingenuity and focus.

The goal of innovation management is to trigger, generate, control and steer new ideas through an organization and to bring the outcome to the market. Innovation management depends on a balance coalition between innovators and those that provide direction and stability in organizations. In order to properly manage creative activities, managers must locate and remove the blocks to innovation, they must provide motivation and establish organizational arrangements that are supportive to individual and team innovative behaviour.

*Velimir Srica*

## Innovation and technological change

Innovation and technological change tend to accelerate over time. There have been a succession of new technological styles, which in the past have appeared at approximate intervals of half a century; the latest of these involves the introduction of information and communication technology (ICT). When, as now, a new style appears, change becomes particularly rapid and unpredictable. Further rapid changes are likely to result in the next two decades from the introduction of biotechnology and changes in input costs due to the developing ecological crisis.

Four main types of technology strategy can be distinguished: offensive, or innovation in its strictest sense; defensive, an early response to the offensive innovator, requiring parallel independent development of technology capability; imitative, or the adoption of the innovations of others with the potential for independent development; and dependent, or innovation without such potential. Offensive innovators tend to be leading firms in 'sunrise' sectors in 'core' countries, while the masters of innovation tend to be found in newly-industrializing areas such as east Asia. Requirements for success in high technology include an organic style of management and, in large firms, central coordination through decentralized execution of strategy.

Technological collaboration is vital today, even for large firms. Inter-firm collaboration includes buyer-supplier collaboration, including that practised by Japanese firms in the vertical system of *keiretsu*. Recently, the conventional model of the large innovative firm has been challenged by new organizational forms, including dynamic networks and new forms of coordination within firms. Large firms are now decentralizing and flattening their hierarchies so as to produce a network of business units in many ways analogous to small firm networks.

The financing of technological change is particularly difficult in the USA and the UK, given the endemic short-termism of the stock exchange-based systems dominant there. Internal financial controls can also induce short-termism and 'sectionalism' which can also hamper innovation. Internal venturing and 'intrapreneurship', and external finance through venture capital, can provide alternatives.

*Andrew Tylecote*

## Insurance

Insurance is a means by which individuals and organizations seek to protect themselves from risk. Originally deemed desirable in order to help spread the burden of losses in risky industries, insurance has become compulsory for many activities (such as owning and driving a car) in many countries. Today, insurance represents a multi-billion-dollar worldwide business.

There are many different types of insurance, reflecting the different needs of individuals and organizations. The most common are property, liability, life, motor, and marine, aviation and transport (MAT). Insurance is provided by insurance companies or, uniquely in London, through syndicates of private underwriters in the Lloyd's market.

While insurance is based on an ability to calculate risk, the insurance industry faces a number of key issues which could upset this probability in the near future. Crime and insurance fraud are growing in sophistication, while past problems such as environmental pollution are having an impact on insurance today, and future issues such as genetic testing may affect insurers still further.

*Malcolm Tarling*

## Integer programming

When optimizing the allocation of resources, managers sometimes find themselves facing discrete units of resources to allocate. For example, managers usually allocate whole units of a plane, bus or truck, not some portion of each that can be determined on a continuous scale. Many of the optimization procedures from the field of operations research focus on continuous scale allocations. To augment those continuous scale optimization procedures for discrete or integer-value problem solving, integer programming was devised.

Integer programming is a mathematical procedure that is used to study constrained optimization problems. It is a special case of linear programming. Integer-programming models contain mathematical constraints, an objective function, decision variables and parameters, like linear-programming models. Unique to integer-programming models is the fact that one or more of the decision variables are limited to integer values. To derive these integer values a variety of integer-programming methodologies have been developed. Some of the integer-programming methodologies are highly efficient in achieving a solution and others can require considerable computational effort to arrive at a solution. A variety of software applications exist that contain a variety of the existing integer-programming methodology. From the beginning of integer-programming history to today, integer-programming methodology has been applied in a variety of problem-solving situations, including businesses in both service and manufacturing sectors, as well as the government, health care and agriculture industries.

*Marc J. Schniederjans*

## Intellectual property

The term 'intellectual property' has traditionally been used to refer to the rights conferred by the laws of copyright, patents and trade marks. However, more recently it has been used to refer to a broader range of rights. In 1968, the World Intellectual Property Organization defined 'intellectual property' as including the rights relating to:

- literary, artistic and scientific works
- performances by performing artists, phonograms and broadcasts
- inventions in all fields of human endeavour
- scientific studies

- industrial designs
- trade marks, service marks and commercial names and designations
- unfair competition
- and all other rights resulting from intellectual activity in the industrial, scientific, literary or artistic fields.

Each aspect of the subject of intellectual property is concerned with marking out, by legal definition, types of conduct which may not be pursued without the express consent of the rightful owner. There are four principal areas of intellectual property: patents; copyright and designs; trade marks and trade names; and confidential information.

*David Llewelyn*

## Interactive programming

Organizations, both in public and private sectors, must develop their activities in an environment characterized by an ever increasing complexity. This stems from many interrelated factors, among which mention should be made of growing economic competition in a global economy and innovation in information technology, namely in terms of advances in computer processing power and multifaceted modes of communication. In this context, most of the important real-world problems are complex and ill-structured, in the sense that an elegant algorithm from the toolbag of operations research and management science (OR/MS) cannot be readily applied. Decisions to be made regarding the actual problem must not just use traditional optimization techniques, mathematical programming algorithms and/or heuristics, but also incorporate subjective inputs from decision makers. These subjective inputs represent a set of preferences, opinions, values and perspectives of reality which embody a personal model of reality on which the decision maker leans to evaluate the potential alternative actions.

The underlying cooperation between decision makers and computer/management scientists leads to an evolutionary, adaptive procedure through which decision makers gain new insights into problems that contribute to making decision situations more understandable and enhance learning about the problems, improving skills for suitable use of knowledge. The interaction with decision makers should guide them through their own creative search processes, making new insights and intuitions emerge in a process of continuous redefinition of the problem until an equilibrium among all components of decision making (criteria, alternatives, representations and evaluations) is reached.

Besides allowing for a division of labour according to what each one makes best (the computer to perform fast and accurate computations and the decision maker/manager to make judgements), interactive programming enhances the creative nature of this division by requiring from the decision maker an active role in obtaining new information. Interactivity contributes to grasping the underlying order of the domain in which decision makers must 'produce' their decisions and changing the boundaries of this domain in the light of what is found throughout the decision process.

*Carlos Henggeler Antunes*

## Interest groups

Interest groups represent one way for organizations such as firms to manage their external political environments, although in practice many organizations use formal groups as one among a range of strategies with which to influence public affairs. Interest groups range from private groups organizing firms through to public groups open to individuals wishing to join. Organizations are significantly easier to organize than individuals.

The influence of an interest in public affairs depends mainly upon its ability to make itself indispensable by bringing key resources which governments need. Interests in possession of a sufficient quality of these become 'insider' groups with government, and form closed policy-making communities, whereas others find themselves excluded. 'Insider interests' enjoy monopolistic access over public policies, particularly in 'low politics' fields involving relatively technical issues, whereas in 'high politics' fields involving politicized issues they operate on more of a 'level playing field' with other types of interests. 'Outsider' interests therefore seek to disrupt closed 'policy communities' by seeking to politicize issues. A further factor governing the influence of interest representation concerns the extent of crowding, so that in Brussels, for instance, there is now one person working in the 'lobbying' sector for every European Commission official. There are now increasing signs of public authorities seeking to manage their interactions with outside interests.

*Justin Greenwood*

## Interest rate risk

A firm or an individual faces an interest rate risk when there is a need to borrow or lend money at a future date. Interest rates, both real (net of inflation) and nominal, are volatile. One of the important tasks of financial management is to reduce the exposure of the agent to interest rate risk. If a firm needs to borrow money at a future point in time it can 'hedge' its exposure to an increase in rates in a number of ways. The principal instruments available for the hedging of interest rate risk are: 'forward contracts', which are agreements made now to borrow or lend money in the future at a fixed agreed rate of interest; 'futures contracts', which are standardized forward contracts traded on a futures exchange; and 'option contracts', which give the holder the right to borrow or lend at a fixed rate, but in contrast with forward contracts the holder of the option is not obliged to borrow or lend at the agreed rate if market interest rates change.

Borrowers often require money over longer periods of time (for example, from five years to twenty-five years). To hedge over longer periods borrowers can use an interest rate 'swap contract' or an interest rate 'cap contract'. A swap is a portfolio, or series, of interest rate forward contracts covering successive borrowing periods. Likewise, an interest rate cap is a series of interest rate option contracts. Most interest rate risk management is done through swap and cap contracts.

Many hedging contracts are made between banks and corporate clients on what is known as the over-the-counter market. These contracts are often specially structured to suit the needs of the corporate client. Many are known as 'exotic' or 'complex' derivatives. Examples are diff swaps, binary options, pay-as-you-go options and zero-cost options.

*Richard C. Stapleton*

### International business, future trends

Major forces are in operation today that are transforming both the manner in which international business is conducted and the environments in which the firm operates. Managing in this evolving global business environment requires a new kind of leadership response that reflects sensitivity to the challenges of continuous change. Competition has become increasingly global in scope and more fierce in nature. Business executives are being forced to re-evaluate the very assumptions and values upon which their organizations were founded. These assessments are providing the impetus for new managerial strategies that are reshaping the structure and processes of the business enterprise.

The challenges and opportunities of international management will become more integrated and interdependent as technological advances bring the world closer together and information becomes more readily available and instantly accessible. The unique cultural, political, legal, economic and technological challenges of international management will be addressed between topic areas and across functional dimensions. The traditional functions of marketing, finance, manufacturing and human resource management will become more interdependent and less distinct as separate entities. Information will provide the interdisciplinary link and integrating force that makes this possible.

As organizations integrate around information and become more dependent on global information networks, management layers will continue to dissolve. More flexible organizational structures will evolve that are no longer dependent on the hierarchical management assumptions of the past. The challenge for future leaders is to integrate and manage across these forces of change.

Information will play a key role in this transformation process. Tomorrow's leaders will manage organizations in which the creation of wealth will depend on how well the information asset is managed. The success or failure of the global organization will increasingly be evaluated in terms of its ability to lever and manage information.

The dynamic environmental setting of international business and the role of information technology as a driving force set the stage for new paradigm shifts in international management. Information has evolved as a central core asset that is essential to the effective management of all corporate initiatives. Quality management and the emerging global workforce are two prominent areas in which information will play an important role.

*P. Candace Deans & David A. Ricks*

## International business, legal dimensions of

The international executive crossing national boundaries must necessarily be concerned about the legal context for activities planned abroad. A number of issues may need to be taken into account. For example, home-country laws may apply extra-territorially to firms when they go abroad. Not all countries use the same accounting and taxation systems, and financing documents and commercial paper used in the home market may not be valid or enforceable abroad. In common law countries such as the USA and the UK, firms are generally free to undertake any activity not specifically prohibited by law, but elsewhere activities may need to be authorized by specific enabling legislation. Laws governing a company's trademarks and technology may vary from country. Finally, the firm may not be free to send home-country nationals to run sales offices or manage production and distribution in a foreign country, but must instead hire local managers.

This complexity brings up the fact that the global manager or marketer needs to be familiar with the national laws of each country within which the firm does business. Some countries have centralized legal systems, others such as the USA have federal systems with state law added to national law. Home-country common-law trained lawyers may not be familiar with all these jurisdictions, necessitating the employment of foreign lawyers in each jurisdiction. Lawyers trained and practising in these different legal systems may also have quite different roles from lawyers or solicitors in the home market. Last of all, the firm needs to examine the legal assumptions underlying its business strategies, which may have been formulated with the home market legal environment in mind; will these assumptions stand the test of foreign law?

*Robert J. Radway*

## International business elites

The international business elite is usually said to comprise the controllers of businesses deriving a substantial part of their revenue from operations outside the country of origin. These persons hold positions on boards of directors, of their own or other companies, or as chief executive officers of such internationally operating companies. The elite may also include those holders of a range of positions who constitute part of the top management team. Many such people will be the controllers not of the parent company but of subsidiary companies or of operating divisions doing business across national borders. The international business elite may also include members of the international capitalist class where they represent families whose capital is made up of businesses with significant international operations. A further fraction of the elite is composed of persons who act as directors of internationally orientated multinational or transnational corporations but who hold no executive positions in any of the companies concerned. Representatives on the board of directors of international companies who are the controllers of participatory banks (which are themselves multinational operators) may also be included.

To this list may be added two 'subsidiary' groups. The first is composed of the owners and controllers of (relatively) small international companies which act as specialist service providers to the core international firms. Included here are international lawyers, patent specialists and international firms of accountants and consultants.The second group includes managers who are pursuing international careers but who as yet have only reached the recruitment stratum for the main boards. These people contribute the *future* international business elite and frequently link national businesses, including the family-owned, to the international arena.

Considering the enormous economic importance of transnational corporations and their very rapid growth in numbers over the last few decades there have been surprisingly few studies of who their controllers are, of how they reach their positions, or of the connections between the different members of the 'group' and between these and other leading elites in the countries in which they operate. Very little is known about their views on key issues of business or public policy and even less about the articulation of their views into any kind of international business world view. While most major business schools now offer courses on 'international business' and consultants of every hue advise corporations on different aspects of creating multinational management teams, very little attention has been paid to the careers of such managers and the paths leading to the top of the international business hierarchy and hence of world business. An examination of the rather fragmented evidence concerning these elites does, however, highlight two distinguishing characteristics: the extent and significance of structural links maintained through international interlocking directorates, which indicates considerable linkage but not necessarily control; and the social characteristics of holders of top international business positions, both current personnel and their likely replacements in coming decades, which shows very limited origins, education and experience.

*Jane Marceau*

## International business negotiations

The growing interdependence in the world economic arena has led to the formation of collaborative agreements between entities from different nations. A major requisite to the formation of such agreements is the successful negotiation of the terms and conditions for their establishment. Depending upon the type and nature of the investment, these negotiations take place with one or both of the following entities: (1) the various governmental ministries and agencies which have jurisdiction over different aspects of inward foreign direct investment, such as the extent of foreign participation permitted in the venture, the raising of capital in the local money market, the remittance of profits and dividends, and matters pertaining to technology transfer; and (2) the local partner or partners, in the event of a cooperative venture, over the terms and conditions of the agreement, such as percentage of equity ownership to be divided between the foreign and local investors, who assumes management control, pricing of output/services, staffing of key managerial positions, the nature of products and/or services to be provided by the venture, and the life of the venture. Even after the establishment of the collaborative agreement, the partners need to negotiate on issues that may arise in the relationship, and thus maintain peaceful co-existence between them. Should relations between the partners deteriorate to the point of irreconcilable differences, that is, one or both partners see termination of the contractual agreement as the only viable option, the parties still need to negotiate with each other on the terms of dissolution. In short, international business negotiations are crucial at entry, exit and throughout the relationships between the host and home country partners.

*Rosalie L. Tung*

## International marketing

International marketing is about the development of foreign markets for the longer term. It is a later stage of internationalization, involving direct investment in a foreign presence, that is accompanied by experience gained through simple exporting. Standardization becomes an important issue, although the focus must still be on the customer; international marketing offers possible benefits and economies of scale, but only if the customers continue to buy. International segmentation strategies are needed to determine customer wants and needs in different countries. In international marketing no two markets are the same, just as in the domestic market no two customers are the same. One of the most common mistakes in international marketing is to assume that market segments within the same general areas exhibit similar characteristics. Even where this is broadly true, the generalizations may serve to conceal real and existing differences.

Developing market entry strategies must take a number of factors into account. First there is logistics: how are the products brought to market? The level of product and brand customization necessary in this segment must be analysed, distribution channels must be selected, and pricing and promotion strategies must be developed that are appropriate for the country in question.

*Stan Paliwoda*

## International operations

In the literature on production and operations management, little has been written about the international aspects of the field. How a company with operations in several countries should structure its operations is a question which still, to a large extent, remains unanswered in literature. It is nevertheless an important question today, as many companies become more global in their operations and as even domestic companies are faced with global competitors.

Managers have identified the lack of an adequate manufacturing strategy as one of the main barriers to the effective management of their international manufacturing operations. How to set up and manage an effective and efficient network of plants is a key issue.

The decision to site plants overseas in the first place may be driven by several factors, most notably access to low-cost production inputs (labour, materials, energy and capital), proximity to a market or proximity to sources of innovation and technological change. Depending on the dominant need, several decisions have to be made. The first is, how many plants should the company have? This in turn depends on a decision on optimal plant size. Second, the firm must decide where plants are to be located, and finally, it must be decided what level of competence each plant will have.

Each plant is in itself a building block which has to fit in the overall 'architecture' of the international network. This network architecture can be designed in two ways: there can be a product focus, in which each plant is responsible for a particular product or product group, or there can be a process focus, in which each plant concentrates on a distinct phase of the production process.

International operations pose major problems for managers, including how to improve the overall productivity of the network, how to optimize the flow of information and goods within the network, and how to transform each plant in the network into a 'virtual' plant, in which the company is able to transform raw materials into value, rather than just products, for the customer. It can be seen that success in managing international operations depends above all on a clear-cut manufacturing strategy.

*Arnoud de Meyer & Ann Vereecke*

## International payments

Statistics on international payment flows were compiled long before gross national product data were gathered. Since governments historically have controlled foreign trade by imposing taxes and/or quantitative restrictions, and these controls require bureaucratic record keeping, data on international transactions, both real and financial, actually precede data on domestic output.

Balance of payments (BOP) represents the most comprehensive information available on the involvement of the domestic economy with the rest of the world. The International Monetary Fund defines BOP broadly as a record of the economy's international transactions. BOP data are used widely for economic policy decisions and for predicting trends in credit and foreign exchange markets.

World trade and payments have undergone significant structural change since the liberalization of trade and capital flows in the 1950s, and these developments have implications for how BOP data should be compiled and interpreted. For example, the BOP focus on cross-border exports and imports masks the fact that much trade is now intra-firm in nature as multinational corporations supply and source from their overseas affiliates. Second, BOP does not distinguish between a country's competitiveness as a location of production on the one hand, and the competitiveness of firms owned by the residents of that country on the other.

The increasing internationalization of production and finance requires a reassessment of how data on international payments should be compiled and analysed. While BOP data represent important raw material for analysis and forecasting, they need to be supplemented by data on indebtedness, exchange rates and sales of foreign affiliates in order to more accurately judge the present and future economic performance of a country.

*Gunter Dufey & Rolf Mirus*

## International trade and foreign direct investment

During the past two centuries, the free trade paradigm based on the principle of comparative advantage has profoundly influenced national trade policies. This principle demonstrates that dissimilar national production possibilities are the basis of international trade that is gainful to both trading parties. Trade enables each country to specialize in making and exporting products in which it is comparatively efficient while importing products in which it is comparatively inefficient. As a consequence, the productivity of national economies is higher than it would be in the absence of trade.

The conventional explanation of comparative advantage is the existence of dissimilar factor endowments (broadly, land, labour and capital) across countries. But economists have now come forward with other explanations of comparative advantage deriving from international technology gaps, increasing returns and product differentiation. The old and new trade theories are complementary, offering collectively a better understanding of trade than the conventional theory.

Foreign direct investment (FDI) is an ownership interest (equity) in an enterprise located in one country that is held by residents (usually another enterprise) of another country. FDI is the distinctive feature of multinational enterprises (MNEs). Hence, a theory of FDI is also a theory of the MNE. Multinationals are the foremost agents in moving factors of production and technology from one country to another. In so doing, they strengthen the international economy by improving the allocation of resources worldwide. Also, MNEs are the key actors in international innovation, spreading new ideas and technology across countries.

A theory of FDI needs to explain how direct investing firms can compete with local firms in host countries, why firms choose to enter host countries as direct investors in production rather than as exporters or licensors, and why firms choose to invest in particular host countries. The traditional theory of international capital movements (portfolio investment theory) cannot give satisfactory answers to these questions; indeed, by assuming perfect competition it rules out the existence of FDI. New theories of FDI centred on monopolistic competition and transaction costs agree on the importance of market imperfections (departures from perfect competition) to explain direct investment.

It has become evident that we need a new paradigm that explains trade and direct investment at both national and enterprise levels. Prospects for creating such a paradigm over the next decade are good. Both trade and investment theories recognize the significance of market imperfections. Another contribution to constructing a new paradigm is Porter's 'diamond'. A single paradigm integrating trade and investment theories would offer better guidance to national policy makers and international managers than the current mix of seemingly unrelated theories.

*Franklin R. Root*

## Internet and business

The Internet is a vast network spanning many countries and subscribed to by many different organizations. It is now widely used by commercial organizations in their business activities. The Internet has its origins in the military and academic research networks first established in the USA in the 1960s. As a result, the standards governing it were developed jointly between a number of institutions, and no one company controls the service.

Services offered on the Internet include electronic mail (e-mail), file transfer, terminal emulation, newsgroups and the World Wide Web. Connecting to the Internet requires an address, and consideration must be given to the amount of traffic this site will receive. The Internet has enormous business potential; by the year 2000 it is estimated that 15 per cent of all US retail sales will be electronic, and access is equally available for large companies, small companies and individuals. The future will see the Internet grow to become a major factor in both domestic and international business.

*Jason Wallace*

## Inter-organizational relations

In a 'society of organizations' the economic success and survival of profit-making organizations, as much as for non-profit organizations, increasingly depends on the quality of the relations they maintain with other organizations. These inter-organizational relationships, which above all provide access to external resources, can be of two sorts: a rather market-like nature may prevail, or, increasingly evident, they may resemble relations within organizations, in terms of the intensity of communication, exchange of personnel or level of trust. These two types of relationships, although they often coincide in practice, are of a very different nature, and hence have been analysed within the traditions of two different lines of theoretical thought: economics and inter-organization theory. However, both lines of thought lack a processual understanding of the formation and management of inter-organizational relations. This is why the development of future inter-organization theory should focus upon the processes of interrelating and coordinating organizations, yet without ignoring the enabling and restraining effects of existing inter-organizational structures on inter-organizational interaction.

*Jörg Sydow*

## Interpersonal skills

Some approaches to the study of social interaction are only concerned with observable behaviour, what interactors actually say and do, whereas others are also concerned with the cognitive processes that guide behaviour. Training can improve the interactors' ability to relate effectively with others. While the focus of most training interventions tends to be observable behaviour, the beliefs that interactors hold about themselves and others also deserve attention. These beliefs can influence both the way interactors interpret circumstances and the way in which they decide to behave in the light of these interpretations.

Interpersonal skills have a hierarchical structure which has provided a basis for a micro-skills approach to the development of interpersonal competence. This involves isolating and practising sub-skills and then synthesizing them into larger units of behaviour.

*John Hayes*

## Inventory and just-in-time models

The management of inventory is a problem common to all business organizations. Basically, inventory is a resource idle for the present but useful for the future. If it is for the future, then why store it now physically and incur costs? Why not procure it only when needed? These questions lie behind the philosophy of 'just-in-time' procurement.

The most common problem faced by managers in this context is how to determine the optimal quantity of inventory to order and the optimal reorder point (the level of inventory which signals the placing of an order). In response to this problem, many mathematical models have been formulated, which are either deterministic or stochastic. One of the oldest deterministic models is the simple economic-order-quantity (EOQ) model, which is however based on simple assumptions such as constant demand rate, no shortages and unlimited capacity.

Models such as this are unrealistic in that they do not allow for the uncertainty that occurs in real-life management. Just-in-time management faces the problems of uncertainty head-on. Its core philosophy is the production of the necessary products to the necessary quantity, at the right place and the right time. The system adjusts the timing of operations 'just in time'. Warehouses are no longer needed because products are produced as and when needed. This requires a continuous production system, which has its own control problems; many firms use the Japanese control system known as *kanban*, in which each product is coded for inventory control during the production process. Queuing models are used to describe the flow of *kanbans* in the system as well as the inventory generated.

*Mario Tabucanon*

## Inventory management

Inventory is the physical goods purchased by a firm in anticipation of being sold to a customer, that has not yet been sold; it includes the value of raw materials and purchased parts, as well as value that is added through labour or processing. Examples run from coils of steel at a car parts factory, through partially assembled printed circuit boards at a computer assembly plant, to packaged snacks at a retail shop. Inventory includes goods in transit from one owner to the next.

An item purchased at retail by a consumer will have been part of many inventories at a number of firms as it was produced, packaged, distributed and finally sold. Even an apparently simple product like a packaged disposable razor will, in its various parts, have been through a steel producer's raw materials inventory, a plastics producer's work-in-process inventory, and a printer's finished goods inventory, before becoming part of the razor manufacturer's raw materials, purchased parts and work-in-process inventories. From there the packaged disposable razor became part of a finished good entering a physical distribution inventory on its way to a retail inventory.

National accounts are kept of manufacturing and distribution/retail inventory levels because of their important role in national economic activity. Growth in national inventory levels can be a harbinger of economic recovery; too much growth can foreshadow economic decline. A key parameter within most large national econometric forecasting models is the history of aggregate inventory levels by industry.

Inventory is typically the second largest asset, after plant and equipment, on the balance sheet of a manufacturing firm. It is usually the largest asset for a distribution or retail firm. Although inventory is defined as an asset, it is a particularly fickle item on a firm's balance sheet: inventory problems are a leading cause of bankruptcy, particularly among smaller firms, where inventory growth, in items that customers do not want, results in a cash crisis.

*Linda G. Sprague*

# J–L

## Japan, economy of

Since the end of the Second World War, the Japanese economy has sustained a high rate of economic growth, and by 1990 its per capita income surpassed that of the USA. Factors that contributed to the success of the Japanese economy – especially the role of the government, the role of business groups, and the relationship between management and labour – have been the focus of many articles and books.

The period before the first oil crisis of 1973 is commonly known as the period of high-speed economic growth. During this period Japan maintained a high investment/gross domestic product ratio, while domestic saving levels were also sufficient for high investment to be made possible without the accumulation of foreign debts. Improvement in human capital, developed through a solid education and on-the-job training, was also an important factor for growth.

Industrial policy, in common terminology, is a wide-ranging combination of policies that influence the level and composition of industrial investment and production. In Japan it is generally interpreted as the nurturing of specific industries through subsidized (policy) loans from the development bank: for example, in the 1950s and 1960s, the coal, steel, shipbuilding and petrochemicals industries. Imports were strictly controlled until the early 1960s, and raw materials and intermediate goods, as opposed to consumption goods, were favoured.

Japanese monetary and fiscal policy was flexible but prudent enough to produce high growth without excessive inflation (except in 1974–6). During the 1950s and 1960s, monetary policy maintained a fixed exchange rate. However, in 1974, in order to control inflation, tight monetary policy was introduced. Inflation was quickly reduced, at the cost of a sharp decline in output. After 1975, monetary policy focused on keeping the inflation rate low.

Fiscal policy was fairly conservative in the 1950s and 1960s. The budget was essentially balanced every year until 1965, when government construction bonds (for infrastructure projects) were issued. Pure deficit-financing bonds have been issued as of 1975. Government deficits grew rapidly in the second half of the 1970s, but fiscal austerity during the 1980s reduced the issue of deficit-financing bonds to zero by 1990. However, the slump in the first half of the 1990s, forced the government to issue new deficit-financing bonds.

Economic institutions and structural configuration are important in evaluating performance. Some critics argue that Japanese institutions and business practices are unique among the industrial countries, although close examination has revealed similarities with the USA and Europe. Various forms of loose relationships between corporations (*keiretsu*) have been of particular interest to researchers.

The yen has appreciated with respect to the US dollar since 1971. In mid-1994, the yen became 100 to one dollar, and then in the spring of 1995, the value reached 80 yen per dollar. In less than a quarter of a century, the value of the yen against the dollar more than quadrupled (less than one quarter of 360 yen now purchases one dollar). Even with this appreciation of the yen, Japan has maintained large external surpluses throughout the 1980s and 1990s, except for brief periods immediately after the two oil crises.

The Japanese economy in the second half of the 1980s was known as the bubble period – sharp increases in asset prices, such as stock prices and land prices. In many places land prices tripled or quadrupled over a few years. However, asset prices declined in the first half of the 1990s, and by 1995, price levels had returned to pre-bubble levels. This had various consequences, including the appearance of a large number of non-performing loans among the commercial banks.

*Takatoshi Ito*

## Japan, technology diffusion in

Japan is widely regarded as the most successful of all nations in importing technology. It was the first non-Western nation to use Western industrial and military technologies to become a world power. Japanese firms are now well entrenched in positions of international leadership in high technology industries and, although it is now a leader in creating new technology, Japan continues to be the world's largest importer of technology.

Two factors account for much of this success. First, the Japanese population is unusually competent and motivated to use foreign technology. It is well-educated by world standards and has been so since even before Japan was opened to world commerce in the nineteenth century. Throughout their modern history the Japanese have believed that the best way for Japan to protect its culture is through the effective use of foreign technology. Second, Japanese business firms, trade associations and the government have been particularly well structured to import, adapt and improve foreign technology.

*Leonard H. Lynn*

## Japanese financial markets

During the high growth era of 1955 to 1973, the Japanese financial market used to have a character very different from those of the USA and the UK. First, financial intermediaries dominated the corporate financing pattern, while the securities market was less developed. Second, the money market developed in an unbalanced way, due to the underdevelopment of the open market and the importance of the inter-bank market.

Since the early 1970s, significant changes have occurred in the nature of the Japanese financial market through large flotations of bonds caused by a large government deficit, internationalization and the deregulation of the financial market. As a result, Japan's financial market has become comparable with those of the USA and UK, although a few differences still survive. In this transforming process, the Japanese financial system has been facing critical problems: one is the problem of stabilizing the financial system, closely related to that of bad debt; the other concerns corporate governance in so far as the monitoring capability of the main bank has declined, but an alternative system has not been established.

*Hideaki Miyajima*

## Japanization

'Japanization' is the process by which Japanese industry is influencing the policies and practices of Western industry. This influence comes about in two ways, through Japanese direct investment in Western economies and through the emulation of Japanese practice by Western companies. Japanese industrial practices such as total quality management, just-in-time methods, work teams and models of buyer-supplier relationships are now widespread in the West. However, not all Western companies have been able to imitate these practices successfully, particularly those in the organizational–political and human resource field. There is currently widespread debate about the effect and benefits of Japanization on individuals, firms and Western economies in general.

*Nick Oliver*

## Job design

At its most basic level, job design refers to changing the actual structure of the jobs that people perform. Unlike other change strategies that focus on training employees or altering the context of work, job design focuses squarely on the work itself, on the tasks or activities that individuals complete in their organizations on a daily basis.

Five approaches to job design can be distinguished. Industrial engineering aims to maximize the productive efficiency of individual employees by eliminating unnecessary work; this was the approach adopted by Taylor. Motivation–hygiene theory, or job enlargement, seeks to deal with some of the negative consequences of standardized work by adding more tasks; one of the pioneers of this theory was Herzberg. Job characteristics theory is based on the measurable characteristics of different jobs and the view that people may respond differently to these, taking a psychological approach to job satisfaction. More recently an interdisciplinary framework has been developed which combines mechanistic, motivational and biological approaches to job design.

The four theories above relate to individual jobs. The fifth approach to job design is to design jobs for teams, based around concepts of group tasks, group composition and group norms. Each of the five approaches has its strengths and weaknesses, and it is clear that considerable research is still required to examine how these approaches work in different cultures.

*Yitzhak Fried, Anne Cummings & Greg R. Oldham*

## Job evaluation

Job evaluation is a technique that systematically compares jobs with each other to produce a rank order on which pay differentials can be based. A job evaluation scheme can be used to compare jobs across a whole country or an entire industry in that country, but normally it is confined to a single organization. In that organization it would be unusual for all jobs to be covered by job evaluation. Typically only some occupational groups are covered and there will generally be different schemes for categories such as manual, non-manual, professional and managerial staff.

Employers will normally have some of the following objectives in seeking to introduce job evaluation: to establish a rational pay structure; to create pay relationships between jobs which are perceived as fair by employees; to reduce the number of pay grievances and disputes; to provide a basis for settling the payment rate of new or changed jobs; to provide pay information in a form which enables meaningful comparisons with other organizations

Job evaluation is often introduced to bring some order into a pay structure. Payment for different jobs may appear to be arbitrary or to have little logical justification. It may have evolved as a result of *ad hoc* decisions sometimes made under pressure and without consideration for the wider consequences. As a result management will face grievances and possibly disputes.

Most of the reasons given for introducing job evaluation are concerned with raising the efficiency of the organization or improving relations with employees. However, the decision may, at least in part, be taken in response to external pressures or constraints. In both the USA and the UK some organizations introduced job evaluation following the imposition of national pay controls. Pay increases could be justified only where a change in the work could be demonstrated clearly. The systematic nature of job evaluation allowed such changes to be legitimized and it was therefore in the interests of both management and unions to agree upon a scheme.

Job evaluation has also been introduced in response to equal pay policies and legislation. Where an analytical scheme is operated without any gender bias it will normally be accepted that men and women are being paid equally for work of equal value.

*Alan Arthurs*

## Just-in-time philosophies

Interest has focused on just-in-time manufacturing (JIT) largely because of the success of Japanese manufacturing. JIT has demonstrated the potential to simultaneously improve quality, reduce costs and shorten delivery times. Much has been written about the simplicity of JIT, but achieving that simplicity is a complex and demanding process and the success rate is low.

The most often quoted philosophy of JIT is the elimination of waste, and this was the spur behind the development of the first JIT system by the Toyota corporation. A corollary to this, however, is the concept of high value-added flow; all activities in the production process are now geared to adding value for the customer. A JIT system requires complete integration of all parts of the plant; other familiar concepts from Japanese manufacturing such as total quality management and flexible work rules can be seen as critical components of this system.

JIT is not always suitable, and is generally only appropriate when a production line is producing both a relatively high volume and a low number of product configurations or models, making mixed model production feasible; its introduction may require a reduction in the number of models, which can have an impact on firm performance in markets where high degrees of customization are demanded. There are serious obstacles to the introduction of JIT, which requires changes in organization, systems, cultures and attitudes across the company. However, JIT also offers significant benefits in terms of reduced costs and inventory.

*Robert F. Conti*

## Labour markets

The labour market as presented in its conventional textbook context is often described as the process through which the various attributes of the worker are transformed into the requirements of the employer. Taken as a generalization, this focuses attention upon one of the most fundamental linkages between people that has existed in society since time immemorial; namely, the employment relationship. For employment provides far more than the means whereby the vast bulk of individuals can find the economic means of survival. It also shapes the organizational future of key elements in society such as families. For it is on the basis of available discretionary income, after all costs have been met, that the quality of life of most of a nation's population is maintained.

Any attempt to define precisely the various dimensions of labour market theory and practice is rather like trying to hit a moving target. The concept of deriving the value of a product from the labour which went into it can be found in medieval writers, while the classical and neo-classical economists define labour as one of three forces of production. The schools of thought which have emerged since have been many and varied, and while they occasionally overlap there are also significant differences. Theories of labour markets include rational expectations theory, implicit contracts, efficiency wage models, insider–outsider relationships and transaction costs theory.

The globalization of the economy and the consequent restructuring of capitalism have profound implications for labour markets and labour market theory. If, as seems true, we are moving away from the concept of the market as a coordinating mechanism, and beyond the firm as a functional agent in industrial sectors, and towards the concept of the business organization as a series of interrelated productive activities, then we are also moving towards a paradigm in which human capital will be of maximal value. One major question is whether these new organizations will be predominantly technologically determined or socially ordered. This question in turn has a strong impact on current arguments about labour market flexibility.

*Alan Williams*

## Labour process

The concept of the labour process, which is found in parts of the organizational behaviour and industrial relations literature, is taken from Marx's political economy and refers to purposeful activity in which a natural object or raw material is transformed into a useful product which satisfies a human need. The elements of which the process consists are human labour, the object on which work is performed, instruments or tools and a purpose or goal. Different class regimes or modes of production create different labour processes, involving distinct ways of combining human producers, instruments, raw materials and purposes. Tools and raw materials can be owned in common or privately; producers can be free or enslaved, skilled or dedicated to one process in a complex production system. The intention of production can be cooperative, to create useful goods for a whole group or society to share. It can equally be personal, providing subsistence for oneself or one's family. Or, as in the case of capitalism, it can be organized for private need, to satisfy the owner of the instruments of production, raw material and finished product.

*Chris Smith*

## Land economy

Land economy is an interdisciplinary approach to the study of the management and development of land and natural resources. The subject draws together principles of economics and of law and applies them to the analysis of land use and economic activity from the perspectives of individuals and organizations in both private and public sectors. The term originated in Cambridge University in the 1960s but the subject has much deeper roots in the UK, and the parallel broad subject area of land economics has even stronger academic foundations in the USA.

From an initial concern with rural land resources, land economy has evolved to embrace urban land use and regional development and is addressing a range of contemporary issues, from concerns about urban regeneration and environmental destruction to the performance of land markets and their relationship with the rest of the economy, and the role of land tenure in agrarian reform and economic development.

*Derek Nicholls*

## Law, commercial

It is sometimes argued that commercial law consists of no more than a simple aggregation of the different rules which govern particular forms of commercial contract and that there is no place for general principles of commercial law. Such a view is unacceptable because the concern of commercial law should be on the focus of the commercial sense of the transaction as well as on the parties themselves. In this regard it is important to identify and refer to the principles of commercial law which are essentially tools in serving the needs of the business community. At the same time, in articulating these principles it has to be recognized that they encapsulate values, and what is entailed in the judgement process involving commercial law is the need to balance these competing values, the relative weight of which varies from legal system to legal system and from one age to another.

*Iwan Davies*

## Law, contract

A contract is a promise between two or more people to do or not do something. More specifically, a contract is a *legally enforceable promise*. That is, when the promise that underlies the contract is perceived to have been broken (breached), the injured or innocent party can call upon the sovereign power of the state to effect some sort of remedy. In essence, the power to contract gives a kind of legislative power to the promisor (the one who makes the promise) and the promisee (the one to whom the promise has been made). By contracting, the promisor and the promisee impose legal obligations and rights upon themselves. Not all promises are enforceable, however. Contract law is that body of principles and rules which specifies what kinds of contracts are enforceable by the state's legal apparatus.

The idea of contract was present in ancient legal codes. The earliest of Roman codes, the Twelve Tables (450 bc/sc), is said to have contained the provision that *'Cum nexum faciet mancipum que, uti lingua nuncupassit, ita jus esto'* (As a man shall declare in a legal transaction, so shall the law be).

The concept of contract arose in its fullest sense only after the development of market economies and the extension of economic activity beyond families and neighbours into distant locales. The fluctuating nature of the market led to legal changes: early laws of contract emerged from actions for debt and focused on enforcing instantaneous exchange ('I will trade you one cow for five bushels of oats'). As commerce came more and more to involve promises of future performance – ('I will buy your crop of oats for such and such a price when it is harvested') – the old laws were found to be ineffective in forcing people to keep their promises when changes in market values induced them to seek bargains more to their advantage.

*Lisa J. McIntyre*

## Leadership

It has been claimed that in 1896 in the USA, the Library of Congress had no book on leadership, but within one person's lifetime, eighty-five years later, over 5,000 entries on leadership were noted by Bass in the early 1980s. This explosion of interest has included an enormous diversity of activity by people known as leaders. Fiedler and Garcia have listed as examples of leadership Henry V's victory at Agincourt against overwhelming odds; Washington, who defeated better-equipped English forces; and Iacocca, who produced the dramatic turnaround of the Chrysler Corporation. They then went on to show the macabre side of leadership by including Hitler. Looking at more recent events, one could add successful business tycoons like Robert Maxwell in the UK, Alan Bond in Australia, and Ivan Bosky in the USA, who all allegedly defrauded millions of people who had fallen under their leadership spell.

With such a wide range of examples to illustrate a phenomenon described in a single word, one has to ask whether the leadership concept has practical utility for understanding organizational behaviour. The answer is a qualified 'yes'. The qualification implies that some usefulness can be extracted from the available evidence, but great care has to be taken not to overstate the explanatory thrust of a term which has given rise to thousands of different definitions and a variety of *post hoc* explanations covering both good and evil.

The literature can be divided into two main streams: universalist approaches and situational approaches. The former include great person theories, personality theories, psychoanalytic theories, charismatic, transformational and transactional theories, organizational economics, grid theory and popular descriptive theories. Situational approaches are, in general, of more recent origin and are based on the assumption that different styles of behaviour, including leadership, are appropriate for contrasting varieties of real-life situations. These approaches are sometimes called contingency theories because they attempt to specify the effect of contingent situations on different behavioural responses. Psychologically orientated theories tend to concentrate on intra-organizational contingencies, like the nature of the task, while sociological theories tend to stress the effect of factors external to the organization, like turbulence of the environment.

The contrast between generalistic and contingency approaches is important and the thrust of evidence in support of the latter lends itself to a more realistic prescriptive approach to leadership. At the same time it must be recognized that there is often a degree of overlap between the two schemata.

*Frank Heller*

## Linear programming

Mathematical and other quantitative techniques have been used to solve problems from business and industry since the beginning of the Industrial Revolution. However, such methods had little impact on management's ability to analyse and improve an organization's current and future operations. All this changed in the last half of the twentieth century with the development of linear programming. Linear programming has proved to be the pre-eminent mathematical procedure with the broadest range of applicability to business and industry. Linear programming is a rare mathematical topic in that its deep theoretical results and related computational procedures combine to yield solutions to decision problems that have direct value in improving the day-to-day effectiveness of an organization.

Early applications of linear programming were confined to the military, for example crew training and aircraft deployment, maintenance scheduling, airlift routing, and contract bidding. Industrial applications of linear programming were pioneered by Charnes and Cooper in their joint work with Mellon on oil refinery scheduling. Since that time, just about all areas of industry, business and government have benefited by having linear programming applied to their activities.

*Saul Gass*

## Logistics

The term 'logistics' is used to describe the activities required to plan and carry out the movement of goods from a material or manufacturing source to the point of consumption. Historically, logistics has been primarily a military activity, the purpose of which was to provide food, clothing, supplies and equipment to troops in the field as well as to transport the troops themselves. The importance of logistics in effective operations is today well understood by military commanders.

While logistics functions have not always been as visible and well defined for commercial and non-profit enterprises, transportation, storage and customer service activities are still necessary. In the past, however, top management did not always understand the importance and competitive impact of integrated logistics. More recently, widespread acceptance of operating philosophies such as just-in-time, total quality management, customer satisfaction and customer responsiveness have led to greater emphasis of the role of logistics in achieving the corporate mission. Well-planned logistics operations are necessary for timely shipment arrival and delivery of undamaged products and, as a result, satisfied customers. The importance of logistics is reflected in the considerable attention paid to this subject in both academic and management publications.

In any transaction, customers desire nine 'rights': the right product, the right quantity, the right quality, the right place, the right time, the right form, the right price, the right packaging and the right information. Logistics plays a major role in delivering these 'rights' to customers. Because of its importance in creating customer satisfaction, logistics plays a prominent role in the marketing mix. A useful model for understanding this is the logistics value chain, which represents the institutions, inventory and information flows required to effectively and efficiently serve customers. Value chain integration, performance measurement, information technology and time-based strategies are all important components of logistics. Globalization is posing new challenges for the management of logistics, both through global sourcing of materials and products and the need to deliver finished products or services to consumers in global markets.

*Donald J. Bowersox & David J. Closs*

## Logistics in manufacturing management and operations

Over the last quarter of the twentieth century logistics and associated activities have become the subject of much study and research. An increasing number of business organizations have recognized logistics as a major strategic variable. Companies like Rank Xerox, Digital, Nissan, Benetton and 3M have invested in developing responsible logistics systems. There can be no doubting the role that logistics has played in their success in the marketplace.

Perhaps the simplest definition of logistics is that it encompasses the movement of materials, parts, inventory and information flows through an organization and its marketing channels so as to fulfil consumer needs in a cost-effective manner. Many different logistics strategies can be adopted, depending on the production system in use. The value of logistics, however, is universal, as demonstrated by Porter in his model of the value chain.

Essential elements of logistics include purchasing, materials management, distribution, maintenance and information flows; the last are critical to the efficient management of logistical flows. In recent years electronic data interchange (EDI) has become a valuable logistics tool in this respect.

The increasing trend towards globalization has shifted still more emphasis onto logistics. The rationalization and concentration of manufacturing in fewer centres has created the need for more physical distribution over greater distances; economic integration on a regional level has created the need for regional logistics strategies. One response has been international strategic alliances between manufacturers, distributors and retailers, drawing all parties closer and improving information and logistical flows.

*Kulwant S. Pawar*

# M

## Maintenance systems

Maintenance is often thought of as a necessary evil in the efficient operation of a production facility. The most difficult operating question with regard to maintenance is whether to make the required repairs before the equipment fails, and support a policy of preventive maintenance, or to wait until the equipment malfunctions and support a policy of corrective maintenance. The former implies that production may be interrupted to perform maintenance, the latter assures that production will be interrupted when there is a failure. In either case the usual determining factor is the comparative costs of the maintenance and lost production. Often the costs are weighted against the risks involved, the probability or likelihood of failure, and decisions about maintenance policies are determined on the basis of the trade-offs required.

There are three basic approaches to maintenance policies: preventive, remedial and conditional. Preventive maintenance refers to maintenance work performed before the equipment fails, and may be major, such as a complete overhaul or replacement, or minor, such as a simple repair. Corrective or remedial maintenance is maintenance that is done when a piece of equipment breaks down. Depending on the need and the criticality of the equipment, this work can be performed immediately after it breaks down or can be placed in a queue to be worked on at a later date based on a scheduled interval. If there is standby equipment and there is no immediate urgency for a repair, then the maintenance crew follows a specified schedule of rounds.

Conditional maintenance is another possible maintenance policy. This involves an inspection and evaluation of the state of the equipment to determine if it should be repaired or not. It may mean that a piece of equipment remains in service for a certain number of hours, then is removed from service at a specified time and replaced, repaired or over-hauled.

To determine the type of maintenance policy to adopt, it is important to know the cost of preventive maintenance, the cost of breakdown repairs and the probability of breakdown after an overhaul or repair. For this reason maintenance systems require a solid base of historical data in order to be reliable in predicting the need for maintenance. The need for machine histories, parts inventories, labour statistics and work estimates has led to the development of computer-supported maintenance systems that can manage the various inputs to the system.

*Kathie S. Smith*

## Make or buy strategy

Make or buy – the choice facing management is whether to provide goods and services from within the firm or to buy them from outside suppliers. This may apply to processes, parts and sub-assemblies in manufacturing industry, or it may apply to supporting services in any business venture.

A consistent approach to the making of these decisions in line with the overall business strategy is a prime requirement of successful business management. A make or buy strategy is essentially a framework within which such decisions can be made; a framework which ensures the consistency of the many individual decisions that are made in the normal operation of the business.

This issue has been of perennial concern to business managers; reference and research can be traced back to early business journals. Very often this takes the form of case examples or surveys which offer no generic guide to good practice. More recently, the associated issues have been approached theoretically from various academic disciplines including engineering, economics, and strategic management. This has enriched the discussion of what might constitute best practice and leads to the possibility of devising a methodology whereby firms could systematically derive their own make or buy strategy.

Coming to conclusions in this area is not a simple process, and many aspects should be considered. The optimal strategy will vary from industry to industry and with prevailing economic conditions. However, the successful company will have a structured approach to the issue and be in a position to review its strategy constantly, taking into account the many contingent factors.

*David Probert*

## Management in Africa

In order to analyse and understand management practices and organizational processes in a diverse continent like Africa, it is necessary to consider at the onset the socio-economic and cultural environment within which industrial enterprises operate. Such an understanding is useful because management policies and practices are influenced by culture and a deep-rooted belief system among Africans.

Modern organizations in Africa fall into three distinct broad categories. The first comprise public enterprises, in which the State controls 50 per cent or more of the share capital. Organizations in this category are set up to discharge specific functions and attain objectives which are more readily achievable outside the civil service system. In practically all African economies, this is the dominant type of organization in the modern sector. The second category includes private indigenous enterprises, an area in which African entrepreneurs are dominant. Enterprises in this category are comparatively small in size and tend to dominate certain industrial sectors such as commerce, but many such businesses exist. A large number of the indigenous businesses can be said to belong to the informal sector, where elementary management principles are not consistently followed. This informal sector occupies a prominent place in the economies of the region, and has been particularly prevalent since the beginning of the 1980s. The third category includes foreign subsidiaries or joint-venture organizations.

Management in Africa has a number of distinguishing features. First, it is strongly rooted in cultural beliefs and traditions, and tends on the whole to be strongly authoritarian. Planning in African organizations tends to be minimal. Human resource management is seldom formally integrated with corporate objectives; trade unions often have limited powers and little effectiveness. The authoritarian style also tends to hamper effective communication. There is a need for a new style of management education in Africa which will take the strengths of traditional culture and harmonize them with best practice from the West in order to break down some of these barriers.

*Tayo Fashoyin*


## Management in the Arab world

The Arab world is extensive but management in Arab countries has been relatively little studied until recently. Hofstede's typology provides a useful framework and, more recently, Hickson and Pugh have examined the impact on Arab styles and cultures of management on the Bedouin and tribal ancestry, the religious framework of Islam, the common experience of foreign rule and the access to oil and natural resources leading to rapid economic development. Some Arab countries, however, are not oil-rich and not all have had the same experience of foreign domination. In particular there are strong differences between the largely French-influenced countries of the Maghreb and the largely British-influenced Middle East.

New typological frameworks are emerging based on empirical studies. There has been an emphasis on education and training and management development, particularly in the oil-rich areas exposed to Western influence. In many the spur to research has come through the political requirement of nationalization, the replacement of ex-patriot managers with nationals. This is increasingly true in the Gulf States.

Studies show that Arab countries, particularly in the Gulf, tend to have highly trained managerial cadres. The apparently restrictive requirements of Islamic finance and banking have not hindered economic development. Leadership control through close supervision and an absence of delegation have not inhibited effective performance. There is currently strong emphasis on the role of women and of family-owned businesses. Considerable evidence is building up that Arab management will present a 'fourth paradigm' and is *sui generis*. New studies of the impact of Islamic and Arab behaviour and belief patterns on motivation and organizational styles are, however, needed.

*David Weir*

## Management in Australia

Like most advanced industrial societies, Australia has experienced a steady growth of employment in the service industries, which now account for more than 75 per cent of the paid workforce. Although agriculture, mining and manufacturing still occupy a central role in the Australian economy, as a source of employment they have declined steadily in recent years. Unemployment rose to around 10 per cent during the late 1980s and early 1990s.

The Australian management environment has been significantly affected in the past few decades by the injection of overseas investment. Some industries are almost entirely foreign-controlled: 90 per cent of vehicle building, 75 per cent of pharmaceuticals and aluminium. Apart from the large-scale, predominantly foreign-owned corporations, Australia also possesses a large number of small Australian-owned enterprises. The typical firm in Australia is family-owned or owner-managed and employs fewer than 100 people. Only 600 enterprises employ more than 1,000 people. Yet half the value added by the manufacturing industry is contributed by the largest 200 firms, half of which are at least one-quarter foreign-controlled. The decisions of these top 200 corporations greatly affect Australian industry because they employ about half of the total workforce engaged in manufacturing and account for 60 per cent of the fixed capital expenditure. These firms also exercise considerable influence on the national economy through their pricing and investments as well as their general competitive capacity. In industrial relations matters, large firms set the pattern for smaller ones.

Although located in one of the fastest-growing economic regions of the world, in recent years the Australian economy has not fared as well as some of its trading partners. According to the IMD-World Economic Forum's 1994 *World Competitiveness Report*, Australia was ranked thirteenth out of twenty-three OECD countries, compared with tenth place in 1989. While Australia scored well for business efficiency, with comparatively good levels of productivity, its managers were regarded as deficient in long-term orientation, strategic skills and international experience. A 1995 report commissioned by the Australian Government, and known as the Industry Task Force on Leadership and Management Skills (the Karpin Report), argued that a lack of depth within the ranks of Australian management had contributed to poor economic performance. Furthermore, Australia's history of protectionism and prevailing educational culture had resulted in limited attention being paid to personal and integrative skills of managers. Accordingly, the Karpin Report called for a programme of management reform that would lead to employment growth and improved living standards. Key proposals in the Karpin Report included upgrading management education at all levels, workplace reform and developing a positive enterprise culture through education and training.

*Russell D. Lansbury*

## Management in the Benelux countries

The Netherlands, Belgium and Luxembourg are the 'Benelux' countries. The Netherlands and Belgium have strong historical ties and were once one kingdom. After their separation in 1830, French culture became dominant in Belgium. Since the industrialization of (the Walloon part of) Belgium early in the nineteenth century, the two countries have grown even further apart – the Netherlands remained an agrarian and trade-orientated country, in fact, until after the Second World War. The industrial relations system still reflects these differences. Management culture in the two countries differs as well, Dutch managers being more 'feminine' and tolerant, and less inclined to keep a power distance between themselves and their subordinates, in Hofstede's terms. There are, however, many similarities, which gives the name 'Benelux' a realistic flavour.

*Albert L. Mok*

## Management in Brazil

Brazil is a modern industrialized country which nevertheless retains many of the values of an agrarian society. A large proportion of the population does not have even a basic education. Culturally, Brazil is very diverse with a mix of African, European and native Indian populations. Although the management culture of Brazil has common features with that of other developed nations, it also has some special characteristics reflecting the educational limitations of the country and its internal turbulence, both economic and political.

Authoritarianism is one of the most important features of hierarchical relationships in Brazilian society, and in management this results in a directive management style with little or no consultation. At the same time management in Brazil is characterized by informality, with priority given to social contacts rather than tasks and to personal rather than formal communications. On the one hand informality contributes to increased competitiveness by fostering innovation and speeding up communication. However, informality also results in a lack of concern for formal information and written reports, which results in inefficiency and waste of time and resources. Despite these problems, however, Brazilian management style reflects both the country's diversity and its particular competitive advantages.

*Suzana Braga Rodrigues*


## Management in China

Chinese management has its roots in ancient thinking and practices, especially in values, performance evaluation, personnel selection, quality control and project management. Four major philosophies, Confucianism, Taoism, Buddhism and Legalism, have helped to shape Chinese society and all have had their impact on the management of organizations, which is characterized by teamwork, orientation around relationships and multi-level regulations. Since 1949 public ownership has been the mainstay of the economy, but since the beginning of economic reform in 1979 other organizational types have emerged. At present there are four types of ownership: state-owned, collective, joint venture and private.

Historically China has tested several models of management system, from 'three-man management', through 'one-man management' and 'director responsibility under Communist Party committee leadership' to the 'director responsibility' system. This last is now a major part of the Chinese management structure. The reforms have meant great changes in areas such as reward systems, responsibility contract systems, personnel management, teamwork, leadership, managerial decision making, joint-venture management, technological innovation and organization structure.

In the late 1990s China was now moving towards a more decentralized, market-oriented, innovative and international stage, with consequent changes for management. As Chinese management undergoes systematic reform, there has been a significant move towards a holistic means of coordinating subjects of management, and of integrating culture, organizational reform and management principles. The framework of the socialist-market economy established in 1993 has as its goal a modern enterprise system with Chinese characteristics.

*Zhong-Ming Wang*

## Management in developing countries

It may be argued that in any business, regardless of location, there is the need for well-developed strategies and proper strategy implementation processes. While this is true, it is also necessary to recognize that strategy definition and implementation are inextricably tied to the business environment, and that environment is fundamentally affected by a country's level of development and by the dynamics of the development process.

One reason for focusing on developing countries is their absolute and growing importance in the global business arena. Almost 80 per cent of the world's consumers are in developing countries and almost all of the population-based market expansion in the twenty-first century will occur there. Although poorer, the developing countries' economies are growing faster than those of developed countries. Developing countries are an increasingly significant part of the global economy, as recipients of growing foreign direct and portfolio investments and as competitors in export markets. The proliferation of business opportunities in developing countries, their growing competitive significance, and the contribution that businesses can make to these nations' development, make them a priority item on the agenda of forward-thinking business executives.

Since the business environments in developing countries are different along several dimensions from those in developed countries, it is necessary to understand the forces shaping the lesser developed countries' environments and the resulting distinctive issues that must be dealt with when managing there, particularly the challenges of dealing with much greater instability and uncertainty.

*Tomás O. Kohn & James E. Austin*

## Management development

Management development covers a wide spectrum of activities ranging from self-development through improving communication and presentation skills or specific skills such as managing information in the office, performance appraisals, financial management, managing other people, managing in different cultures and aligning the capabilities of managers with changes in the strategies and structures of the organization.

Global flows of currency and information impact directly on management development, which was originally defined during earlier periods of relative stability when it was possible to screen out uncertainty rather than engage with it. Management is in transition from the command and control structures appropriate to relative stability to the distributed decision-making structures necessary in rapidly changing conditions. Managers now require new approaches to decision making in uncertainty, and they must also do much more to create an atmosphere where people can cope with uncertainty not only in making decisions but also in the patterns of their working lives. Best practice in management development integrates the development of individuals within the design of the organization.

*Gillian Stamp*

## Management in eastern Europe

The collapse of communism in brought with it the blurring of the notion of eastern Europe, which for decades had been used in an economic and political sense to indicate the planned economies of the German Democratic Republic, Bulgaria, Czechoslovakia, Hungary, Poland and Romania. This blurring took place for three reasons.

First, the political system of these countries lost its communist homogeneity as different levels and forms of democracy started to evolve in Bulgaria, the Czech Republic, Hungary, Poland, Slovakia and Romania. The political changes also brought closer to eastern Europe countries such as the Baltic states (Estonia, Latvia and Lithuania), post-Soviet states (for example, Belorussia, the Ukraine and Moldavia) and some countries from southeastern Europe (for example, Slovenia, Albania, Croatia, Bosnia and Serbia). Second, the relatively similar economic systems, based upon planned economy principles, collapsed. Market reforms and transformations were initiated in all post-communist countries but their shape and direction differed. Third, with the disintegration of the umbrella system of communism, cultural diversity, regional conflicts and ethnic clashes immediately came to the fore in some countries in the region, former Yugoslavia being the extreme example. Homogeneity was replaced by such rich diversity that many researchers and managers have great difficulty in accepting the fact that these countries are now more unlike than like. Nevertheless, there are some common threads in the development process in these countries, mostly because of the common communist legacy of economic recession, political fragmentation and lack of management skills on the global and local levels.

Today, management across eastern Europe is an underdeveloped practice due to the lack of its relevance for the success of firms during the communist era. However, the gap between management in eastern and western Europe is slowly closing, thanks to constant and severe pressure from the turbulent business environment, the presence of management benchmarks created by multinationals and successful private entrepreneurs, and the growing strength and diversity of management education in the region.

*Krzysztof Obłój*

## Management education, future of

Management education is a highly competitive field in which many changes are rapidly occurring. The future of management education requires examination from a strategic point of view. An appraisal of those factors most likely to have the largest impact on management education, exploring differences between European and US management education and looking at the most important trends in today's marketplace – internationalization, executive education and partnerships with business – provides the basis for a strategic prescription for the future.

There are major differences between European and US management education, particularly in the areas of Master of Business Administration (MBA) programmes, the level of practical experience provided to PhD graduates, academic nomenclature and other areas such as income, status and roles. In both regions, however, there are general factors which will have an impact on the future of management education, including the ageing of the population, the dispersion of population and jobs, the increasing importance of women in the workforce, economic trends, political changes and technological advances.

Keeping track of these issues and responding to them in increasingly competitive conditions will be critical to the survival of many educational programmes. Having a grasp of an institution's competencies and understanding one's position in the marketplace sets the stage for an educational organization to control its own future.

*Peggy Simcic Brønn & Peter Lorange*

## Management education and development, international

International management development is a structured system for selecting, evaluating, tracking and training managers on a worldwide basis. Identifying and developing leaders is a key priority for globally-orientated firms, as there is a growing shortage of managerial personnel capable of meeting the requirements of these firms for technical competence, international expertise and global perspective. The development of global strategies, expansion into wider global markets and the need for international or global expertise through all levels of the managerial hierarchy have combined in such a way as to require greater attention to the development of a managerial and executive workforce which will be capable of meeting these organizational demands.

Within those global and multinational companies already successfully competing in the world marketplace, new management development programmes are being launched to meet these needs. These programmes are designed so as to integrate an international and global perspective into managerial and executive development.

The key to international management development is the human resource staffing cycle. Within this cycle, goals can be set for management development on the strategic, managerial and operational levels. Career planning is an important aspect of development; overseas assignments are a particularly useful way of enhancing managerial careers and developing international expertise. However, even sophisticated international management development programmes face problems, such as the potential 'cloning' of executives and the problems of relating performance to potential. However, international management development is and will remain an increasingly important aspect of corporate strategies as companies become more and more focused on the global marketplace.

*Edwin L. Miller*

## Management education in Africa

Most African countries badly need trained managers in order to overcome their numerous economic and social problems; however, many African countries also lack high-quality management education provision. Many African management training institutes have been heavily criticized for failing to make a significant impact on either individual or organizational performance. One particular problem lies in the fact that many current programmes are adapted from Western models and lack specific African focus or relevance.

There is a need for alternative approaches to management education which may be more in tune with African cultural values. In particular, Western educational models which rely heavily on classroom teaching are increasingly seen as having little value in an African context. Traditional African models of learning such as apprenticeship and other forms of on-the-job training might be more relevant and more useful in Africa today than the formal, institutional programmes currently in existence.

The term 'management education' is used here to cover a range of educational strategies whose aim is to enhance managerial capabilities. These include institution-based and classroom-based courses leading to formal awards in management subjects, classroom-based short courses for practising managers, in-house workshop-type activities intended to improve specific skills, work-based approaches such as Action Learning, and on-the-job training. Hence management education as defined here subsumes a variety of educational activities which might in other circumstances be labelled as management training or management development.

*Merrick L. Jones & Peter Blunt*

## Management education in Asia

In most Asian countries, formal management programmes are offered primarily at universities, polytechnics and professional institutes. The range of programmes on offer covers a broad spectrum and caters to all types of students. Mid-career managers, especially those from non-business backgrounds, enrol in short courses to learn about finance or marketing; ambitious executives study for MBA degrees on either a full-time or a part-time basis; other managers enrol in distance learning programmes or open universities in order to learn at their own pace. Prospective academics can pursue a PhD degree either locally or abroad, and researchers are encouraged to publish their findings in international journals. In some countries, secondary school curricula may also include business subjects such as accounting or commerce.

As a result of rapid economic growth, family firms particularly in east and south-east Asia are expanding their activities. Most corporate founder-managers have learned to manage through experience, and most continue to involve members of their families. However, many are now beginning to employ marketing, finance and other professionals to manage their operations, and consequently are recruiting young people who have some form of formal management education, especially those who are multilingual and have a global perspective. The development of this new generation of professional managers is particularly important as many Asian companies begin to expand into international markets.

Asian companies doing business in the USA or other Western countries prefer to recruit managers who have had a business education in North America, Europe or Australia; large Japanese and Korean companies in particular often send their managers to Western countries to pursue further studies and to establish contacts. Asian companies also seek MBA graduates, from foreign as well as local universities, for senior positions. Many Asian universities sponsor their young academics for doctoral studies overseas, while others have started their own PhD programmes.

*Chwee-Huat Tan*


## Management education in Australia

Though small by world standards, the Australian economy is none the less a strong one. It is also undergoing many changes both internal and external, particularly in its increased focus on the Asia Pacific region. These developments have considerable implications for the education and training of managers.

Management education in Australia began in the 1920s, with the first MBA programmes appearing in the 1960s. Two different models of management education were followed, that of the USA and that of the UK. The Australian government has undertaken reviews of management education in Australia in 1970, 1980 and 1992, but the recommendations of all three have yet to be implemented in full. At present, Australian management education still falls short of the high standards set in other countries. The 1995 Karpin Report has spelled out ways in which these defects may be overcome.

*Bernard Barry, Peter J. Dowling & Graeme Tonks*

## Management education in central and eastern Europe

In Europe prior to the Second World War, management education was mainly carried out by schools of engineering (polytechnics) or commerce. The countries of central and eastern Europe broadly followed this model. The communist system also developed its own model of management education, the primary purpose of which was to train bureaucrats and managers of state-owned enterprises. In most cases the communist parties maintained a tight hold over management education, but in the 1970s partial liberalization allowed Hungary and Poland to begin developing some Western-style programmes.

Following the break-up of the Soviet bloc, foreign aid has played an important role in the further development of management education in central and eastern Europe.

Characteristic features of management education in central and eastern Europe include skyrocketing unsatisfied demand, severe constraints, low institutionalization, sources of financing and associations and groups of management educators. The massive increase in demand for management education following the fall of communism in 1989 means that the situation in this field is constantly changing.

*Andrzej K. Kozminski*

## Management education in China

The growth of Chinese management education reflects China's economic development during the twentieth century, particularly during the period of economic reform which began in 1978. The rapid changes in the economic system during this period necessitated a major expansion of the management education system. Three strategies were adopted to build up a basic infrastructure for the provision of management education. First, the economic ministries launched training programmes for senior executives and managers in newly-established training centres and institutes. Second, the already-existing industrial management departments in the universities were expanded into business schools with various degree courses such as undergraduate and MBA courses. Finally, the major developed countries including the USA, the EU, Japan and Canada set up joint management programmes in China to transfer modern management skills directly from the West.

The development of management education in China has been affected significantly by ideological and cultural factors. Subjects based on exact sciences or natural sciences tend to be given higher priority in management education curricula. People-related subjects are still controversial, and there are unresolved issues relating to value and cognitive style. The major challenge for Chinese management education is to learn advanced management from Western sources and then to adapt it to a context which is both Chinese and socialist.

*Derong Chen*

## Management education in developing countries

Management education in developing countries in Africa, Asia and Latin America is influenced by a number of factors which both determine the form such education takes and strongly influence its chances of success. One major influence is the environment within which management education is delivered, which is itself a function of variables such as governance, culture and resource availability. Other factors include the models and methods of management education employed, teacher qualifications and experience and the nature of institutional structures for the delivery of management education. Taking these factors into account, there are a number of ways in which management education in developing countries could be improved.

Much has been said and written about the poor management of organizations in developing countries. Public organizations in particular have been and continue to be criticized for inefficiency, waste, over-staffing and ineffectiveness. These claims have considerable validity (although poor performance is by no means uniform) and organizational dysfunction in developing countries is a serious impediment to development. Lack of management capability is one of many factors contributing to this condition.

In contrast with the industrialized nations, most management education in developing countries is directed at public sector rather than private sector managers. The private sectors of many developing countries are of small size and simply do not employ as many managers as do the frequently overstaffed public sectors. While this balance is likely to change as more and more developing countries are persuaded to reduce the size of their governments and encourage private sector growth, the speed of this change will vary considerably from one country to another. A further reason for the prominence of public sector management education in developing countries is that, even under conditions of smaller government, the public sector will clearly continue to be crucial to effective national governance through its responsibilities for policy implementation in areas such as education and health, regulation and protection of the environment, and the creation of environments which are conducive to entrepreneurial activity. Effective public sector management is indispensable to sustainable economic and human development, and its needs take priority over those of private sector management in developing countries.

*Peter Blunt*

## Management education in India

Indian management institutions offering teaching and/or training programmes were first established in the 1950s. Their numbers have since grown, and Indian management education is now poised for spectacular growth thanks to widespread acceptance of the need for formal management education in both the business and not-for-profit sectors, and to an open-door entry policy for new institutions. Indian management schools are not insular; many are members of national and international networks. Some are of world class, and their diversification into different sectors has created the potential for a rich cross-fertilization of ideas.

However, while the opportunities for management education are many and varied, there remain nagging problems about educational quality, relevance to the needs of 'customers', inadequacies in pedagogy and subject areas, and mismatch between the career aspirations of management students and the management needs of the country. There are considerable differences in quality between the top schools and the rest, and there are also variations among the top schools like the Indian Institute of Management at Ahmedabad and others. Notwithstanding these problems, Indian management education is growing rapidly and becoming more innovative. The latest trend, distance education through computer networks and satellite-based transmission, has the ability to bring high quality management education to the doorsteps of many institutions and individuals.

*Pradip N. Khandwalla*

## Management education in Japan

The uniqueness of management in Japan lies in its encouragement of people in any organization, whether they are entrepreneurs, managers, administrators or other professional specialists, to become organizational persons prior to becoming managers. This is a basic concept, common to all education and training programmes conducted by employers.

Management education is seen as being part of general workforce education, with the strategic potential to train not only managers but the entire workforce. Most management education used to take place in-house; the emphasis was on job rotation by company order, on-the-job training (OJT) by seniors, promotion within the company and seniority-based compensation, as well as on selecting new intakes of university graduates. Systematic OJT and job rotation took place at every stage of the manager's career. In-house education and training also included some off-the-job training (OffJT). The primary aim of in-house education was to foster generalists who could deal with any managerial issue, not just specialist issues. Managers in the fast track had to be generalists; to be a specialist meant not being in the mainstream. However, these general management skills tended to be specific to the organization.

In the 1990s Japanese management has an abundance of middle-ranking managers but a shortage of entrepreneurial qualities and skills. Japanese organizations which used to aim to improve the administrative skills of their managers are now having to work to increase their strategic and entrepreneurial abilities. Managerial skills are moving from internal and organization-specific skills to universal and market-orientated skills. As a result, large Japanese organizations are depending more on OffJT for management education than before. Self-development programmes are also encouraging managers to take courses dealing with personnel management, planning and accounting. However, Japanese organizations still have strong confidence in such policies as selective recruiting among university graduates, OJT by seniors, job rotation for generalist training and organizational skill formation.

*Yoko Sano*

## Management education in North America

Formal management education in the USA has a history of more than 100 years and involves an immense number of degree-granting institutions (over 1,200) and students (who receive more than 250,000 baccalaureate and 80,000 master's degrees each year). Management education enrolments grew fairly steadily during the first part of the twentieth century up until the Second World War, and then expanded rapidly immediately following the end of the war. Growth rates increased again from the early 1960s through to the 1980s, largely due to the increasing number of women entering undergraduate and Master of Business Administration (MBA) degree programmes. However, by the early 1990s growth had slowed considerably and a period of consolidation then began.

Since the basic model of management education established in the 1960s still seemed to be working well in the early 1980s, business schools had little incentive to make any major changes. Enrolment levels were high and growing and graduates were being placed in high-paying jobs with relatively little difficulty. By the end of the decade, however, numerous criticisms were being directed at this model from a variety of sources, both internally within the academic community and externally in the business community and the business press. The critics argued that the existing business school model was outdated, was not doing a good job of serving the needs of employers, and was not well suited to the challenges of management and the business world of the future.

In the 1990s, as a consequence not only of these criticisms but also of the rapidly changing and increasingly global competitive context in which businesses were operating, management and business schools began both collectively and individually to change. The chief accrediting agency for business schools in the USA, the American Assembly of Collegiate Schools of Business (AACSB), adopted a fundamentally revised set of accrediting standards in 1992 that allowed its members greater flexibility in areas such as curricula and the balance between teaching and research. In addition, a number of leading schools independently initiated substantial changes in their curricula and their overall approaches to the delivery of management programmes. The most significant challenge for US business schools in the immediate future is how to respond to a variety of demands and expectations from multiple constituencies. The business world and its needs are changing rapidly, and so too is the world of higher education.

*Lyman W. Porter & William Broesamle*

## Management education in Russia

The traumatic political changes in Russia during the early 1990s had a major impact on virtually all aspects of Russian society, with management education being no exception. The break-up of the Soviet Union and the abandonment of communism in 1991 marked the beginning of a transition towards a market-orientated economy in Russia, which has in turn necessitated a massive programme of re-education for thousands of managers.

There were a number of management education programmes in Russia during the Soviet period and most managers attended one form of programme or another, but these programmes lacked practical content and had little impact on the Russian economy. Since 1991 management education has become more market orientated, with new types of business schools and Western involvement in a number of management programmes. At present business schools in Russia face many challenges, some of which are linked to the country's economic problems; however, business schools should continue to have a high profile and there are opportunities for them to help shape the emerging market economy and assist Russia's growth and development.

*Sheila M. Puffer*

## Management in Europe

It is difficult to make generalizations about management in Europe because, although in the latter half of the twentieth century Europe has become more integrated, there still remain differences between countries. Nevertheless, generalizations can provide some value, particularly when comparing management in Europe with management in the USA and Japan.

By comparison with Japan, management in Europe tends to be more individualist and more focused on the needs of corporations and individuals than on the needs of the country. The result is that those in Europe are not given to stoicism, preferring instead to articulate dissatisfaction. The European view of business is that economic success is meant to enhance the wealth and welfare of citizens, not the grandeur of the state. Managerial processes tend – by comparison with Japan, at least – to reflect the acts and decisions of individuals rather than being collectivist processes. There is a sharper separation between the interests of business and government; European corporations are distinct and identifiable, and are more strongly differentiated from the state sector. By the same principle, trade unions are based on an aggregation of individual interests.

Comparisons with management in the USA are more complex; European companies tend to be at one and the same time more conservative and less systematized than their US counterparts. They exhibit more complex and variable attitudes towards organizational conflict and change. There are also differences between the two in the ways in which corporate strategy is perceived and communicated, and European companies tend to have longer time horizons. There is less emphasis on management systems and more on individual judgement and discretion; attitudes towards measurement, in particular performance appraisal, are more sceptical in Europe than in the USA.

In personal terms, European managers tend to be less single-minded than their US counterparts and more likely to recognize secondary (non profit-related) goals; there is an emphasis on 'being' rather than 'becoming'. Other differences include more variable and qualified attitudes to inter-company mobility, a more conditional view of the rights of the individual and less utilitarian attitudes to language, again all part of an outlook which is more conservative and less systematized.

In terms of relations with the external environment, European corporations are likely to have more relations with government and accept a degree of government involvement in the capitalist economy than are US companies. There is a greater acceptance of trade unionism and the recognition that unionism will contain an ideological component. There is also more acceptance of worker democracy. As a result, European companies are more likely to accept negotiation and compromise in labour relations.

These international comparisons highlight the fact that there remains a large degree of heterogeneity in management in Europe. The most obvious aspect of this heterogeneity is the difference between eastern and western Europe, itself in large part the legacy of communism. However, there are also many differences in management values, style and practice between western European countries, as evidenced by a number of empirical studies and surveys.

An important issue arising from this heterogeneity is the need to manage diversity. This is a concept particularly familiar to Europe: for the member countries international markets and exports have always been of primary importance, forcing cooperation and integration. Given this need, some measure of success must be acknowledged.

*Peter Lawrence*

## Management in France

France is often perceived as a nation of contrasts and exceptions. Despite (or perhaps because of) the long shadow cast by her history and traditions, the French are perpetually engaged in a process of modernization. Innovative ideas, new technologies, brash new departures in architecture, all are welcomed yet translated into a characteristically French idiom. France as a country leans towards long-term planning (as witnessed by the five-year economic plans of the 1950s and 1960s which survive in the regional planning process and the strategic emphasis on telecommunications, nuclear energy and aerospace), yet French managers are adaptable, willing to accept change and have a reputation for rapid, improvised solutions. Moreover, the French are markedly individualistic yet have a strong tendency to centralize decision making.

A view frequently held by the French business world maintains that the role of the centralized state in coordinating and directing economic growth and development – so-called *dirigisme* – has been crucial to the post-war success which has transformed France from an economic backwater into a leading industrial nation, whose gross domestic product (GDP) per capita is the seventh highest in the world and the third highest in Europe. France is often seen as the home of protectionism and interventionist industrial policy. Indeed, the state–industry partnership has produced excellent results in select fields such as high-speed trains, Concorde, Airbus, Ariane or Minitel. However, although this interpretation highlights a traditional French preference for institutional solutions promising order and logic rather than the vagaries of market mechanisms, it exaggerates the power of the French state *per se*. A specific management style for both the economy and firms can be seen but is the result of an extensive intermeshing of the political, administrative and business domains. Such a style allows solutions which may be seen as characteristically French solutions and which have few parallels around the globe.

*Joseph Szarka*

## Management in Germany

Management has many different meanings: it may be used to focus on structures for designing performance-orientated achievement processes based on the division of labour (organizational aspects) or on action concepts for performing tasks involved in such achievement processes (functional aspects). However, irrespective of its usage, management is always the attempt, or the result of the attempt to reconcile, in the employment of resources, the cultural guidelines of both individual and collective action with the requirements of an actual or potential market. The content and form of management emanate from strategies whose visionary core and fundamental criteria cannot be separated from the cultural environment in which the actors are embedded and to which they feel committed.

When determining the peculiarities of German management it is vital to investigate the cultural or environmental characteristics in which it is rooted and which constitute its basic form. This is particularly important in view of the tendency towards standardization of managerial action, a tendency strongly influenced by the requirements of worldwide competition. For an analysis of German management it is appropriate to consider the problem from five interrelated perspectives: its economic and ethical basis; the legal framework, which limits individual and collective decision making; the organizational structure of management; managerial qualifications; and those concepts that determine managerial action.

These necessarily affect the application of management tasks in various areas, such as: identification of priorities (for example, in Germany technological standards tend to dominate the production process whereas in the USA the emphasis is on market orientation); the timeframe for planning (for example, medium- or long-term planning in Germany versus short-term planning in the USA); conflict resolution (for example, of conflicts between the economic point of view and employee interests).

*Rainer Marr*

## Management in Hong Kong

A key to understanding the practice of management in Hong Kong is to appreciate the hybrid, cosmopolitan and pluralistic nature of its economic life and society. While the legacies of Chinese tradition and Confucian ethics continue to have a major influence on work and business, the territory has grown to represent an almost neo-classical model of a 'free enterprise' capitalist economy within which individualistic striving and an ethos of competitive advancement and entrepreneurship are cherished.

This paradox has emerged in part because of the bureaucratically competent administration instituted by the British after colonization of the territory in the mid-nineteenth century. This regulatory framework provides a solid basis for the otherwise traditionally informal processes of management in Hong Kong, which permit firms a much needed measure of flexibility vital to their survival in the increasingly competitive marketplace.

A system of such a hybrid nature has meant Hong Kong is particularly receptive to innovation, whatever part of the world it may stem from. Coupled with a government policy of 'positive non-intervention' and a substantial measure of foreign investment, these factors have combined to sustain the appearance of the 'Hong Kong miracle'. Both geographically and demographically, Hong Kong suffers from a scarcity of resources. The resultant increases in business costs have recently seen levels of local and foreign investment drop considerably and the mass migration of professional, managerial and skilled workers overseas. In addition, there has been the question of Hong Kong's political future and the need to prepare for Chinese sovereignty in 1997, and its far-reaching economic metamorphosis, emanating from the modernization of the Chinese economy and the boom in the east Asia region.

*Ng Sek-Hong*

## Management in India

Indian managers run their organizations according to a pattern derived from their cultural, political and economic background. Although both Eastern and Western traits can be found in management behaviour, the diversity of Indian culture makes for a distinct style characterized by centralization of decision making, vertical hierarchies, confrontational management–employee relationships, and dual discipline and control strategies.

The Indian economy was for a long time protectionist, shielding firms from fierce competition. As a consequence, there has been no incentive for managers to invest in product improvement; the domestic market is captive. Reinforcing this, many strategic and operative decisions, such as plant location, production technology, pricing, staffing and industrial relations, are determined by established state regulations.

The introduction of economic reforms in 1991 has brought change to India. Aimed at liberalizing the market, these reforms have opened up the country to foreign competition. In the future organizations will be forced to develop and progress if they are to survive.

*Monir Tayeb*

## Management in Indonesia

Indonesia is a multi-ethnic, multi-cultural society struggling to become an advanced industrialized country. Consisting of over 200 ethnic groups, each with their own distinct culture, 'Indonesian' culture is also strongly influenced by various religions (Hinduism, Buddhism, Christianity and Islam), the Dutch (since colonization), Japan (since the occupation) and the West. Increasing industrialization has meant a fusing of 'national' values (including regional and local values) with 'international' values.

No specific management science or style has developed in Indonesia. As a colony, the management of various enterprises lay in Dutch hands. After independence, however, the Indonesians took over, forced to learn through direct experience. Growth in industry has resulted in a demand for managers, with a parallel interest in management education (US-orientated), which has become increasingly popular.

In its search for a style of its own, Indonesian management has two main orientations. One is pragmatism: let management be applied by managers based on individual conditions and cultural values. The other is nationalism: the development of a management science and style based on the Indonesian state philosophy, the *Panca Sila*.

*Ashar Sunyoto Munandar*

## Management information systems

The subject of management information embraces many recent developments in acquiring, processing, using and transmitting information, all of which are profoundly affecting modern business and management. The subject includes not only the information needed by management in decision making, but also information processing and information technology, which have become intertwined with almost all aspects of economic and social activity. The scope of information in management is therefore almost limitless, and includes strategy, the value chain, marketing, manufacturing and production, human resources and finance.

Computer-based management systems include management information systems (MIS) proper, which perform routine business processes; database management systems; visual interactive modelling; intelligent systems; executive information systems; enterprise information systems; and group decision support systems. Knowledge-based systems characterized by the use of artificial intelligence are also being increasingly used; these systems include expert systems, natural language interfaces, vision systems, robotics and neural networks. Virtual reality systems are also being developed for a variety of purposes.

Advances in information technology are continuing to increase the power and reach of management information systems. There are, however, associated costs, in terms of alienation, information security and impacts on employment.

*Alan E. Singer*

## Management in the Irish Republic

The Irish Republic was a late developing economy, with most industrial development occurring since the 1960s. As a small, open economy, the

Irish Republic is highly dependent on foreign trade and sensitive to developments in the world economy. Since the mid-1960s, government policy has focused on attracting foreign direct investment to the Irish Republic (using generous tax and financial incentives) and on building the physical and human capital support infrastructures.

A short account of management in the Irish Republic will almost invariably include some generalizations. There are wide variations in practice between indigenous and foreign-owned companies, and between small and large companies, in the Republic. However, some general themes can be picked out. One recent development is the trend towards more professional management. Traditionally, management practice in the Irish Republic has been based more on pragmatism than professionalism, with common sense and experience being considered more important than education. However, there is evidence that this is changing, mainly as a result of the influence of foreign multinational corporations. There are also some general cultural characteristics which can be identified, including an attachment to hierarchy, a high degree of uncertainty avoidance and a frequent unwillingness to delegate authority. The Irish Republic is a common-law country and its laws governing business entities reflect that background.

For those seeking a career in management, there are three major career routes in the Irish Republic: the specialist route; the business qualification route; and the generalist route. Due to the preference for experience, most Irish managers, especially in indigenous companies, do not have formal management qualifications, although more are now seeking them. Irish managers are currently facing a variety of problems, most notably the need for quality improvement and the need to develop innovative personnel policies which will improve the competitive position of Irish enterprises.

*Patrick Gunnigle & Michael Morley*

## Management in Israel

Management in Israel has been very much shaped by its history. The emergence of the country was characterized by enormous difficulties, with the need to create something new out of nothing. Entrepreneurship, innovation and the ability to improvise were vital during the establishment phase and throughout the first few decades of Israel's history.

One of the most pressing needs for Israel was the absorption of new immigrants and, ideally, doubling of the population within a few years. This was a huge project, with important social consequences. The first wave of immigrants, the Ashkenazim, came from Europe. However, this was not the case for the majority of immigrants. Known as the Sephardim, they arrived after the Europeans and came primarily from the Arab countries. With the advantage of a more modern education and the first opportunities for jobs, the European immigrants naturally took the best positions. Thus, although there is no class system in Israel in the way there is in the UK, the Sephardim have found themselves making up the body of the working class, while the Ashkenazim tended to be white-collar workers and managers. As years have passed, however, the distinction has become increasingly blurred.

The creation of the state of Israel, following the Holocaust, was characterized by wars with neighbouring Arab nations (and later the Arab boycott) and by the support of many of the eastern bloc countries for the Arabs. This created a common feeling among Israelis that 'all the world is against us', that Israel must fight its way through alone. Management style is characterized by such values.

*Yehuda Baruch*

## Management in Italy

A number of factors exist which distinguish Italian management from its counterparts in northern Europe and North America. Italian managers tend to view their organizations as 'families', with corresponding authority relationships. They have a preference for personal rather than work-specific relationships, and their ability to innovate, adapt and operate flexibly is well developed. Italian managers are also considered to be less formally trained than some of their international counterparts although Italian companies have achieved considerable success in the post-Second World War period, with design and styling underpinning the success of Italian products and services.

Within Italy itself differences also exist. Italian management reflects the historical and regional diversity which has had a significant influence on business culture in Italy. This comprises a number of contrasts: the economic and cultural divide between northern and southern Italy; the persistence of a large public sector of industry operating alongside privately owned organizations; and the economic influence of large domestic multinationals and the relatively large number of small companies.

These differences help give Italian management a distinct flavour of its own. However, this is currently under threat as Italian business and management undergo a period of substantial flux, the result of social and political trends and the rising impact of European and international developments.

*Vincent Edwards*

## Management in Japan

After the Second World War, the strength of company culture as a binding factor in Japanese organizations became increasingly powerful. This was particularly true for larger companies. The new organizational homogeneity, coupled with cultural homogeneity, gave a centripetal and cohesive nature to such cultures. Under the *ringi* system of decision making and the influence of *nemawashi*, the value premises of company members have accelerated in their convergence towards an identical organizational value.

This organizational value has resulted in strong decision codes for members of a company, who thus reject anything or anyone different. Although the *ringi* system and the reliance on the formation of consensus dominates Japanese business practices, these have not been extended to include foreign managers or workers of subsidiaries in foreign countries. This is not only due to language difficulties experienced by Japanese managers: company culture also plays a part. There is often conflict between a domestic unit and a foreign unit.

This cultural and organization problem is not limited to the international operation of Japanese companies, but also affects mergers between Japanese companies. For the Japanese, fusion and real integration of two different cultures is not complete until the existing members of the two organizations have gone. Until that time, any department of the new company effectively retains two departments within it, one from each company.

*Naoto Sasaki*

## Management in Latin America

Latin America is on the verge of significant changes in the next century. The region as a whole is currently experiencing growth, and inflation has fallen substantially. National economies have moved towards greater integration into the global system, and are also more politically and economically integrated at the regional level.

It is generally agreed that Latin America has the potential to transform itself into one of the most dynamic regions in the world. However, economic growth has yet to show benefits in terms of decreasing poverty and inequality. Latin America's economic volatility and political instability reflect the region's struggle for identity down through its history. Politically, Latin America has been marked by alteration between military coups and populist government. Vacillation between capitalism and socialism was in the past encouraged by the major world powers during the Cold War, but was grounded also in attempts to deal with the deep inequalities present in many nations. Economically, Latin America's quest for identity leaned on the one hand towards nationalism and on the other towards modernism; the Latin American protectionist ethos has always drawn support from populist as well as leftist tendencies.

Studies of Latin America suggest that one important reason for poor economic performance in the region lies in its colonial legacy of state bureaucracy, which has permeated the public and private sectors for centuries. The culture of authoritarianism served as a justification for an elitist orientation which viewed citizens and employees as a passive recipients of their policies and decisions. Industrial relations usually rely on state intermediation; unions have been kept under control either through repression or cooptation. Relationships in Latin American societies have been defined by bureaucratic control and patronizing authoritarianism.

Management in Latin America is marked by contradictions. Studies show that although society is promptly seduced by innovations and novelty, most private enterprises are still managed traditionally and invest little in human resources training and development. Organizations show excessive preoccupation with formal bureaucratic control, but decisions are bounded by personal relationships. Latin American governments and organizations are driven by short-termism; they do not usually make plans in advance, or organize their time according to these plans. Studies also show that Latin Americans differ from their counterparts in Asia in the USA in terms of negotiating styles; they are less group-oriented and meet their potential partners with only vague ideas of their preferences and little planning. Though there is concern with rules and norms, these are generally dismissed in practice.

After the so-called 'lost decade' in the 1980s, and as a result of neo-liberal policies recently introduced in various countries, foreign investors began in the 1990s to turn their eyes to Latin America. The region's future will be largely determined by its economic capacity to generate sustainable economic growth.

*Suzana Braga Rodrigues*

## Management in Malaysia

In discussions of management in Asia, Malaysia presents a singular case because of its unusual sociocultural features: the former British colony of Malaya until independence in 1957, in which bureaucracies and labour management systems were modelled on Western practices; a multi-ethnic society; a modern economy overlaid, since the 1980s, with a state-directed campaign to impose Japanese management practices.

Malaysia, consisting of the peninsula above Singapore, boarded by the Straits of Malacca and the South China Sea, and the states of Sabah and Sarawak in the northern half of the island of Borneo, has a population of 20 million, of whom 47 per cent are urban residents. Malaysia is a constitutional democracy, with a bicameral parliament consisting of the House of Representatives and the Senate. The King, or Yang di-Pertuan Agong, presides over the legislature and is elected every five years from the Conference of Rulers, the nine sultans or other royal heads of Islam in their respective states.

Management in modern organizations in Malaysia takes place in the context of a literate labour force with strong government support for manpower training. Since the colonial days, Malaysia has had a well-established infrastructure of road and rail systems, ports, electricity and water supply, health care facilities and, more recently, telecommunications. About 10 per cent of the labour force are unionized, largely in industrial unions, although the government has been encouraging enterprise unionism since the early 1980s.

Malaysian management styles are also influenced by state policies which have promoted rapid export-oriented industrialization since 1970, with resulting high levels of foreign investment. These two factors have placed heavy demands on the quality and supply of local managers and on training programmes.

*Wendy Smith*

## Management in Mexico

Management in Mexico is different from management in other countries primarily because of workforce and infrastructure characteristics. The management of people, materials and technology are shaped by these characteristics. People management is influenced primarily by the culture and the background and skills of the workers, the high turnover rate and Mexico's unions and Federal Labour Law. The management of materials is influenced by Mexico's weak supplier base and weak infrastructure which make it difficult for organizations to coordinate tightly activities with suppliers. The management of technology is influenced by society's traditional ideas about businesses, the high cost of debt, the low-skilled workforce and a shortage of maintenance parts. These forces act against the adoption of advanced technologies.

*John J. Lawrence*

## Management in North America

In the aftermath of the Second World War management in North America was the kind of management held in the greatest respect; in many ways it set the standard of excellence for the entire world. North American multinational corporations dominated the international marketplace in a number of industries, from copiers and computers to industrial equipment and transportation vehicles. By the 1970s, however, this dominance had begun to fade, and during the 1980s it became clear to North American managers that dramatic changes were needed. US managers also recognized the need to develop learning organizations in order to stay ahead. In order to maintain their status, to be world-class organizations, management needed to change, not simply react.

In Canada, given the high level of US investment – indeed, the high levels of cross-investment on both sides of the border – a business culture has developed which is very similar to that of the USA.

Important developments in North American management since 1980 have included downsizing, the use of advanced information technology and total quality management, as well as specific concepts such as empowerment, continuous improvement and re-engineering. The total quality approach in particular has dramatically changed North American management, but it is now recognized that this is just the starting point for moving into the twenty-first century. US and Canadian management is attempting to move towards what are becoming known as learning and world-class organizations. The world-class organization is built on customer focus, continuous improvement, flexibility, creative human resource management, an egalitarian climate and strong technological support.

These new paradigm organizations incorporate total quality but go beyond it, and are increasingly being adopted by North American managers to regain lost ground and strengthen their position in the domestic and global economy. There will continue to be a great deal of focus on external market conditions. Not all organizations can achieve world-class levels, but even to survive they will need continually to fend off competitors and maintain local markets.

*Fred Luthans & Richard M. Hodgetts*

## Management in Pacific Asia

Since 1960 world business has had to come to terms with the increasing weight and significance of the economies of Pacific Asia as the region has evolved into a major centre of gravity in its own right. This development contains two related aspects: first, the power of this new competitive force is such that it presents serious challenges in world markets to the European and North American enterprises which dominated those markets in earlier periods; second, Asian success is based on alternative forms of managing and organizing to those found in the Western textbook. The more recent emergence of China as a potentially major player and the additional potential lying in Vietnam indicate the dynamism and rapid rate of change which must affect any view of the region's economic and managerial development.

It should be noted at the outset that management in Pacific Asia encompasses considerable regional diversity and variety, from the highly developed Japanese economy through the newly industrialized and developing countries to the socialist survivors such as Vietnam and the rapidly evolving China.

From this multitude of contexts, however, there can be seen three common traits: paternalism, personalism and collectivism. All Pacific Asian cultures are more or less authoritarian in social structure, and paternalism, deriving from Confucian values, is an important determinant in shaping social and organizational hierarchies. Coupled with this, personalism refers to the reliance on specific individual relationships. Finally, Asian societies tend to be collectivist, promoting the interests of the group over the individual.

Three main successful forms of Asian business have emerged: the large Japanese corporation, the Korean *chaebol* and the Chinese family business. It remains to be seen how all three of these will change in the face of increasing pressures towards globalization and the adoption of Western management methods, particularly in China.

*S. Gordon Redding*

## Management in the Philippines

A first-time traveller to the Philippines could look at the surface characteristics of the business community and quickly arrive at the conclusion that it is thoroughly Westernized in its manner and attitude: the country's economic infrastructure is patterned along American lines, and English is the primary language of commerce. However, anyone wishing to do business in the Philippines will soon find it necessary to look more deeply into its history, culture and value system. In many respects, although the country seems to be highly Westernized, it is in fact uniquely Filipino in its way of doing business. An understanding of these Filipino characteristics will be important in arriving at an understanding of management as it is conducted in the Philippines.

*Rodolfo P. Ang & Ellen H. Palanca*

## Management research, management of

Looking upon management research as part and parcel of a business school's business calls for systemic monitoring of its contribution to the development of management science. Processing it among other organizational activities of prime managerial concern requires learning capacities whose enhancement is effected through continuous self-evaluation.

Gauging the value added to business performance by management education is not an easy task. However, in the modern age of knowledge, such assessment must be attempted and there is a need for a systematic approach by business schools in this area. in particular they need to move from periodic reviews to continuous learning, and towards a process of organizational self-examination. Criteria for such evaluation ought to include results (value added to knowledge), instrumentation (the range and reach of methodological development), throughput (the quality of the research process), institutional programming and commitment, and externalities including side benefits of experimental learning, contribution to the overall institutional development and cross-fertilization through networking and partnerships. From the above it is evident that there is a strong need for internal and external partnerships.

*Alain Bultez*

## Management in Russia

Managers of enterprises play a key role in the success of Russia's macroeconomic reforms. The decisions and actions they take in their organizations in response to incentives and obstacles have the potential to affect the health of the Russian economy, both domestically and internationally, as well as the material and psychological well-being of the Russian people. In short, because of their major impact on the economic progress of the nation, managers have an important function in the Russian economy and society as a whole.

At the same time, the role of the manager in Russia has undergone dramatic changes in recent years. Prior to the collapse of the USSR, managers in Russia were educated in a system dominated by the Communist Party, where the manager's roles were seen to be the implementation of the Party's policies, the fulfilment of production and other economic targets and ensuring the social and economic welfare of the workers. The end of central planning meant that managers suddenly had much greater autonomy, but the emerging private sector has also meant much tougher product and labour markets. At the same time the government privatization schemes which distributed shares to employees have tied the hands of many managers. It will take many years for a market-oriented economy to take root in Russia, and managers will continue to have to feel their way until an appropriate economic, political and social infrastructure has been created.

*Sheila M. Puffer*

## Management in Scandinavia

Viewed from the outside, Scandinavia could easily be considered an almost Utopian cluster of peaceful, harmonious and stable countries in an otherwise chaotic world. In any presentation of the Scandinavian welfare states and their mixed economies, emphasis is usually put on the cooperation between different institutions in what is sometimes labelled a 'negotiating economy'. The art of peaceful inter-organizational cooperation, characterized by close relationships between business, labour and government, has been widely appraised and is judged to be the very foundation of what has often been labelled the 'Scandinavian model'.

In general the Scandinavian model is defined as having stable labour relations based on two powerful bargaining groups – employers and employees – agreeing on how to distribute the results of industrial productivity; reforms in working life, introduced and supported through the bargaining system rather than by legal regulation; and strong governments, usually Social Democratic, in alliance with the trade unions, committed to an extensive welfare and social security system with full employment as a key objective. The emphasis of the model is on common participation – government, employers and employees – in order to reach ideological and value-determined social democratic goals that probably have more to do with improving world security, reducing wage differences (especially between men and women) and creating meaningful jobs for the unemployed than with promoting productivity and profit.

Scandinavian values with regard to people and worker empowerment also possess a distinctive style, and are perhaps best reflected in the Work Environment Act (WEA) which was passed in Norway in 1977 (similar laws were passed in Sweden and Denmark). This law is possibly the most ambitious of its kind in the world and defines health as including both mental and physical well-being. It is part of a long-standing attempt to create a more egalitarian society and a more human social order by improving the total work environment. There is a sharp contrast between this and the Occupational Safety and Health Act (OSHA) of its US counterpart, which is primarily oriented towards protecting workers from physical dangers and injuries, and relies on clear unequivocal rules (so anything not specifically prohibited can be done). The WEA instead tries to create a dialogue based on shared principles, a goal that requires autonomy, decentralization, participation, local control, cooperation and worker empowerment.

*Pat Joynt & Tor Grenness*

## Management science

Management science may be defined as the application of scientific method and analytical reasoning to the decision-making process that concerns executives in managing business and industrial systems for which they are responsible. These systems may belong to any industrial sector involved in the provision of products and services, so that management science may be applied to a wide variety of managerial activities concerned with the deployment of limited financial, physical and human resources to achieve certain goals. Thus, management science has been practised in a wide variety of industrial and business enterprises in the private sector and it has also found numerous applications in the public sector, at the level of both local and national government.

Management science has its origins in the formal techniques of operational research, which began its development in the UK in the late 1930s. There are very few differences in theory between the two disciplines. In practice, however, formal techniques play a very small part in management science investigations, which by their nature have to start with real problems that demand solutions and not with a toolkit. Even techniques such as linear and mathematical programming, which dominate management science literature, are not in common use in business and industry. Managers are increasingly relying on information analysis and strategy formulation based on scientific modelling to guide their actions; it is here that management science, assisted by the phenomenal growth of computing power, can make perhaps its most important contribution.

*Samuel Eilon*

## Management in Singapore

Management practices and styles of business organizations often reflect the culture of the society in which these organizations exist. In Singapore, there is a variety of management practices and styles which can be attributed to two major factors. The first factor is Singapore's multi-cultural immigrant origins: the business culture has been strongly influenced by the Confucian values of many of these immigrants. The second factor is Singapore's open, pragmatic and pro-business policies of attracting foreign investors and multinational companies. These two factors contribute to the array and richness of management practices and styles in Singapore.

As Singapore experiences change and modernization, existing management practices and styles are also transformed and modernized. Changes in management are inevitable in order that business organizations in Singapore, whether they are small and medium enterprises or multinational companies, may continue to be competitive in the increasingly competitive global business environment.

*Joo-Seng Tan*

## Management in South Africa

South Africa's re-entry into competitive global markets in the 1990s has created new managerial challenges. Although the legacy of apartheid is being eroded, little more than 10 per cent of South African managers are black. However, employment discrimination is being replaced by policies and practices aimed at recruiting and developing black managers. Management development, changes in corporate culture and black advancement have all become more prominent.

Following Western approaches to management there is an emphasis on general management at middle to senior levels. These skills are acquired through career path planning experiences such as job rotation, project assignments and cross-functional appointments; the completion of a general management education programme such as an MBA or of a shorter executive development programme either at one or more of South Africa's seven business schools or one run by management consulting firms; by ad hoc, informal work exposure; or by a combination of the above.

Decades of economic isolation have created tough but inward-looking managers in South Africa who are hands-on and results-orientated. Managers tend to be individualistic and directive in their styles, with a masculine orientation. Other than in the retail sector, fewer than 15 per cent of managerial jobs are held by women. Managers are appointed to such positions following five to ten years work experience in a particular functional discipline occupation such as engineering.

*Frank M. Horwitz*

## Management in South Korea

The spectacular economic success of Korea in the past few decades can be traced to a number of factors, one of which is the competitiveness of Korean companies. The Korean management system has three major sources of influence. The first is Confucianism, which was the state philosophy of Korea for more than 500 years, beginning with the Yi Dynasty in 1392 and ending in 1910 when Korea was annexed by Japan. The profound influence of Confucianism on the values, attitudes and behavioural patterns of Koreans has apparently spilled over into the Korean management system. The second and third sources, Japanese and US influences, are more recent. Korea was a Japanese colony from 1910 to 1945; after the Second World War, influences from the USA outweighed those from Japan until 1965, when Korean–Japanese relations were normalized. Since then, many Korean companies have developed close business ties with both nations. The USA is seen as a key market for exports, while Japan is relied upon as a source of intermediary products needed to manufacture those exports.

Based on these sources of influence and Korea's own historical traditions and experiences, Korean companies have developed their own management system, sometimes known as 'K-type management', that includes top-down decision making, paternalistic leadership, clan management, *inhwa* (harmony-oriented cultural values), flexible lifetime employment, personal loyalty, compensation based on seniority and merit rating, high mobility of workers and expansion through conglomeration. In spite of various inherent problems and a constant pressure for change, the Korean management system has maintained its own uniqueness.

*Min Chen*

## Management in Spain

In structural and strategic terms, Spanish management is relatively fragmented. It has had to evolve in an economic, social and political environment that has witnessed phases of discontinuous and uneven development. In recent years, accelerated levels of economic growth and economic internationalization have exacerbated the degree of fragmentation within capital and management structures. In addition, there are within the country competing management styles and practices. The unifying characteristic, if anything, is an attempt to bypass certain types of external, state and industrial relations regulation. This has been achieved to some extent through both the use of traditionalist, paternalist organizational and employment methods and the copying of modern (some would say 'postmodern') managerial styles and practices. This is an intriguing characteristic due to the way modern bureaucratic forms of regulation were developed under the Francoist dictatorship (1939-75) and during recent modernization projects of a partially 'social democratic' nature.

Another important factor is that management in Spain has had to work within a historic legacy whereby business elites have been unable to develop national projects and state relations that are popular in political terms. That is to say, the failure of the Spanish Right and its reliance until recently on militarist elites at moments of social and political crisis has undermined the attempt within organizations to develop long-term, modern and participative forms of management practice: hence, a more paternalistic model of management relations has tended to prevail. Given the degree of political stability in recent years and the process of internationalization, external points of reference have been sought regarding management practice. Such a transformation in management finds its origins in the Francoist regime's renovation programme of the late 1950s that opened Spain up to more international economic influence and moved the emphasis of policy making to a new range of business elites. Such contextual factors are central to any analysis of the nature and orientation of management in Spain.

*Miguel Martinez Lucio*

## Management in Switzerland

Switzerland is the most prosperous country in Europe and is one of the best managed. It has many large multinational companies and, in spite of its small population, has an impact on international business disproportionate to its size. In spite of a lack of natural resources it has grown rapidly economically by seeking export markets for both manufactured products and services, value-added via quality, and by investing in people. Yet its very economic virtues are now potential vices, as its structural problems grow by the year.

In the late 1990s Switzerland has still not decided whether to join the EU. Swiss-French cantons favour the idea, but the Germanic areas were less keen. Big business is, as elsewhere, much more enthusiastic about a larger market, although the existing trading arrangements give Swiss firms a great deal of tariff-free access to European consumers. The Swiss currency is free-floating; it is much in demand as a safe currency hedge, but the price is a high cost-structure for manufacturing and service industries such as tourism. Structural problems, akin to those in Germany, have eroded competitive advantage and productivity growth has been slow. Managers in Switzerland face many challenges in the coming decades.

*Malcolm Warner*

## Management in Taiwan

The business environment in Taiwan has certain common features with other East Asian business environments. Confucian values are strongly in evidence, and personal relationships are the means by which business is done. The business landscape in Taiwan varies widely, from world-leading multinationals to small family businesses, but all rely on a network of personal contacts to succeed in their family businesses. State-run enterprises have in the past been a key factor in the government-led revitalization of the Taiwanese economy, and large private firms maintain close relations with the government.

Taiwan's stunning economic development was marked by a low volatility of growth rates and peaceful labour relations. Taiwan's main challenge in the 1990s, as perceived by the government, is to regain international status and upgrade its domestic technology. There are plans to make Taiwan an international hub for finance, telecommunications and transport in an effort to rival Singapore and Hong Kong. This requires modernization of the economic infrastructure. The latter may be facilitated by the return of increasing numbers of students from the USA, who may have the skills needed to transform the Taiwanese economy still further.

*Johanna Böstel*

## Management in Thailand

Management in Thailand has many unique characteristics, derived from Thailand's own distinctive culture and history. Business systems in Thailand tend to be strongly hierarchical and oriented towards social networks. Thai business culture can be defined as characterized by nine types of value orientations: ego orientation, grateful relationship orientation, smooth interpersonal relation orientation, flexibility adjustment orientation, religio-psychical orientation, education competence orientation, interdependence orientation, fun–pleasure orientation and achievement-task orientation. These show how Thai cultural values and expectations affect the whole managerial process in terms of effective communication, motivation, leadership, decision making, problem solving and conflict handling. The strong impact of Thai cultural variables on the management process is important for foreign managers to understand if they are to enjoy a good working relationship with Thai workers, and hence greater organizational success and productivity.

*Suntaree Komin*

## Management in Turkey

Management in Turkey is a typical reflection of the particular geographical status of the country as a passageway between Eastern and Western cultures. Turkey's close economic interaction with the Middle East and the OECD (Organization for Economic Cooperation and Development) countries and the special relationship with the Asian Turkish countries since 1990 is a case in point that reflects the diverse economic and cultural ties of Turkey's managerial class.

Public sector companies were predominant in the Turkish economy until the 1970s, when a number of private sector companies made their presence felt. By the end of the decade the Turkish private sector was among the largest in the world. Management styles in these two areas differ greatly. The public sector companies were set up in the 1930s as the nucleus of the industrialization movement. As such they reflect the cultural influences of the countries from which their technologies were originally borrowed. They also possess the typical bureaucratic structure of a conservative and politics-dominated culture. In contrast, most of the private sector companies date back only as far as the 1950s. Management styles tend to reflect the prevailing culture, which ranges from Harvard Business School education to a fundamentalist orientation.

Financial management, the introduction of new products and the implementation of new technologies are the areas in which Turkish managers have been most successful. The weakest points seem to be teamwork, delegation and restructuring. The beginning of the 1990s has seen a rapidly changing political, economic and social environment which has forced private sector managers to create strategic management systems and to emphasize total quality and teamwork.

Faced with an unstable business environment and the pressure of competition on an international scale, managers in Turkey must adapt. The complex blend of different cultural influences which makes up the country, although the cause of various clashes and frictions, holds great potential – but only if the disparate elements can be combined into a workable form.

*Esin Ergin*

## Management in the United Kingdom

Changes in the economic and occupational orders of the modern-day UK have led to increasing proportions of workers in managerial and professional positions. Although it is difficult to define precisely the nature of the managerial role, definitions of managers taken from occupational censuses suggest that they comprise more than two million of the workforce. This is certainly the case if the two broad categories incorporating managers in central and local government and in large-scale commercial and industrial enterprises are included with those engaged in smaller establishments. There have been a wide range of studies in the UK covering different aspects of the managerial role and, as a consequence, there is an increasingly clear picture of the dominant characteristics of managerial attitudes and behaviour. Indeed, much is now known about patterns of share ownership among managers in the UK, industrial relations experience, job satisfaction and motivation, and views on the role of government and the enterprise culture. Moreover, specific aspects of managerial behaviour with respect to issues such as careers, training and education have increasingly been targeted as areas of particular focus.

The rise of managers as an occupational group in the UK during the nineteenth and twentieth centuries is usually attributed to the growth in size and complexity of industry, coupled with the expanding administrative activities of the State. These led to a separation of ownership from control and the emergence of management as a separate, specialist function. Today, as a result of the increased complexity of organizations and industry, British managers, like managers in other countries, are engaged in a wide variety of disparate functions. One consequence has been the increasing professionalization of the managerial role, along with the development of professional bodies such as the Institute of Management.

Management of the employee relationship is a major feature of management in the UK. Broadly speaking, it is possible to classify the overall approaches of UK managers into two types, pluralist and unitarist. Pluralism recognizes a coalition of diverse individual and group interests in the firm and is broadly associated with the recognition of trade unionism. Unitarism focuses on a unified authority structure within the firm and emphasizes common policies and objectives.

Another salient feature of management in the UK is a convergence of styles between private and public sectors. The future of UK management encompasses five key issues: the development of the corporate state and enterprise culture; continued professionalism and management development; trends in ownership and control; the evolving employment relationship; and the increasing internationalization of management. In general, it is clear that British managers have a special role in shaping the future of the country's organizations and society.

*Michael Poole & Richard Scase*

## Managerial behaviour

Studies of managerial behaviour have been made since the early 1950s. Two major aspects of this area of research should be noted. One is the confusion of terminology and the other its complexities. There has been confusion between managerial behaviour, managerial work and managerial jobs so that inappropriate generalizations about one of these have been made from a study of another one.

The methods and findings of the main researchers who have done most to develop our understanding of managerial behaviour and managerial jobs are summarized, starting with Carlson in Sweden in the early 1950s. From these we have learnt that the managers who were studied – and that wording is significant because of the dangers of generalizing to managers in other cultural settings – acted in a more reactive way than Fayol's analysis of managerial functions would imply. Their working pattern was fragmented. The social aspects of management were highlighted in a number of studies. The managers spent the majority of their time talking and listening. They were part of a social system and sought to secure the cooperation of others through networking, trading and negotiating. These are just some of the generalizations made.

Studies of differences in behaviour have taught us that there are wide variations both for the same manager from one week to another and, more importantly, between managers in similar jobs. There are also wide differences between managers' jobs even in the same country. These differences are greater when comparisons are made across countries. Much of the literature reflects an Anglo-American bias.

The complexities of studying managerial behaviour have gradually been revealed. First, we have not been able to define what is distinctively 'managerial' about managerial work. Second, how researchers seek to answer the question 'what do managers do?' depends upon their perspective. Managers can be thought of as working in the organizational interest and/or in their own interest. They may also be seen as developing an ideology of management and acting as the agents of capitalism. Third, recording managerial activities poses considerable methodological problems, which may not be recognized, including the fact that the categories used for work content reflect the researchers' perception of management tasks. Fourth, the potential area of study is very wide. Future studies should take account of these complexities, but what is most needed is imaginative thinking and attention to the nature of the context within which the managers are working.

The main practical implications of studies of managerial behaviour are to improve our ability to select and train managers appropriately, and to recognize the differences in job requirements. Most researchers have also drawn conclusions for improving managerial effectiveness.

The early research into managerial behaviour arose partly from simple curiosity: What are all those managers actually doing? There had been a long history of studies of workers' behaviour and of the nature of workers' jobs, but not of managerial behaviour or managerial jobs. There were, of course, also more specifically academic concerns in studying managerial behaviour, such as identifying common managerial activities or distinguishing the differences in managerial jobs. There were, too, practical interests such as offering guidance for management selection and training, and suggestions for improving managerial effectiveness. These practical concerns are still a reason for seeking a better understanding of managerial jobs and of managerial behaviour.

*Rosemary Stewart*

## Managerial theories of the firm

Managerial theories of the firm are economic theories of how the behaviour of modern management affects the working of the economic system. These theories have been the subject of considerable research in business and management literature. Managerial theories of the firm themselves fall into three broad categories: discretionary theories, in which it is assumed that managers, without a direct stake in the firm and free from strict supervision by the owners, will take decisions based mainly on price and cost; growth-oriented theories, which start from the same basis but assume the long-term goal of managers is the growth of the enterprise; and bureaucratic theories, which assume that the owners of the firm also control it and seek strategies which reduce risk. These managerial theories stand in opposition to neo-classical theories of the firm, which imply that management-managed firms are directed in the sole interests of their shareholders.

*R.L. Marris*

## Manufacturing strategy

It is usual for the manufacturing function of a manufacturing company to: control 90 per cent of the firm's installed capital; be responsible for 70 per cent of revenue expenditure; hold 80 per cent of the firm's net assets; and employ over 50 per cent of the firm's workforce. Manufacturing has a critical influence on product quality and cost, order lead time, delivery time and the speed of introduction of new products. To achieve competitive performance in these areas requires, among other things: sound capital investment; sensible make versus buy decisions; human resource policies that encourage employees to give their best; and manufacturing control systems that facilitate the flow of material and orders. These are examples of some of the elements of a manufacturing strategy. However, manufacturing strategies do not exist in isolation, and need to be placed in the context of the other strategies found in organizations.

The content of manufacturing strategy includes the establishment of manufacturing objectives and the recognition of manufacturing strategic decision areas. Formulating a manufacturing strategy requires first the identification of markets, competitors and current performance; second, an identification of opportunities and threats; third, an assessment of current strategy; and fourth, the generation of a new strategy to meet requirements. Strategies then need to be evaluated for comprehensiveness, consistency, the extent to which they have been articulated and communicated, and the contribution they make to competitive advantage. Future developments in this field will focus on the application of a resource-based perspective within manufacturing strategy and on improvements to the application or process of manufacturing strategy formulation.

*John F. Mills & Ken W. Platts*

## Manufacturing structure, types of

The structure of manufacturing continues to grow in importance as the end of the twentieth century approaches. Manufacturing itself, the 'forgotten function' of the firm, has been lavished with attention in recent years, primarily because of global competitive pressure among the industrialized – including the newly industrialized – countries of the world. Coupled with this global competitive trend has been the widespread rejection, or at least questioning, of popular notions of a service-dominated 'post-industrial' economy. The success of Japanese manufacturing firms in the 1980s has been a significant factor in the rebirth of manufacturing because, in the process of matching or surpassing so many previous industry leaders, many Japanese companies have demonstrated the strategic importance of manufacturing as a force in competitive excellence.

Although it remains to be seen if this widespread attention to the manufacturing function will have a lasting impact on individual firms struggling with global and domestic competition, the assumption driving much of this ferment is that manufacturing has regained its place of parity as a competitive weapon along with marketing, finance and research and development (R&D) in the globalizing firm. Even when changes lead to competitive gains, productivity and accounting measures tell only part of the story. Recent economic gains in the USA, for example in computer chips and other industries, have still not redressed the trade imbalances with Japan, and furthermore, these gains have been accompanied by the dislocation of millions of people in the workforce. The economic recovery from the recession of the late 1980s and early 1990s was uneven in terms of employment; construction and service employment recovered significantly, while manufacturing and mining were actually losing jobs in 1993.

Regional economic conditions and social or political differences notwithstanding, the refocusing on structure has emerged primarily from discussions of manufacturing strategy, those patterns of consistent actions observed in a firm that are used to gain competitive advantage. In most current treatments, manufacturing strategy is considered to be more than just a way of filling customer orders better and faster than competitors. Although this primary purpose remains, manufacturing has also become viewed as a significant, pro-active long-term plan, born from strong corporate cultures that value creativity.

Manufacturing structure in this context includes the elements of capacity, facilities, technology and vertical integration. Each of these has a long-term impact on manufacturing structure and therefore strategy, and each requires substantial capital investment to introduce or alter. Finally, there is an important infrastructure–structure convergence between quality and technology which also must be considered.

*John E. Ettlie*

## Manufacturing systems, design of

While the design process is well recognized in most manufacturing businesses, design is normally associated with the products that a company sells rather than the facilities used to make them. In fact many companies have factories which have evolved through incremental modification rather than any form of conscious holistic design. This may appear surprising but is understandable in those firms producing a wide range of products from a single, flexible manufacturing facility. The broad capability of such factories insulates them from changes in the design of a product or, at least, allows change to be limited to a small part of the total system. On the other hand, mass production systems have always been 'designed', usually in response to the introduction of a new product. Such systems are so tightly integrated that the complete facility must be designed as a single entity to ensure that its constituent elements work properly together. During the 1980s competitive pressures led to wider acceptance of the idea that all manufacturing systems, even traditional batch or jobbing factories, must be designed, rather than allowed to evolve haphazardly.

In its widest sense, the term 'manufacturing system' is taken to incorporate all the people, facilities and services needed to produce a product or range of products. The scope of this viewpoint is significant since it extends beyond the narrow boundaries of traditional production engineering responsibilities such as machine tool and process selection, plant layout and job design. In particular, responsibility for organizational issues and for the design of information and control systems represents an increase in the range of skills required of the practitioner. The comprehensive nature of the approach means that the scope and scale of the task can be daunting and a number of consequences flow from these circumstances. First, it is clear that all but the smallest redesign project will be beyond the capability of any individual, in relation to both the skills required and the volume of work involved. Thus a group of people drawn from related technical and operational functions in the business is normally set up as a project team with manufacturing systems engineers providing the core coordinating competencies. Second, since the scope of the project is likely to be so large, some kind of formal procedure is needed to guide and control the design process. Such a procedure is known as a design methodology.

*Doug Love*

## Marketing

There are many different definitions of marketing, reflecting the fact that marketing is a complex subject with diverse origins. Despite, or perhaps because of, these complexities, marketing is a subject of great importance; it represents the interface between the organization and the consumer. Marketing analysis is critical to developing an understanding of the market and where opportunities lie; the elements of the marketing mix, combined in a marketing strategy, allow companies to meet market needs and their own goals.

Marketing has many diverse roles, but one pivotal aspect relates to continuing the growth of economies while at the same time ensuring continuance in individual standards of living. Determining needs and wants, backed by purchasing power, must indicate how management should deploy its scarce resources to maximize customer satisfaction. In addition, by thinking ahead and predicting people's future needs and wants, management can act to ensure future satisfaction.

Marketing is an essentially simple proposition that supply is a function of demand and is therefore subservient to it. Demand is the controlling factor, and analysing and understanding demand must underlie all marketing functions. Successful marketing depends on coordinating four managerial aspects of demand, market research, product development and design, influencing demand through means such as product design or advertising, and service, including distribution and after-sales service. These elements must be combined into a marketing 'mix' suitable to the particular situation at hand. The mix represents a combination of the important forces emanating from the market which bear on the marketing operations of the enterprise and the procedures and policies of its marketing programmes.

A key aspect of marketing is the analysis and research phase, when marketers attempt to understand what it is that consumers want. The aim is to try and identify particular consumer segments whose needs can be met. However, marketing analysis runs up against intangibles such as consumer buying behaviour, which can be understood in general terms but cannot be predicted exactly.

Having defined a segment, the marketer must then develop a strategy to meet that segment's needs. At the heart of marketing is the principle of consumer sovereignty, which insists that all marketing is focused towards meeting consumer needs.

*Michael J. Baker & Elaine M. O'Brien*

## Marketing, cultural differences in

The great French philosopher-mathematician Pascal once said that there are truths on one side of the Pyrenees that are falsehoods on the other. This metaphor for the effects of national boundaries on culture and perception aptly sums up the challenges facing managers who must undertake marketing on a global basis.

The rapid integration and growing interdependence of markets in the world economy has created a truly global marketplace, necessitating changes in marketing, market research, product development and distribution strategies. Not surprisingly, many companies have failed to adapt to these changes, and the literature on this subject contains many examples of marketing *faux pas*. The most common difficulties faced by global marketers relate to advertising in different cultural environments, as advertisements which were successful in one area fail to have any impact in another or fall foul of local restrictions on advertising media and content.

Another common problem relates to the differences in consumer tastes around the world. Companies which attempt to market globally must realize that not every product is going to be acceptable in every culture; an extreme example might be the marketing of shaving cream in countries where men do not customarily shave. Packaging, labelling, distribution and sales all raise their share of marketing problems.

Despite these formidable challenges and the many failures which have occurred, however, cross-cultural marketing can be effective and successful. Recently a survey of Muscovites showed that McDonald's in Moscow had replaced Lenin's mausoleum as the most popular place to visit, by a ratio of three to one. By understanding local cultural preferences and finding ways to meet them, marketers can overcome cultural barriers and succeed on a global scale.

*Robert T. Moran*

## Marketing, foundations of

Marketing can be conceptualized as both a philosophy, which holds that an organization's human and physical resources should be deployed to serve customers, and as a technology which provides tools and techniques to improve business performance. The fundamental domain of marketing is the exchange relationship, the core of which is the transaction between buyer and seller. Also within the subject of exchange, marketing concerns itself with the institutions and mechanisms which facilitate exchange, the social norms and implications of marketing activity for society, and the legal, moral and ethical dimensions of the marketing process.

The philosophy of any subject is the set of principles that provide the rationale for the existence of the discipline. In marketing, this philosophy can be viewed from different but related perspectives. First, there is the seller's perspective. The prominence of marketing in business is largely the result of its contribution to managerial performance and its ability to explain what, where, when and how sellers carry out their part of the exchange. This positivist approach has been supplemented by the development of marketing management as a process, or normative approach, which examines what firms and their managers should be doing in order to be more effective.

A second perspective is that of buyer behaviour. Using this perspective, marketers seek to understand why, where, when and how buyers make purchases. Although this may seem to be part of the same process, it has been argued that consumer behaviour and the study of the consumption patterns of individuals, groups and organizations should be an independent subject, separate from marketing management. The emergence of consumer protection legislation and consumer advocacy groups confirms there is often a mismatch between the parties in the exchange process, which needs to be addressed.

A third perspective examines the processes of marketing exchange from an interaction perspective, which views the buyer and seller as interdependent rather than independent, appreciates the similarity of their tasks and assumes purchases are part of an ongoing relationship rather than single, discrete events. This perspective thus tries to reconcile the twin goals of individual consumer satisfaction with organizational needs for survival, growth and profitability. Although the concept of interaction has existed in industrial and organizational marketing for some time, it is receiving increased attention as a way of understanding marketing processes for all types of exchange.

*Bill Donaldson*

## Marketing, green issues in

Green marketing can be seen as one of a number of issues of social importance to businesses, such as social marketing, societal marketing and sustainable development. Adopting green marketing strategies involves modifications to many elements of a company's overall marketing strategy. Companies need to ensure that their products and/or services are produced and delivered in such a way as to meet environmental concerns; this involves both strategic and operational changes. Companies also need to perceive themselves as environmentally orientated and socially responsible, and begin to act accordingly. Environmental strategies cannot be adopted in isolation; they are by implication part of the fabric of corporate strategy, and must be addressed by and receive support from managers at the highest levels.

The future of green issues in marketing will depend on a number of key issues, including developments in the global environment and the responses of various interest groups. Increased environmental legislation will play a vital role in the activities of the marketing function. As environmental pressures on producers continue, green marketing can be expected to become a much more prominent element of marketing activities in the future.

*Andrea Prothero*

## Marketing communications

Marketing communications is sometimes described as 'promotion'. That much less self-explanatory description has the sole merit of emphasizing that it is one of the 'four Ps' of the marketing mix. In the view of many writers it is the most important element, since it is through communication that customers are given significant information about the product, its price and its availability, and encouraged to respond in a way that meets the communicator's objectives as well as their own.

There are many different forms of marketing communication. All work in much the same way, however, and all can be measured in various ways to determine their effectiveness. Which methods of communication are adopted will depend largely on the product or service being offered, the behaviour of customers, and the market or segment in which the current marketing programme is being carried out. The nature of the audience is particularly important, and this will vary according to time and place.

Managing marketing communications is problematic under any circumstances because of the difficulties of ensuring and measuring effectiveness in the absence of an appropriate model for understanding customer responses. Great care must be taken when selecting the agencies to which communications functions are delegated, and in delivering the right kind of guidance in the briefs given to the latter. There are many variables, not least of which are the cultural and market variables encountered by companies operating around the world. Marketing communications remains one of the most important, and one of the most problematic, areas with which marketers must deal.

*Keith Crosier*

## Marketing environment

All businesses operate within an environment which directly or indirectly affects how they function, just as all consumers live in a cultural and social environment which to a greater or lesser degree determines the ways in which they behave as individuals. The marketing environment is made up of a combination of both internal and external elements which affect the firm's operations.

A business organization's marketing environment may be defined as those actors and forces external to the firm's marketing management function but which may affect the latter's ability to successfully develop and maintain transactions with its customers. The factors affecting how well a company meets its customer needs are therefore a combination of the external forces which dictate the operating environment of the organization and the internal organizational pressures which determine the nature of responses to those forces.

Internal environmental forces tend to be of a more controllable nature than external forces. The external environment consists of a number of factors which may have varying degrees of influence at different stages in a product's life or a company's development. All relevant external forces should be analysed as part of an ongoing planning process, in order that the company may identify any changes within its operating environment which could result in either a threat to its present position or an opportunity to gain competitive advantage.

*Elaine O'Brien*

## Marketing ethics

Marketing ethics can be defined as both the study of the moral evaluation of marketing and the standards applied in the judgement of marketing decisions, behaviours and institutions as morally right and wrong. It refers to a discipline and to the subject matter of that discipline, the 'rules' governing the appropriateness of marketing conduct. It is a subset of business ethics, which in turn is a subset of ethics or moral philosophy. More simply, marketing ethics is about the moral problems facing marketing managers. It includes, for example, the ethical considerations associated with product safety, truth in advertising and fairness in pricing, and is an integral part of marketing decision making.

Much of the discussion of marketing ethics by academics and practitioners is centred on ethical dilemmas, issues that arise when an obligation to one group of people conflicts with an obligation to another, suggesting a difficult choice between alternative courses of action. For instance, a company's relationship with its customers may conflict with its relationship with channel intermediaries when it finds opportunities to supply customers directly; wholesalers that have developed the business initially could be denied margins on future transactions, but customers may be better served. Fundamentally, these ethical issues are about the incorporation of values such as honesty, trust, respect and fairness into marketing decision making. The end result should be more consistently 'good' marketing decisions, good in the sense of promoting the welfare of and having respect for those affected by the decisions.

The attention given to marketing ethics reflects marketing's unfortunate status as the functional area most frequently associated with unethical practices. Accordingly, marketing ethics is a subject area in its own right, with frameworks specific to the evaluation of marketing.

*N. Craig Smith*

## Marketing function, management of

The marketing function is one of the most important functions in any company, forming the interface between the company and its customers. There are many different ways of organizing and managing this function, and the company's ultimate choice of a marketing structure will depend both on its own traditions and goals and on the market it is in.

Most commonly, some or all marketing functions are handled by a marketing department. The structure of this department will again vary, depending on the nature of the company and its markets, but typical marketing responsibilities include gathering and analysing product information, developing new products, building customer relationships and developing and increasing corporate revenue through sales. Marketing is ultimately about enhancing the profitability of the company, and marketing departments should be structured in such a way as to carry out this task efficiently and effectively.

*J.R. Bureau*

## Marketing information systems

An information system is a combination of work practices, information, people and information technologies organized to accomplish organizational goals. As a sub-system of the much larger management information system (MIS), the marketing information system (MkIS) is growing in use, popularity and complexity as the combined technologies of computers and telecommunications continue to advance. While paper-based systems do exist, the majority are computer-based, although the sophistication varies by company, product and market. Some authors prefer not to differentiate between an information system and a decision support system. Rather, they prefer to consider all information systems as decision support systems of varying degrees, along a complexity continuum. The majority of writers and practitioners split the broad category of MkIS into the following three classifications according to organizational level and the amount of decision support offered:

1  *Transaction processing system.* A system that produces summary information from the raw data. Such a system is used by junior management to manage the day-to-day business of the firm.

2  *Marketing information system.* A system that provides middle management with reports based on summary information. Such a system allows 'what-if' analyses to be carried out as well as *ad hoc* interrogations and report production.

3  *Marketing decision support system.* A system that allows senior management to model market behaviour to investigate the effects of alternative courses of action, conduct 'what-if' analyses and to 'drill down' to lower levels of data.

All three of these closely related systems should be supported by one unified base of operating data. This eliminates the risk of multiple updates, reduces error and ensures that all personnel accessing the system are using the same data. Thus, updates made to the daily sales figure for a particular product in a particular outlet, for example, are summarized in real time and can be presented in a management report and further summarized, again in real time, for executive query analysis. Additionally, each level creates a link between often disparate information sources and the decision maker. Such a system is a classic example of an 'open system' where there are known and unknown inputs to the system as well as environmental disturbances. Consequently, there are both known and unknown outputs from the system.

An advanced MkIS can consist of eight sub-systems, each associated with a particular area of marketing: sales, forecasting, marketing research, pricing, distribution, promotion, new product development and product planning, but linked to each other as well as to critical non-marketing areas, for transfer of common data.

*Kenneth R. Deans*

## Marketing management, international

The term *international marketing* generally includes three separate but related marketing activities: foreign entry, local marketing and global coordination. In the foreign entry context, the marketer is usually seen as an exporter; marketing decisions include which countries to enter, and which modes of entry should be used. Questions of foreign market potential, identification of appropriate foreign representatives, tariff and non-tariff barriers and the use of trade facilitators are paramount.

Local marketing deals with the management of marketing in a foreign country. To some extent these marketing activities resemble those in any other country, and from this angle international marketing is often viewed as simply another application of standard marketing principles. However, the local marketer faces an environment which can be different in important respects from that at home. It thus becomes necessary to sensitize the local marketer to the basic assumptions on which marketing principles are founded, and to question these critically in the context of the foreign environment.

The global coordination aspect of international marketing deals with the problems a marketer faces when trying to generate cost savings and market synergies from the operations of a multinational corporation. Managerial problems include the identification of appropriate levels of standardization for various marketing activities, and the motivation of local subsidiaries in accepting globally standardized marketing programmes.

This three-part division has a correspondence in company growth. Smaller firms intent on international expansion will often begin by exporting, attempting to establish a market presence abroad with the help of independent agents and distributors. As involvement abroad grows, questions naturally arise as to whether the company should take greater control of the marketing effort in important countries and markets. Establishing a sales subsidiary and sending some expatriate managers abroad to manage it might facilitate greater control, but also creates a need to learn more about the foreign market. Finally, once the company has entered many markets and has some control over the marketing effort in each, the issue of better coordination of the global marketing effort becomes salient.

Historically speaking, global coordination is a fairly recent phenomenon. Multinational companies have traditionally treated each country as a free-standing profit centre. However, with the emergence of global communication facilities, the rapid diffusion and application of new technology and the success of global products and services in markets open to foreign competition, global coordination has become both possible and necessary. Strategic alliances and other collaborative efforts are making it possible for even smaller firms to consider global coordination of manufacturing and marketing.

*Johny K. Johansson*

## Marketing mix

The term 'marketing mix' is used to denote the mixture of controllable demand-impinging instruments – those making an impact on demand – used by a firm (or any other organization) such as advertising, dealer margins and customer service. These elements can be combined into a marketing programme, with the intent of stimulating a certain level and type of response from the target market. There is an endless list of possible instruments which can be used in this way; these instruments are usually categorized under four headings, *product, price, distribution* and *communication*.

The marketing mix is often equated with its most popular categorization, that of the four Ps, which is essentially the same categorization given above but with mnemonic headings: *product, price, place* and *promotion*. The four Ps classification allows for a quick intuitive understanding of the marketing mix concept as well as easy remembrance of its main categories. For more thorough analysis and planning, however, a more rigorous scheme is preferable.

The basic elements of each of these four categories can also be enhanced by additional promotional instruments, which have no power themselves but can be used to complement and sustain the basic marketing mix over relatively short periods of time. For example, temporary price reductions can be used to gain short-term advantage without cutting prices on an ongoing basis.

*Walter van Waterschoot*

## Marketing planning

Marketing planning is a logical sequence of activities leading to the setting of marketing objectives and the formulation of strategies and tactics for achieving them, together with associated financial requirements. Planning is necessary because of the complexity caused by the many external and internal factors that affect an organization's ability to achieve its objectives. The purpose of marketing planning is first to analyse this complex environment, and then to identify and create opportunities for sustainable competitive advantage.

There are two outputs from the process of marketing planning: the *strategic marketing plan*, covering a period of between three and five years, which outlines a unit's position in its market relative to competitors and defines market needs, company objectives and strategies and the resources required to achieve the desired results; and the *tactical marketing plan*, which covers a twelve-month period and details the schedule and costs of the specific actions necessary to achieve that year's objectives in the strategic marketing plan. The degree of formalization of the process depends on an organization's size and complexity, but the process itself is universally applicable regardless of circumstances.

The marketing planning process starts with financial objectives, proceeds to a marketing audit, and then goes on to define marketing objectives and strategies for the stated period. Managers throughout the organization are involved at this stage, to ensure that the plan can be resourced effectively. The final output of the process is the development of tactical marketing plans (corporate headquarters will often consolidate these into corporate plans). At the start of the organization's fiscal year the tactical marketing plan is implemented and then measured throughout the year, with the process repeating itself in the following year.

*Malcolm McDonald*

## Marketing research

Marketing is a process of exchange between two parties, with the producers of goods and/or services on the one side of the exchange, and consumers on the other. The physical and psychological distances between these parties have increased over time, and communications between them have become ever more complex. Factors which have contributed to this widening gulf include increasing technological complexity, the rise of the global organization, deepening consumer experience and discrimination and the increasingly fragmentary nature of markets.

The primary focus of marketing is on the consumer, but before producers can understand the preferences and aspirations of consumers, the system must fashion an 'open channel' to the latter so that their needs and wants can be understood clearly and without ambiguity. Marketing research is a collection of techniques that enables producers to ensure that the needs of current and potential consumers are identified, avoiding the corrupting effects of measurement and/or sampling error and bias, in such a way that the appropriate data can be fed into a company's information system. This data may then be used as a basis for organizational strategy and decision making. Marketing research has many uses, the most common of which include investigating customer requirements, providing inputs into new product development, assisting in the design of pricing policies and distribution strategies, and providing a basis for managing communications and promotions.

*John R. Webb*

## Marketing strategy

Any discussion of international business and management is bound to include numerous references to the concept of strategy and its application at both the corporate and functional levels. The boundaries between corporate and marketing strategy are often blurred and indistinct; also, there is no definite agreement on the nature of marketing strategy, or on whether or not the concept is distinguishable from that of strategic marketing.

Despite this lack of agreement, it can be argued that marketing strategy possesses many features in common with corporate strategy, and that in smaller organizations the two are largely synonymous. Only in the case of large organizations comprising two or more strategic business units (SBUs) does the distinction between corporate and marketing strategy have any practical relevance. Using the SBU as the unit of analysis, it can then be argued that commercial organizations have only a small number of basic strategic choices. These generic strategies include (1) aggressive growth objectives through high value positioning, (2) steady sales growth through selective targeting and premium positioning, (3) steady sales growth through selective targeting and average positioning, (4) steady sales growth through selective targeting with high quality products, and (5) defensive objectives through cost reduction and productivity improvement. Strategic marketing planning is a discrete process, for which there are a number of analytical frameworks including the growth vector matrix, the product life cycle concept and portfolio analysis.

*Michael Baker*

## Markets

What defines a 'market' for a good or a service? This question has been hotly debated by economists and lawyers for many years, particularly in the context of antitrust litigation. It is generally agreed that the market for a good includes the good itself and all close substitute products whose prices act as a constraint on the price of the good in question. The definition of the market is of fundamental importance in terms of the ability of firms in that market to exercise control over the prices they set. The scope of the market in terms of the number of products and the number of buyers and sellers in it, together with the ease of entry to and exit from the market, and the flow of information within it, all determine how much control individual players will have over prices, and how producers and consumers will divide the surplus generated by the transactions that occur.

Economists have identified different types of market structures, which differ in the extent of market power associated with each. The two extremes are perfect competition, where no market power exists, and pure monopoly, where complete market power exists. In between are a host of oligopolistic markets dominated by a number of large firms whose ability to set prices and extract rents will depend on each other's pricing decisions. Oligopolistic firms usually sell highly differentiated products, which allows them some limited control over prices, but the limited substitutability of their rivals' products prevents them having full control over prices. Economists divide oligopolies still further, based on whether firms in the industry are cooperating (cooperating oligopolies, better known as cartels) or competing (competing oligopolies). In most western countries, both monopolies and cartels are illegal, though there are some exceptions.

The types of market structure are too numerous to be analysed here. However, it is clear that each type of market structure is associated with a different degree of market power exercised by incumbent firms, ranging from the greatest power in the case of pure monopoly to the least in the case of perfect competition.

*Kimya M. Kamshad*

## Markets and public policy

The nature of private exchange has long been subject to governmental influence. Indeed, the competitive market itself can be understood as a public commodity which would probably be under-supplied if left totally to the private sector. Over the last century, however, government regulation designed to correct perceived imperfections in the operation of competitive markets has become increasingly common.

Guided by models derived from welfare and industrial economics, policy instruments to correct a variety of market failures – ranging from cartels, to environmental pollution, to insufficient public information on the quality of universities – have been instituted by governments in the USA and Europe. While these models are applied routinely by policy analysts engaged in regulating private industry, two distinctive contributions have suggested the utility of these models and the supporting research to the field of management. First, the work of Porter turned the framework of industrial economics 'outside-in', revealing how knowledge of industry structure, including government regulatory policies, can be critical to gaining and sustaining comparative advantage in competitive industries. Second, Wolf suggested that perceived failures in competitive markets must be balanced against the potential failures of government bureaucracy and inefficient governmental provision. Consequently, a new wave of policy instruments has evolved, designed to de-regulate industries, privatize government and create new markets. Both these new policy instruments and traditional regulatory policies will alter the structure of the markets in which businesses and industries compete. Therefore, knowledge of the relationship between markets and public policy is of substantial interest to those involved in management.

*David D. Dill*

## Market structure and conduct

A proposition which has received much attention from economists is that market structure influences business conduct and, hence, business performance. There are two important possibilities: first, that persistently high profits are the result of the market power associated with highly concentrated industries (those industries where a small number of firms account for the bulk of industry sales); and second, that concentrated market structures have a beneficial effect on the extent of technical progress. Given the importance currently attached to such issues, it is the latter which receives most attention, but relatedly, the implications of *labour* market structure, and in particular trade unions, are also important.

Despite a large volume of research exploring the links between market structure and conduct, unequivocal conclusions are difficult to discern. In part this is due to the fact that economically meaningful, theoretical constructs such as concentration and profitability can be defined in a variety of ways. Estimation is further hampered by data limitations, and in particular the relatively short time limitations (often a single year) available for analysis. Thus, discrimination between the market power and efficiency hypotheses of the persistence of excess profits becomes extremely hazardous, since technical progress and reverse linkages by their very nature involve much longer time periods than are typically covered by most datasets. Individual case studies and the development of long-run datasets therefore appear to offer the most scope for future empirical work in this area.

*Kenneth D. George & Paul L. Latreille*

## Markov processes and applications

Many real-world phenomena evolve randomly over time. Examples range from the motion of a small particle floating in a glass of water to the number of customers waiting for a teller at a bank and stock-market prices. When it is desirable to make predictions about the future behaviour of a random process (stochastic process) it is necessary to construct a model that can be analysed mathematically. A Markov process is a stochastic process with the property that if the present state is known, additional information about past states will not affect predictions about future states. In other words, the future is independent of the past if the present state is known.

The state space of a Markov process is the set of values it can potentially assume. For example, the state space for a queue-length process might be

{ 0,1,2,...}, while the state space for a model of stock-market prices might be the continuous interval $(0, \infty)$. In many cases, the state space is finite. Even when the state space is finite, it is often quite large. For example, the state space for a model of a factory might specify which machines are working and which are not. If there are $N$ machines in the factory there are $2^N$ states.

There are two important kinds of quantities that can emerge from the analysis of a stochastic process: 'transient' and 'limiting' (or 'steady-state'). 'Solving' a Markovian model means determining (or approximating) transient and/or steady-state values associated with the model. Transient quantities describe the process during a finite (possibly random) time frame, while steady-state quantities describe long-run averages. Depending on the application, the important quantities to predict may be transient or steady-state or both.

The analysis of Markov processes is typically much easier than the analysis of non-Markov processes due to the fact that the mathematical equations governing their behaviour do not include as many variables. It is therefore very common in practice to approximate a real-world stochastic process by a Markov process in order to gain insight from its model. The study of time series includes stochastic processes that are not Markov processes, for example, Gaussian or stationary processes.

*Burton Simon*

## Material requirements planning and manufacturing resource planning

Material requirements planning (MRP) is a management information system providing a basis for production decisions when what is manufactured has a composite structure and when lead times are important features. MRP is a manufacturing control system dealing with the production of assembled products, which are made up of sub-assemblies, components, raw materials, etc., usually known as items. Taking the production period into account, required raw materials and sub-components will be needed ahead of times at which the production of a particular item is completed. The MRP system calculates the amounts of produced and purchased items needed at different times and proposes a plan for when this production is to be carried out taking these lead times into account. MRP is particularly well suited for production systems in which lot sizes are large and the products are made up of parts and components on many different levels, and where product demand behaves irregularly. Production involving extraction, in which several products are derived from the same amount of raw materials – as in some process industries, for instance refineries – is not equally suitable for applying MRP.

The basic procedure of MRP is to start from a master production schedule for the planned external deliveries of each final product (in MRP called end item) from the system over a series of periods. This schedule generates a sequence of gross requirements, which are then compared to scheduled receipts and available inventories for each externally demanded item. An ordering sequence covering these net requirements generates the internal demand for the immediate need of sub-assemblies and other components making up such parent items.

The purpose of MRP is to determine the requirements and to schedule for the manufacturing and purchasing of items in order to accomplish the needs set out in the master production schedule. MRP uses the master production schedule to project the requirements and to compare these with actual inventory levels on a time-phased basis. Ideally, the MRP system will ensure that materials and components are available in required quantities at the requested time to make it possible to manufacture the end items as given by the master production schedule. The output of the MRP is in the form of action notices, which are inputs to the manufacturing execution function of shop floor control.

Apart from the master production schedule and the bills of materials, other inputs to an MRP system are data from inventory records, and the planning factors, which include production lead times and rules for lot-sizing and for the choice of safety stock levels. In capacity requirements planning systems additional inputs are needed, such as work centre capacities (capacity bills) and production routing data with operation lists and operation times. An MRP system cannot function unless it has accurate bill of materials and inventory files, as well as a realistic master production schedule.

*Robert W. Grubbström*

## Mathematics in finance

Traditionally, the main mathematical tools used in finance were the techniques of compound interest. However, since about the mid-1960s many other techniques have been introduced to help understand the functioning of capital markets. The valuation of options, in particular, requires special methods from stochastic calculus. Calculations of compound interest make it possible to work out how money grows, how loans are repaid and what is the value of cash flows which will be received in the future. They also make it possible to compare interest rates which may be quoted under quite different conventions. These techniques are also referred to as 'discounted cash flow' (DCF) methods.

In addition to compound interest calculations, other parts of mathematics are particularly useful in finance. Matrices make it possible to represent entire tables of data using algebraic notation, and also to describe algebraic operations on them. This has many applications in finance, particularly related to portfolios consisting of a large number of securities. Matrix algebra is also extremely convenient for describing the calculation of mean-variance efficient portfolios.

Calculus deals with calculating the rates of change of functions (differentiation), and also the areas under curves (integration). Stochastic calculus can be used to consider the behaviour of things which evolve randomly through time such as portfolios or the valuation of call options. Finally, the tools of statistics and econometrics are fundamentally important to understanding the behaviour of and returns on securities.

*Stewart Hodges*

## MBA concept

Since its inception in the USA earlier this century, the master of business administration (MBA) degree has become a widely accepted management qualification. Indeed it is the only management qualification with an international 'currency' or recognition. While there is little agreement on a definition of 'management', and indeed on what ought to be taught on management programmes, younger and even mid-career managers now enrol on MBA programmes in increasing numbers.

While current enrolment figures are not available, there are various indications that MBA enrolment on full-time programmes has declined since the late 1980s. That decline may in part have been due to the recession of the early 1990s; certainly when all modes of study are taken into account, total MBA enrolment is significantly higher than it was five years ago. More broadly, the growth of supply alongside increasing competition implies significant problems and changes within the MBA market during the 1990s and beyond. These pressures will lead the quality business schools to respond in particular ways.

MBA programmes can be classified along two key dimensions, control and internationalization. Two generations of MBA programmes can thus be identified, along with an emerging 'third generation' MBA. The third generation MBA takes account of the judgemental, intuitive and experiential nature of much management practice; it is also, or is becoming, genuinely international. Flexibility, incorporating different learning methods such as distance learning and computer-based learning, is also one of its hallmarks. Changes in content, learning process and delivery systems are required for the third generation MBA to succeed.

*Colin Carnall*

## Meetings and chairing

Meetings are an increasingly integral organizational mechanism. The potential for constructive outcomes may be great but the potential for missed opportunities or negative outcomes is also great. Meetings may vary in their purpose, frequency and formality. They are also costly because of the time involved, which is often that of senior employees, and consequently the skills of effective chairing are particularly important. Key skills involve adequate preparation, effective process control, the containment, and where possible, resolution of conflict and clarity of, and commitment to, outcomes.

Preparation is crucial before meetings: if the duration of the meeting is reduced by effective preparation, the time saved is gained by every person attending. Effective preparation will also improve the prospect of productive outcomes and thus the reputation of the chair. During the meeting it is critical that the chair runs the meeting in accordance with a previously established structure and maintains control over all those present, including themselves. Finally, recording and follow-up procedures should be established to ensure that issues raised are dealt with and to prevent subsequent disputes.

*W. David Rees*

## Mergers, acquisitions and joint ventures

Mergers, acquisitions and joint ventures are business combinations undertaken by companies to achieve certain strategic and financial objectives. Hostile takeovers in some countries play an important role in corporate governance and in resolving the conflicting claims of stakeholders. Business combinations may have anti-competitive implications and, therefore, are subject to antitrust scrutiny. The actual conduct of takeover bids is in some countries highly regulated. Increasingly, business combinations are international. Both large-sample and survey-based studies suggest that many business combinations fail. Managerial surveys provide insight into the causes of failure and a list of critical success factors.

A corporate merger pools the ownership interests of shareholders in two companies, with these shareholders now owning the combined entity. In an acquisition, one firm buys the equity stake or the assets of another firm. The equity bought may be a majority stake exceeding 50 per cent of voting share capital, or a minority stake. Another term often used to denote a majority control acquisition is 'takeover'. A hostile takeover is an acquisition resisted by the target company management. In specific contexts, 'merger', 'acquisition' and 'takeover' are defined precisely but in general they are used, as here, interchangeably.

An arrangement under which two firms cooperate to achieve certain commercial objectives may be called a strategic alliance. The various types of strategic alliance include: supply or purchase agreement; marketing or distribution agreement; licensing of know-how; franchising and joint venture.

Mergers, acquisitions and joint ventures raise important issues for the stakeholders in those firms such as shareholders, managers and employees. Moreover, they have wider implications for the economy, including the level of competition and employment.

*P.S. Sudarsanam*

## Migrant managers

Traditionally, a migrant manager was someone sent from the headquarters of a multinational corporation (MNC) to manage a subsidiary, branch office, plant or other operational unit in a foreign country. Generally, the migrant manager was assigned for a period of from a few months to several years, with the expectation that they would return to headquarters after the foreign stint. Migrant managers, until recently, were almost always nationals (citizens) of the country in which the MNC's headquarters were located and, thus, were known as parent country nationals or PCNs. Rather than assign PCNs who may lack international experience or hire host country nationals (HCNs) who may lack technical expertise, companies recruit managers from third countries (TCNs) with international and technical experience. These multilingual, modern-day itinerant managers represent a new professional cadre who sojourn from subsidiary to subsidiary, as likely to move across corporations as across national boundaries.

Migrant managers are typically male (estimates range from 90 per cent to 97 per cent) and married (75–85 per cent). While they cover a large age range, almost 50 per cent are in their thirties, and the trend is towards a lower average age as firms increasingly send managers abroad at earlier stages in their career. Most managers on assignments over six months have at least some of their family members accompany them. Although women have historically been excluded from foreign assignments due to a variety of prejudices, that picture is changing rapidly. Today, more women are accepting overseas assignments, and they are generally regarded as particularly effective in managing cross-cultural issues.

*Durhane Wong-Rieger & Fritz Rieger*

## Military management

Armies are as old as civilization, and military management can be regarded as one of the oldest managerial professions in the world. In modern times, armed forces are complex organizations requiring very high levels of control and coordination. Much training is provided to serving personnel, especially to officers, in how to manage organizational functions.

Business management theorists have long been interested in the parallels between their field and military management. Business concepts such as strategy, operations, logistics and leadership have been largely borrowed from military management, and books with titles such as *Marketing Warfare* are common. However, there are limits to the analogy. Although many military management and leadership techniques have civilian applications, some do not; business managers with a military background may actually be less flexible and adaptable in some instances than their purely civilian counterparts. The major distinction between a civilian manager and a military commander is that the latter's orders are enforceable by military law. This can make some former officers, used to having their orders obeyed, intolerant of delay or discussion.

*Will Fowler*

## Modelling and forecasting

Econometric models by design attempt to capture or represent simultaneously the data of interest and the ideas about how the modelled economy functions as reflected in that data. Economists have been building such models for several decades. Their primary task is one of identifying a set of parameters or constants that can be seen to characterize the economy being modelled. Such models are thought to represent a cause-and-effect relationship between two types of observable quantities. The effects are the so-called endogenous variables being explained and the causes are the so-called exogenous or autonomous variables whose values are determined by nature. Exogenous variables are determined by events beyond anyone's control or by artificial constructs that by design are completely within the control of governmental policy makers (tax rates, subsidies, etc.). It is the fixed parameters that determine the effects of any changes in the causes. The hope has always been that econometric model builders could succeed in developing a model that would simulate accurately the workings of the economy. Such a model, if the values of all its fixed parameters could be measured, would provide an excellent and reliable tool for forming predictions and forecasts of the future state of the economy or of the effects of changes in government policies.

Forecasting researchers have for the most part been disappointed with the performance of econometrics-based forecasting models. The reason for the unsatisfactory performance has always been considered a puzzle, and few critics have ever thought that the puzzle could not be solved. Nevertheless, as long as econometrics is the basis for building forecasting models, it is very unlikely that the puzzle will be solved.

The obstacle that stands in the way of solving this puzzle is to be found at the very foundation of econometric methodology. It is the fundamental view that sees the task of econometric theory as one of developing techniques to measure the values of *fixed* parameters. While physics may be based on the notion that nature provides fixed parameters such as the gravitational constant, it is questionable whether society can truly be seen to be governed by a set of nature-given fixed parameters. To think that fixed parameters can be the basis for an explanation of all of society ultimately leads to the view that all individuals' actions are pre-determined by the nature-given fixed parameters.

This obstacle leads forecasters to a forced choice. On the one hand, if one recognizes that parameters can be fixed (if at all) only for short periods of time then only short-term forecasts are warranted and only when based on recently collected data. On the other hand, if one builds only short-term forecasting models, then the forecasts will be plagued by the noise inherent in short-term data such as daily records of prices. The noise is the result of unexpected, unusual events that can temporarily distort prices and other data from their usual seasonal or trend-related values. Many forecasting researchers seem to be resigned to the dilemma of either rejecting the possibility of making model-based forecasts or accepting the necessary level of inaccuracy that is inherent in econometrics-based forecasting.

*Lawrence A. Boland*

## Modern portfolio theory

Modern portfolio theory (MPT) is a sophisticated investment decision approach that allows an investor to classify, estimate and control both the kind and amount of expected return and risk. Its roots lie in Markowitz's innovative research in the early 1950s which shows that, by investing in a number of securities (portfolio), an investor can maximize the expected return and minimize the risk. Essential to portfolio theory is its quantification of the relationship between risk and return. The basic assumptions of this theory are that security returns are multivariate normally distributed and that investors are risk averse, thus, they must be compensated for assuming risk and they should attempt to diversify their portfolio rather than hold the single asset with the highest expected return.

These assumptions imply two features of investment decisions under uncertainty. First, the distribution of future returns of a portfolio are only described by the mean and variance of these returns. Second, investors prefer higher expected returns to lower expected returns for a given level of portfolio variance and prefer lower variance to higher variance of portfolio returns for a given level of expected returns.

*M. Ameziane Lasfer*

## Mondragón

Mondragón is an exception to the commonly held belief that worker cooperatives can only survive in special niches, sheltered from the competition of large private enterprises. The Mondragón cooperative complex has survived and grown from its start in 1956 to become one of the main elements in the regional economy of the Pais Basque country of Spain. Its success is rooted in visionary leadership and social invention.

Many critics have argued that worker cooperatives can not succeed because they possess a number of built-in weaknesses that prevent them from becoming important factors in modern industrial competition. Despite this, Mondragón has been a definite success. The key to its continued success lies in its system of financing and control. Mondragón creates no stock; it is instead financed using credit from the initial contributions of members and the future earnings of the firm. The system also has great advantage in the conservation of employment and human resources. The Mondragón experience has been imitated, not only in the UK but in the USA and eastern Europe.

*William Foote Whyte*

## Monetarism

Monetarism is a school of thought in which its members share the view that fluctuations in economic activity are largely governed by fluctuations in the stock of money. While it is broad enough to accommodate disagreements within its ranks with regard to the extent of the influence money has on economic activity, or even the appropriate definition of money that best satisfies the main proposition, the common factor that binds all of the members of this school of thought is the belief that ultimately inflation is caused by excess growth in the money supply. This latter view derives from the 'quantity theory of money'. In its simplest form, it is asserted that a relationship exists between the level of national income (measured in current prices) and the stock of money. Consequently the rate of growth of national income (gross national and domestic product (GNP and GDP), etc.) will be strongly correlated with the rate of growth of the stock of money. If it is additionally asserted that in the long run the real value of national income (national income adjusted for the general price level) grows at a stable rate, then the rate of growth of money in excess of the rate of growth of real national income will result in inflation. In other words, an increase in the money supply will at first benefit economic activity by raising the level of income but over the long period, as real income reverts to its historic rate of growth, the result is inflation. This view is encapsulated in the phrase: 'inflation is caused by too much money chasing too few goods'.

Monetarism has gone through several incarnations. It has a long historical pedigree that strongly influenced pre-Keynesian economic thought. The influence of the monetarist school waned with the development of Keynesian economics. The label 'monetarism' came even later – a term that was invented in the 1960s. It was Milton Friedman who in the 1950s restated the quantity theory as a theory of the demand for money.

Monetarism became influential in the late 1960s and the 1970s, when inflation in the developed countries rose to double digit figures. The British monetarist experiment of the 1980s was the closest that any economy has come to following a monetarist macroeconomic policy. Whether the experiment was a success or not is a topic for future historians. However, a key policy recommendation of monetarism is that low monetary growth is a necessary condition for low inflation. Monetary targets have been developed in many developed economies with this aim in mind. The history of monetary targeting has been mixed, but where it has been successful, as in Germany, the result has been a stable monetary environment and low inflation.

*Kent Matthews*

## Motivation and satisfaction

Work motivation and work satisfaction continue to be major topics in organizational behaviour because it is assumed that they exert an important influence on action and behaviour in organizations. Often called 'soft factors' (as opposed to so-called 'hard factors' such as hardware, costs and benefits and the like), motivation and satisfaction constitute hidden realities in organizations which cannot be measured in a direct, objective way. Research concerning these soft factors does not provide much evidence for a relationship between motivation/satisfaction and behaviour. But despite these not-very-encouraging results, work motivation and satisfaction are regarded as very important human resources in organizations. They are seen as resources one should not only take seriously with regard to organizational culture and identity but also should take into account for managing effectiveness and quality.

Motivation theories can roughly be divided into process-orientated and content-orientated theories. Both types are shown to have considerable limitations, especially with respect to the prediction of action from motivation. Several modern theories of motivation, volition and action are therefore introduced. Some of them are distant ('distal'), others close ('proximal') to action, and some allow for a link between the content, process and action perspective of motivation. It appears that these integrative approaches to motivation and volition of goal-directed action may substantially contribute to a better prediction of work satisfaction, employee withdrawal or job performance.

Work satisfaction is the most prominent result of work motivation, and research continues to produce a large number of results relevant to organizational behaviour. However, while work satisfaction is one of the most frequently studied concepts in industrial and organizational psychology, it also suffers from critical shortcomings. This derives especially from its mostly theory-free concepts and from the very large proportion of satisfied workers and employees in almost all studies since the 1960s (to the extent that more and more researchers speak of an artificial character of these results). To overcome these problems, a model of different forms of work satisfaction can be developed, distingushing forms ('qualities') as opposed to quantities of work satisfaction and allowing the processes behind these forms to be explained. By differentiating between forms of satisfaction (for example, resigned, stabilized, progressive) it can explain the high percentages of satisfaction in earlier studies.

*André Büssing*

## Multinational corporations

Multinational corporations (MNCs), alternatively known as multinational enterprises, international corporations or transnational corporations, are corporations owning and controlling production or other value-adding facilities in several countries. More generally, the term is used to refer to global chains of affiliated companies managed and controlled from a headquarters located in a specific country. The global expansion of an MNC is secured with foreign direct investment (FDI), which is defined as investment made abroad to secure a controlling interest in an enterprise. MNCs are important actors in the world economy, controlling large proportions of global output, international trade and the global pool of technology. Since the mid-1980s their importance in the world economy has risen dramatically with cross-border economic integration being pursued in different regions, due to the opening up of new opportunities and an improved investment climate in many host countries or regions.

MNC operations' motivations can be broadly classified into four types, depending on the nature of the investment being undertaken: natural resource-seeking investments, market-seeking investments, efficiency-seeking investments and strategic asset-seeking investments. A firm which chooses to make investments and operate abroad must possess advantages that can more than offset the handicaps faced in an alien environment and cover the ensuing risks. The ownership of firm-specific intangible assets or knowledge capital which may be in the form of technology, expertise, brand name goodwill and marketing skills is therefore a prerequisite for internationalization. MNCs are generally characterized by high levels of expenditure on R&D, a large proportion of professional and technical employees in their workforce, new and technically more complex products and high levels of product differentiation or advertising. The importance of intangible assets for MNCs means that their market valuation greatly exceeds the value of their tangible assets such as plant and machinery.

*Nagesh Kumar*

## Multinational corporations, history of

Multinationals are firms which own and control income-generating assets, such as factories, in a foreign country. This form of business originated in the nineteenth century and grew rapidly in the context of an expanding world economy with few barriers to foreign companies. In this period, multinationals were most active in natural resources and related service activities, mainly in the developing world.

The First and Second World Wars and the Great Depression slowed the growth of multinationals, and encouraged firms to collaborate in cartels rather than invest abroad. In the three decades after the Second World War multinational growth was strongest in manufacturing, although services became the key growth sector subsequently. Multinational activity progressively came to consist of cross-investment between North America, western Europe and Japan.

The growth in multinational enterprises (MNEs) after the Second World War was fast. As in early periods, but on a larger scale, multinationals transferred the latest technologies and organizational skills between countries. Yet it was only in the 1990s that multinationals approached the same relative importance in the world economy that they had held before 1914. However, there were major differences between the historical and more recent periods. In the late twentieth century, multinationals engaged in the integration of the world economy at a deeper and more complex level than in the past.

*Geoffrey Jones*

## Multinational corporations, organization structure in

To engineer artfully an organization that configures globally dispersed resources to meet the mandates of multinational operations is the frontier of international management. While most international managers find it easier to decide what to do, the point of innovation has shifted to devising a structure of such clarity that the intricate organizational task of mediating worldwide integration versus local differentiation becomes straightforward. The shifting frontier of international business develops this assertion. The unfolding transition from the industrial to information era is transforming wealth creation in the multinational corporation (MNC) from a specialized division of sequential functions to a 'boundaryless' conception of synchronized business processes. The magnitude of this transition is radically redefining the principles of organization in the MNC. Simply put, the bureaucracy of a vertically configured MNC, the mode of the industrial era, is surrendering to the entrepreneurialism of the horizontally configured network in the information era.

*Daniel Sullivan*

# N

## Negotiation skills

Negotiation is a process of joint decision making between people with different preferences. It has been studied by game theorists using an abstract mathematical approach and by other social scientists using a more real-life-orientated approach. The findings of both research streams have contributed to current knowledge about negotiation skills. Each stage of the negotiation process – exploration, bidding and bargaining, and settling – calls for a distinct set of skills. The exploration stage calls for information-gathering and planning skills. Bidding and bargaining call for using either competitive tactics or collaborative tactics, depending on the negotiation game plan. Key skills in the settling stage include recognizing when it is time to move towards agreement and controlling the drafting of negotiation documents. Future work on the topic of negotiation skills is likely to include further investigation of how negotiation expertise is gained, how information processing influences negotiations, and how the effectiveness of various negotiation skills differs across cultures.

*Lisa Hope Pelled*

## Neo-classical economics

Neo-classical economics is the approach to the subject which developed mainly in Europe (and particularly the UK) in the late nineteenth century. It is still regarded as the mainstream of economic thinking and has revived in recent years with the decline in emphasis on Marxist and Keynesian concepts.

Economists who led the 'neo-classical revolution' did not reject classical economics, with its emphasis on the efficiency of markets in allocating resources. Their contribution was to refine the analysis of markets by applying the logic of differential calculus – marginal analysis. The result is a model in which individuals maximize their own satisfaction and firms maximize profits. Provided that there is sufficient competition in all markets, the consequence of this pursuit of individual gain is optimum welfare for the community as a whole.

The logic of neo-classical economics underlies not only much of current political thinking but also much of the conceptual framework applied in 'practical' management disciplines – for example, finance, marketing and business strategy. This is because this logic is mainly deductive – once the assumption of maximization (of profit, sales, output or any other outcome) is adopted, the implications are theoretically irrefutable. Criticisms of neo-classical economics relate mainly to the excessive simplicity of the initial assumptions and/or to the impractical complexity of the derived implications for business decisions.

*Francis Fishwick*

## Networks and applications

The study of networks is necessarily mathematical; but one very appealing aspect of this area is that practical needs have provided the major motivation for research concerning the properties and potential uses of networks. Applications have come from all areas of business, economics and the sciences, and range from finding the most cost-effective way to route shipments between suppliers and consumers to mathematical models for comparing DNA sequences.

Network models have proved to be effective devices for such a wide variety of problems because of the significant research done in algorithm design and computer implementation techniques. Another factor contributing to the usefulness of networks is the remarkable number of problem instances that possess the characteristics of a network. It is very natural to describe a problem as a network and it has a graphical nature that allows even the uninitiated to quickly grasp the nature of the underlying problem.

*James O. Frendewey, Jr*

## Networks and organizations

The topic of networks and organizations seeks to capture both the similarities and differences between firms as organizations on the one hand, and the formal and informal networks which facilitate market exchange on the other hand. The major differences between firms and networks can be found in employment contracts and commercial contracts. The employment contract demands that the employee submits a portion of his or her autonomy to the firm by adopting, within limits, the firm's goal, while the firm is not expected to reciprocate. In contrast, if the parties of a commercial contract lose a certain autonomy, it is not because they submit to a common goal. Any loss of autonomy by one party is reciprocated by all participants in the network.

Firms as organizations are not ultimately about power, which also characterizes networks in the form of monopoly power; firms are rather about fuzzy strategic thinking which necessitates the asymmetrical surrender of partial autonomy of part of the members. Strategic vision is behind the special nature of the employment contract, which in turn acts as the first theoretical distinction between firms and organizations.

*Elias L. Khalil*

## New product development

New product development is an activity vital to the competitive success of companies and the economic wealth of nations. The success of economies has been characterized by healthy product development activity since the beginning of the Industrial Revolution. Healthy product development demands a constant stream of new and modified products which meet customer demands. It is, however, a risky business; the more radical the new product under development, the greater the risk. It is essential, therefore, for companies to define their risk tolerance and be clear about the appropriate level of 'newness' in their product development that they wish to pursue. Once these broad strategic decisions have been taken, the actual process of developing new products can commence.

Many representations of 'how to' develop new products exist and, with minor differences, they all outline how a new product idea must go through various stages of physical development, and functional and market testing, before it can be launched. The tasks involved in each of the stages have to be allocated to certain individuals or groups. This is the process of organizing for new product development. Here again, many models exist, including 'new product committees', 'new venture teams' and 'new product managers'.

There is little doubt that new product development will become increasingly complex to manage, given the rapidity of technological change. In addition, the continual search for competitive advantages will ensure the fast application of emergent technologies in a large number of industries. Companies of the future will have to become adept at monitoring and exploiting technological developments by introducing new products which improve on their predecessors' satisfaction of customer demands.

*Susan Hart*

## New technology, investment in

Managers who are considering investment in new technology for their company are faced with two main problems: selecting the correct technology and ensuring that the investment will be profitable. Traditionally, engineers have concentrated on the first problem and accountants on the second. As a result, having spent considerable effort in selecting a technical specification, engineers have seen financial justification as a final hurdle that has to be overcome rather than an integral part of the selection process. Their attitude has been to try and justify a decision they have already made, rather than to evaluate alternatives.

As technology became more complex and expensive with the development of advanced manufacturing technology and information technology, managers found it increasingly difficult to justify investments because many of the benefits were thought to be intangible. This helped develop the belief that existing accountancy procedures were inadequate when dealing with the complexities of advanced manufacturing technology and information technology. Confirmation of this belief seemed to come from surveys which showed that companies were getting a poor or negative return from their investments. The result was the inability of managers to relate technology to the overall financial needs of their company and a perceived need to develop new accountancy systems.

By identifying and solving the problems that managers encounter when trying to select and justify investment in new technology, it can be seen that there is nothing wrong with existing accountancy principles: the problems have resulted from the incorrect application of these principles. The ability to quantify all the benefits that were thought to be intangible shows that the value of these benefits is much greater than the direct savings that managers had previously concentrated on. In fact, most new technology only makes financial sense when the investment is aimed at achieving these benefits, which were often ignored in the past. The change in objectives from direct savings to company-wide benefits means a change in the technology that is selected.

*Peter L. Primrose*

## Non-linear programming

Non-linear programming (NLP) is a field of study within mathematical programming that concerns unconstrained and constrained optimization problems. The concept of optimization is well known as a principle underlying the analysis of many complex decision problems. In the context of NLP, one approaches a decision problem, involving the choice of values for a number of interrelated variables, by focusing attention on a single objective designed to quantify the performance and the quality of the decision. This objective is optimized (maximized or minimized) subject to the constraints that may limit the selection of decision variable values. A variety of NLP methods and algorithms have been developed and many software packages containing different methodologies are available. Applications of NLP are found in business and management, engineering, biological, physical and social sciences.

*Malgorzata M. Wiecek*

## Non-tariff barriers

Historically, goods in international trade have been subjected to tariffs, that is, taxes on imports. Those paying tariffs to foreign governments would therefore raise prices to cover this additional cost. In turn, consumers would be less inclined to buy imported goods because of their higher prices, reducing their effective demand. In this way, tariffs have long served as barriers to international trade.

Over the decades since the Second World War, however, most states have systematically and jointly agreed to reduce tariffs to historically low levels, and international trade has skyrocketed in volume to reach unprecedented levels today. Simultaneously, however, a variety of non-tariff barriers (NTBs) has sprung up to impede international trade flows. There are six categories of NTBs: strategic goods restrictions; currency devaluations; national standards; voluntary export restraints; domestic subsidies and government procurement rules.

Even as types of trade barriers have proliferated, international commerce has become much more complex in form; cross-border commodity trade is now joined by burgeoning trade in services, and by huge volumes of foreign direct investment and other capital flows. Accordingly, firms have had to develop strategies by which to cope not only with NTBs to trade, but with various barriers to direct foreign investment as well.

*Neil R. Richardson*

## North American Free Trade Agreement (NAFTA)

The North American Free Trade Agreement (NAFTA) is a complex international agreement between Canada, the United States of America and Mexico agreed in the mid-1990s. It provides a set of rules and the institutional framework to govern both the trade and investment relationships of the three countries. It also provides a mechanism for the accession of new members and introduces new dispute settlement procedures (for both trade and investment disputes) not seen previously in international economic agreements.

The key trade-related provisions of NAFTA are the elimination of all tariffs between the member countries (over three timelines) and the introduction of new rules of origin to determine the tariff-free status of certain products such as vehicles and apparel. The key investment-related measure of NAFTA is the introduction of the principle of national treatment, which prohibits discrimination in the application of laws involving parties from the member states, except in certain sectors where the discriminatory laws are listed as derogations from the principle of national treatment.

*Alan M. Rugman*

## Not-for-profit management

The not-for-profit sector has reached an important stage in its development, and has correspondingly been receiving unprecedented attention. The sector includes a diversity of organizations, all of which have five features in common: goals which do not include profit, a formal constitution, separation from government, self-governance and a degree of voluntarism.

Alternative names for the not-for-profit sector include 'the third sector' and 'the voluntary sector'. This last is somewhat misleading in that not all who contribute to it are unpaid volunteers. Charities are the most significant subset within the sector, and are often subject to legal or tax proscription; they are also probably the oldest form of not-for-profit organization. The not-for-profit sector as whole, including charities, accounts for up to 5 per cent of gross domestic product in some countries, and so performs an appreciable role in the economic and social life of these countries.

The not-for-profit sector tends to be highly regulated and characterized by strong levels of government intervention, due to the vulnerability of both donor and recipient. This adds another layer of complexity to the task of the not-for-profit manager, who is often required to introduce efficiency and effectiveness in order to serve as a protection against fraud. The 'three As' of accountability, accounting and (internal) audit form the basis of corporate governance in not-for-profit organizations.

*Gerald Vinten*

## Not-for-profit marketing

The essential starting point for not-for-profit marketing is the cultivation of a corporate customer orientation and mind-set for the development of an effective marketing strategy. Second, not-for-profit organizations need to develop effective strategic plans. Many of these institutions face significant declines in traditional sources of revenue, dramatic changes in their customer mix and bold new competition; they need to reconsider both their goals and the broad strategies used to achieve them. Strategic marketing planning occupies a prominent and very important position in the presentation of the overall marketing concept.

If an organization's marketing programme is to make an impact both internally and externally, it must have sufficient financial and personnel resources to do so. Thus, the acquiring, developing and organizing of such resources is an essential forerunner to the marketing planning process.

All marketing activities must be realistically costed and form part of a planned and timed programme of events. Each individual element of the marketing mix must form part of a coordinated and complementary programme. Finally, evaluation and control is an essential part of a marketing programme as it provides ongoing feedback on the targeted audience's reactions and responses to the organization's marketing efforts.

*Philip Kotler & Alan R. Andreasen*

# O

## Occupational psychology

Occupational psychology is a British term used to describe the study of the behaviour of people at work. Different terms are used in other countries. A psychological perspective on work behaviour offers distinctive insights and perspectives and also offers an expanding range of career opportunities.

The domain of occupational psychology encompasses the following: selection and assessment, careers and career counselling, training and development, design of work and working environment, motivation and performance, individual–organizational linkages, well-being and the quality of working life, and change and transition. Occupational psychology has also been able to contribute to the dual goals of worker well-being and organizational effectiveness. Challenges currently faced by occupational psychologists include the tension between science and application, the pressure to develop and pursue fads and fashions and the need for a more international perspective.

*David Guest*

## Operations management

Operations management encompasses the fundamental action of an organization, the provision of goods and services. It is the field which has evolved from Taylor's scientific management movement to become the sphere of intellectual and practical activity focused on the realization of an organization's productivity and its competitive posture.

The origins of the field date to the nineteenth century, when the factory method replaced craft workshops as the Industrial Revolution gathered steam. Development of the field of operations management has been pushed along by movements and crusades, followed by reactions to previous enthusiasms. Technology has driven both the need for change and the changes themselves. Today operations management is the field within business which most explicitly grapples with the implications of rapidly developing technology for the day-to-day operation of the organization.

The most significant recent advance in the field has been – and continues to be – the adaptation and evolution of concepts and methodologies originally developed in manufacturing environments to suit service operations. Since the late 1950s, manufacturing employment has declined in the Western democracies as manufacturing output has skyrocketed. Employment in service businesses has grown steadily. Even in previously Marxist-Socialist centrally planned economies – where tertiary sector economic activity used to be somewhat suspect – there is substantial movement from manufacturing to service operations. Further exacerbating the movement from manufacturing to service operations is the fact that a decreasing fraction of the workforce within manufacturing firms is actually engaged in direct manufacturing activity.

While economists express concern about the historic lack of productivity management in the tertiary sector, operations managers are learning to adapt their knowledge, tools and techniques to improve productivity in this field. The growing international scope of business will also lead to increasing attention for one of the offspring of both marketing and operations management – logistics and physical distribution systems. The gulf between operations management and marketing is narrowing, as is the distance between operations management and human resources.

*Linda G. Sprague*


## Operations research

Operations research (OR) devotes its effort to understanding the behaviour of operating systems made up of nature, people and machines, where this last term includes not only the artefacts of modern technology but also laws, common practices, human behaviour and social structures and customs. Such systems are common in business, management and government settings. Operations research work includes both developing theories – called models by operations research workers – and applying their knowledge to improving the operations of these systems. Other fields of research allied to operations research include decision support systems, management information systems, operations management and industrial engineering.

Operations research and systems analysis play an important role in helping to ameliorate problems such as how to conduct international businesses so as to benefit not only their staffs and stockholders but also the nations and their citizens that are affected, how to meet the world's energy needs while maintaining the quality of the world's atmosphere, and how to manage sustainable worldwide economic development. Operations research in the 1990s has the capacity to reach out beyond strictly business problems into this kind of broader social arena.

*Hugh J. Miser*

## Optimal-design models

'Optimal design' means different things to different people. In the context of business and management the emphasis must be on the optimal design of the overall system, not just the optimization of a given system. Traditional linear programming cannot design a 'tight' system because the available resources are assumed given. In the modern production environment, which is characterized by high-productivity attributes such as minimal buffers, close-to-zero inventories, just-in-time operations, minimal waste and flexibility of layouts, linear programming is too restrictive and does not appear to be a sufficiently rich and flexible tool to match these requirements.

*De novo* programming, first proposed by Zeleny, concentrates on optimal design under multiple criteria. It is not as restrictive and, furthermore, it reduces the optimal-design problem to the solution of simple linear knapsack problems and thus has the added attractive feature of simplicity in computation.

However, because in *de novo* programming only the objectives or criteria are assumed given and the resources or constraints are assumed as unknowns, new approaches or the re-examination of old approaches are needed. Several new solution methods such as the use of optimal path ratios and fuzzy set theory have been proposed. Another area concerns new interpretations in the light of the new approaches proposed. A good example is the interpretation of the well-known 'shadow prices'. This interpretation is especially complicated due to the fact that degenerate solution is a norm rather than an exception in the *de novo* optimal-design problems.

*E. Stanley Lee*

## Optimality and optimization

The notion of optimality and the process of optimization are pivotal to the areas of economics, engineering, management and business, but also useful in many areas of social and biological sciences. Optimization is closely related to action (or behaviour, human or animal), decision making, choice, judgement and design. Doing, behaving, deciding, choosing, judging and designing in an optimal manner are of (survival) interest and value to both humans and animals.

Any single attribute or criterion is characterized by values that are maximal and values that are optimal while the two do not necessarily coincide. Maximizing the number of lumps of sugar in your coffee or maximizing your own body temperature should make this distinction clear.

The key is to recognize and operationalize the difference between single and multiple criteria in problems of measurement, choice and evaluation or assessment. When there is only a single dimension or attribute chosen to describe reality, then maximization or minimization with respect to constraints is sufficient. When there are multiple criteria (measures or yardsticks), as is true in most situations, then optimality and optimization (in the sense of balancing) need to be developed. Optimality is best understood in terms of the process or behaviour, less so in terms of the quality of a solution or outcome.

Real maximization and minimization (as well as optimization) processes are rarely unconstrained, unlimited or out of context, striving for absolute maxima or minima. Constraints and stipulations reflect the ever-present conditions of scarcity.

*Milan Zeleny*

## Option pricing theory

A European style call (put) option is a security giving the holder the right, but not the obligation, to buy (sell) a pre-specified quantity of the underlying asset, at a pre-specified price (the exercise or strike price), on a pre-specified date (the maturity or expiration date). American-style options confer the same privileges to the holder as the European option, but also provide the owner with the right to exercise the option on or after the exercise date. If an option is not exercised on or before the expiration date, then it expires worthless.

Although options (also called contingent claims or derivative instruments) have been traded for centuries, it was only in April 1973 that the first organized market for trading options opened to trade call options on sixteen common stocks. The initial success of the Chicago Board Options Exchange (CBOE) prompted a rapid increase in the number of stocks with listed options and also in exchanges offering them. During the 1980s this was followed by an expansion in markets to include options on fixed-income securities, currencies and a variety of stock and bond indices, as well as a number of commodities. Although these instruments remain relatively specialized, the theory behind their pricing extends across the whole area of financial economic theory, owing to the fact that option-like structures appear in virtually every part of this vast field. The theory has been used to value shares of a firm, business decisions, risky debt, deposit and pension fund insurance, and wage bargaining as well as currency fluctuations.

*Les Clewlow & Chris Strickland*

## Organization behaviour

Organization behaviour has to be seen as both a practical and an academic field. A discipline in itself, it is also a cross-disciplinary endeavour. Essentially the word 'organization' has two different meanings: one refers to a particular social collectivity and the other to organizational properties of collectivities. The field of organization behaviour is sub-divided into specialist topics according to various criteria. The main ones are: the level of aggregation and analysis; specific aspects of organizational life; goal-, product- or service-related specificities; criteria of performance in organizational domains; particular approaches to theory-building; synchronic or diachronic perspectives.

Sub-divisions cannot be broken up into separate compartments. A satisfactory treatment of one specific topic usually requires reference to other fields. This requirement can be described by reciprocal 'predication', whereby a specific organizational insight emerges on the basis of different insights from other sub-fields.

Despite the co-existence of different theoretical and research traditions, a coherent body of organization behaviour theory can be summarized. Dominant explanatory factors are utilitarian, culturalist and institutionalist approaches. There are also different types of theory distinguished by their epistemological foundations: nomothetic, idiographic and dialectic approaches. Such approaches compete with one another, but they can also be intertwined. Academic advance and innovation in organization behaviour proceeds through the mutual competition and cross-fertilization of distinct approaches. It can be argued that more satisfactory accounts and explanations result when students are competent in different approaches and in combining these to create new fields.

This is also the basis for an effective cross-fertilization between theory, research and practice. A pragmatic, undogmatic handling of theoretical approaches leads to more useful practical recipes, and organization behaviour theory and research thrive where practical organizational experience is systematically integrated into a more properly academic treatment.

*Arndt Sorge*

## Organization behaviour, history of

Organization behaviour as a subject emerged as the analysis of the structure and functions of organizations and of the behaviour of groups and individuals within them. Appearing first in the middle of the twentieth century, it was an interdisciplinary field which drew primarily on sociology and psychology but which also incorporated aspects of economics, industrial and labour relations, political science, production engineering and social anthropology. Organization behaviour was, from its beginnings, open to new knowledge inputs, both theoretical and empirical, especially from the empirically based social sciences. It set out to integrate the respective elements (individual, group and organization behaviour) into a unified field of study, the potential importance of which is based on the fact that organizations face a number of common challenges: to recruit people to work in them; to motivate these employees to pursue common goals; to divide up and allocate tasks; to coordinate the activities of participants; and to acquire and use resources effectively.

Organizations of many different kinds across historical time generated rules to resolve such issues. Organization behaviour represented an attempt to understand why and how organizations developed their regulating features (such as their structure) and to identify the influential factors in this process. Various schools of thought which have emerged include the scientific management of Taylor, management theory as defined by Barnard and Fayol, structural theory as drawn from the work of Weber, group theory based on the work of Mayo, individual theory derived from occupational psychology, technology theory and economic theory. More recently the study of organizations has moved towards cross-cultural analysis, critical theory as well as post-modernism, among others.

*Malcolm Warner*

## Organization contexts and environments

An organization does not operate in isolation. On the contrary, an organization continuously interacts with its environment. In a way, the search for a fit between the features of the internal organization on the one hand and the characteristics of the external environment on the other is the key issue that is implicit (or explicit, as in contingency theory) in much organization science. The bottom line is that an organization has to understand (the dynamics of) its environment in order to be able to adapt to the changing demands of the outside (and inside) world. There are many different ways of scanning the organizational environment. A useful distinction can be made between three differently orientated, although overlapping, taxonomies of the environment: definition-driven classification, issue-driven classification and theory-driven classification. These may structure the way that an environment is scanned.

*Arjen van Witteloostuijn*

## Organization culture

The concept of 'organization culture' has become popular since the early 1980s. There is no consensus about its definition but most authors will agree that it is something holistic, historically determined, related to the things anthropologists study, socially constructed, soft and difficult to change. It is something an organization has, but can also be seen as something an organization is.

Organization cultures should be distinguished from national cultures. Cultures manifest themselves, from superficial to deep, in symbols, heroes, rituals and values. National cultures differ mostly on the values level;

organization cultures at the levels of symbols, heroes and rituals, together labelled 'practices'.

Differences in national cultures have been studied for over fifty countries. They show five independent dimensions of values: power distance; individualism versus collectivism; masculinity versus femininity; uncertainty avoidance; and long-term versus short-term orientation. National culture differences are reflected in solutions to organization problems in different countries, but also in the validity of management theories in these countries. Different national cultures have different preferred ways of structuring organizations and different patterns of employee motivation. For example, they limit the options for performance appraisal, management by objectives, strategic management and humanization of work.

Research into organization cultures identified six independent dimensions of practices: process-orientated versus results-orientated; job-orientated versus employee-orientated; professional versus parochial; open systems versus closed systems; tightly versus loosely controlled; and pragmatic versus normative. The position of an organization on these dimensions is determined in part by the business or industry the organization is in. Scores on the dimensions are also related to a number of other 'hard' characteristics of the organizations. These lead to conclusions about how organization cultures can be and cannot be managed.

Managing international business means handling both national and organization culture differences at the same time. Organization cultures are somewhat manageable while national cultures are given facts for management; common organization cultures across borders are what keeps multinationals together.

*Geert Hofstede*

## Organization development

Organization development (OD) is understood to mean planned change based on the paradigm of action research. OD can thus be described as a learning process. The active development of an organization towards its desired corporate identity succeeds only if this change process is undertaken holistically. From a behavioural perspective this means, for example, that the behavioural conditions that lie within the person (qualifications, motivation) as well as those lying outside the person (organizational structure, technology) must be modified. The process of change is also described as a political process. That is, in which phases of change and for which reasons is the mobilization of power salient? Lastly, the change process is often examined in terms of whether, and how, basic assumptions within an organization can be decoded through analysis of symbols.

Types of intervention include the person-centred approach, the structural approach and the relationship approach. The person-centred approach requires the development of both a social competence that fosters cooperation and a general intellectual competence that promotes innovation. The structural approach requires moves to reintegrate hitherto segregated work sequences and attempts to decentralize decision making. The relationship approach requires team development, role negotiations and survey-feedback methods.

Overall, evaluations of OD bear out the potential fruitfulness of its key approaches. But follow-up studies have thus far shown the outcomes to be widely variable, meaning that the degree of success or failure cannot be precisely forecast in each case. Accordingly, conditions on which OD measures depend for their success are discussed in the latter part of the text.

A new approach to organizational transformation (OT) is beginning to gain acceptance in the literature. OT is a 'harder' concept, often associated with re-engineering, and there is some concern that this could be used, not as a contingency measure, but as a replacement for organization development. Clearly there are dangers in a widespread adoption of such an approach.

*Diether Gebert*

## Organization networks

The field of organization networks is a rich one in terms of research studies. However, there are clear differences in how the network approach has been applied. It has been used primarily for descriptions of how different units relate to each other inside an organization or between relatively independent organizations. In a few studies it has been used for giving normative recommendations. A common denominator is that a network structure is characterized by a set of actors connected by a set of relationships. Each actor is related to a certain number of the other actors. Generally, multiple types of ties between the actors are assumed to exist. Furthermore, relationships are expected to be more or less connected; that is, the outcome of one is dependent on the outcomes in some of the others.

Network analysis has been used both for explaining how large companies can be divided into smaller units working in relation to each other and how sets of independent companies can work together creating larger 'wholes'. In this way network analyses have given results which have implications for several major managerial areas. The most important ones are concerned with the position or strategy of an organization towards surrounding units. Results indicate that the position in terms of developed relationships with important counterparts has important consequences for how the company will function both in terms of cost efficiency and innovative ability. Another area deals with entrepreneurial activities. The existence and mobilization of some key relationships seem to be necessary for a new company to develop. A third area is technological development. Relationships between organizations can function both in a positive and a negative way in relation to technological changes. They can be innovative and organizations can therefore use them to develop their own resources or, on the other hand, they can restrict development potential, relationships having a lock-in effect. Finally, the two most important counterparts to every organization are their suppliers and customers. In this way, organization networks have important consequences for companies' purchasing and marketing activities.

*Håkan Håkansson*

## Organization paradigms
On both sides of the Atlantic, the notion of 'paradigms' in organizational analysis has received much attention since the early 1980s. While by no means invented by the US philosopher of science, Kuhn, the term has become associated with his work on the development of the physical sciences and how old ideas and frameworks for carrying out science become overthrown by the new. The term revolves around the idea of 'classic laws' and 'modes of community life'. This is to say that the paradigm marks out, in an agreed and deep-seated sense, a way of seeing the world and how it should be studied and that this view is shared by a group of scientists who live in a community marked by a common conceptual language and a very defensive political posture to outsiders.

Social scientists alighted on the Kuhnian approach with great enthusiasm in the late 1960s and early 1970s and began to see their own disciplines in this 'paradigmatic' way. The articulation of paradigms which were alternative to the ruling one of structural functionalism began in sociology and then spread to organization theory in the decade of the 1970s. For those opposed to the dominant orthodoxy, the concept of alternative paradigms was very liberating for it established their revolutionary credentials and legitimated them as progressives to whom the future belonged. As a meta-narrative – a story which explained their place in intellectual development – Kuhnianism was a very powerful tool for the younger generation of organization scholars.

Links between organization studies and social theory were laid out, although not using Kuhnianism in anything like a faithful way. The four 'paradigms of social theory' were identified as being constructed from meta-theoretical assumptions about the nature of society and the nature of science. Since organizational analysis was a social science, it was argued, it *must* make these sorts of assumptions irrespective of whether individual authors were aware of them.

Paradigm analysis became the battlefield upon which struggles of an intellectual and power-seeking kind could be worked out, often between young and old. Those who engaged in it were seen as challenging the right of functionalism and functionalists of whatever age to dominate the field. Those who denigrated the very concept of paradigm itself often did so in order to undermine the right of others to have an alternative voice. The debate became acrimonious and hostilities often broke out.

The situation in the mid-1990s is characterized by a decline in interest in the concept of paradigms. The debate moved on to issues of post-modernism in Europe where theoretical and methodological alternatives might still be attempted and to the excesses of population ecology in the USA where the scientization of organization theory reached a new high-water mark. Conservatism once again stalks the land and the next generation of organization scholars are still looking for ways of revolutionizing the discipline and escaping from the dead hand of aged scholars.

*Gibson Burrell*

## Organization structure

Organization structure has been one of the central issues in organization theory in the twentieth century. Three main theories of organization structure have emerged: the archetypical bureaucracy; the stakeholder model; and newer ways of thinking, especially reflexive theories.

Archetypical bureaucracy theory stems ultimately from the theories of Weber. Its features are rationality, task specialization, hierarchy and regularity and there is a strong emphasis on structure as a controlling force. In the stakeholder model, on the other hand, rationality is abandoned and structure becomes the framework in which the various stakeholders – leaders, internal parties, external parties – seek to achieve their own goals.

However, new research on organization structure has focused on variables such as culture, metaphors, learning forms, dynamic organizational variants and fields such as total quality management and the related paradigm shift. Both organization theory and organizational practice would benefit from a critical reflection on the significance and use of the concept of structure. The sociology of knowledge, concerning itself with questioning the way knowledge is produced and used, provides an excellent starting point for such a reflection.

*Cas Vroom*

## Organization types

An organization type defines the general characteristics of a class of organization. A major purpose in defining an organization type is to be able to distinguish one class of organization from another. A typology provides a system of types whereby classes of organization can be distinguished according to their relative position on a number of predetermined variables.

Other terms which are used almost synonymously with 'typology' are categorization, classification, configuration and taxonomy. The term cluster, especially since the widespread use of the statistical technique of cluster analysis, may also be used to refer to empirically derived typologies.

Typologies have been extensively developed in the life sciences as a means of categorizing plants or animals. The social sciences, such as organization theory, have also been active in developing typologies. A major argument for the use of a typology in organizational management and organizational literature is to move away from reductionist theory, with its emphasis upon bi-variate relationships and fragmentation, towards a more holistic perspective. The case for using a typology rests upon the notion that organizations have discrete interdependent structural and environmental elements which tend to coalesce into recognizable patterns making it difficult for just one of these elements to change on its own. An effective typology therefore should have the capacity to provide an economical explanatory theory of why particular features are found.

Two main problems often become apparent with typologies which suggest that a heavy reliance upon typologies in a subject indicates a pre-theoretical stage of development. First, is obtaining agreement among scholars concerning the basis for categorization. This has led to a proliferation of typologies each with its own set of advocates. Second, is the problem of choosing the category within the typology to which a particular member of a population of organizations belongs. For instance, a well-established simple typology makes the distinction between bureaucratic/mechanistic and flexible/organic organizations. To categorize an organization as bureaucratic is to imply that it cannot have some characteristics of the organic category; in practice, however, organizations will exhibit some aspects of both categories.

*Richard Butler*

## Organizational convergence

The subject of organizational convergence is concerned with how far organizations in different countries have travelled along a path to global convergence in operations and management, and conversely how far the influence of specific cultural factors must be understood and planned for if the manager is to be effective in cross-cultural situations.

In international enterprise managers need to know whether the workings of organizations in one country are completely different from those in another. How can knowledge of their home country style of organization and its functioning help them deal with organizations in other places in the world? Are the structures and functioning of organizations in different cultures coming sufficiently close together to permit the development of universally applicable approaches with the expectation of obtaining consistent outcomes? Clearly there are international differences, but the key issue is: how important are they?

For example, are the differences in organizational functioning between the UK and France and Germany, or between the developing and the developed world, fundamentally different and likely to remain so? Or are organizations all over the world converging so that differences in management are becoming less and less important? If differences are becoming less important then managers can rely on a substantial basis of globally established knowledge and skills which they can transfer from one culture to another. The major differences between national groups of managers have been shown to be in their work values, but it is important to remember that values are only one influence on the behaviour of managers. Other factors, such as market pressures and the technological demands of the operating processes, will also affect behaviour. What managers actually do in different countries appears to be much closer to each other than to the values they espouse.

*Derek Pugh & David Hickson*

## Organizational decline and failure

Concern for organizational decline arises from the realization that growth is no longer a permanent feature of the organizational landscape. Organizational decline can be understood as deteriorating demand, deteriorating resources or deteriorating performance. Typically, economists look at deteriorating demand and to some extent performance, sociologists at deteriorating resources. There are several identifiable causes of organizational decline, including age and stage of the organizational life cycle, technological obsolescence, faulty information processing and the tendency of decline, under some circumstances, to be self-perpetuating. Many of the effects of organizational decline are captured in the threat-rigidity hypothesis: to the extent that decline is experienced as threatening, and that constriction of control and of information processing are likely to result. What evidence exists is largely consistent with the threat-rigidity hypothesis: centralization of control, conflict and scapegoating are frequent responses to decline. There are other effects of decline as well. Typically, ratios of administrative to production workers increase under conditions of decline; the administrative overhead is resistant to contraction. And industry-wide decline causes small firms to exit before large ones, consistent with sociological theories of structural inertia and inconsistent with economic arguments suggesting that small firms stay profitable longer under conditions of decline. Managing organizational decline poses profound problems. Decline triggers role conflicts for managers, exacerbates the normal problems of motivating employees and raises questions of fairness and justice that normally have little salience. There are no easy ways to manage decline, but it appears that openness and realism are preferable to the secrecy that usually surrounds decision making in declining organizations.

*Marshall W. Meyer*

## Organizational evolution

Evolutionary thinking was applied to explain developments in societies long before Darwin. However, his success in the natural sciences inspired the application of evolutionary concepts to the social sciences. Basic to all evolutionary thinking is the notion that human practices and norms are the result of human actions, but not of human design.

In organization and management theory constructivistic concepts, which postulate organizations as being subject to rational control, prevailed. However, a number of evolutionary approaches can be identified, which have no more in common than the assumption that the rational design and control of organizations is severely constrained and that managers can only present solutions to a selection process. They vary considerably in the ways in which they model the processes of variation, selection and retention. For example, the population ecology approach, which can be considered the most influential of all theories of organizational evolution, conceptualizes the evolution of organizations in close analogy to biological evolution. By taking collective interpretation schemes as the basic unit of organizational evolution, it can be postulated that the evolution of organizations is characterized by processes which are different from bioecology. Other concepts link the evolution of institutions, including organizations, to the evolution of societies.

Concepts of evolutionary management have been developed in reaction to the growing awareness that organizations are unmanageable, or at least unmanageable in the sense of traditional management theory. They propose that managers assume a new role: that of an 'enabler' or 'facilitator', as opposed to a that of a 'doer'.

*Alfred Kieser*

## Organizational information and knowledge

Throughout the world, economies have been putting more and more emphasis on service industries and especially on information work. The term 'information worker' is used to denote employees who primarily create, work with or disseminate information, including clerical workers who mainly process data or preserve it without attempting to understand it; clerical workers who interpret information and act on it; researchers and others who generate new information; and experts such as lawyers, accountants and consultants who generate new information. Information workers can be distinguished by their formal education and cognitive skills

Information work concentrates in offices, where automation systems facilitate the processing, distribution and coordination of information. Office automation includes systems as diverse as document-management technologies, groupware, personal information managers, project management software, investment work stations, computer-aided design and virtual reality. Organizations that depend most strongly on knowledge and information work are known as knowledge-intensive firms (KIFs). These firms attempt to convert knowledge into capital, though they generally have precarious bases for success.

*Kenneth Laudon & William H. Starbuck*

## Organizational learning

Organizational learning is a relatively recent metaphor for the organization which stands alongside other metaphors, both old and new, such as organization culture, the open system, the machine or the organism. Metaphorical language is one of the most important devices by which knowledge is generated, and it is based essentially on an analogic process which sets A (the already-known term) in relation to B (the term that one wishes to know). In this way cognitive transpositions come into operation which make it possible to imagine and to talk about the object in question (for example the organization) as if it were another already-known object. A metaphor works by matching what is distant with what is close, similar features with dissimilar ones, and it is a cognitive tool which develops creativity and social imagination and reveals the importance of language and symbols in the construction of reality and in the formulation of theory. Organizational learning is a metaphor which matches two concepts – learning and organization – and enables exploration of the organization as if it were a subject which learns, which processes information, which reflects on experiences, which is endowed with a stock of knowledge, skills and expertise. It is a metaphor which problematizes the relationship between organization and knowledge, between organization and the social and cognitive processing of knowledge, between organizational action and organizational thought.

Knowledge is today a vital problem for all organizations because the production of goods and services increasingly involves knowledge; because new information technologies are 'knowledge intensive', and such knowledge has an extremely short life span and is highly innovative; because flexibility is today the most valued of competences. In the post-industrial age, knowledge is a resource just as important as raw materials, economic and human resources, and so on, and may give an organization competitive advantage. The metaphor of organizational learning enables one to view organizations as if they were systems that learn; this perspective may contribute to the design of organizations that do, in fact, learn. The learning organization may stand as a valid theoretical alternative to the rational organization because it replaces the classical concept of the organization which acts according to the principles of rational choice with that of the organization which acts according to principles of experimentation, of trial and error, of success and failure, of discovery and invention.

*Silvia Gherardi*

## Organizational performance

Performance occupies a key interface between organization behaviour, strategy and international management. In organization behaviour, the position of performance in the structural contingency theories and research studies was marginal. Many textbooks omitted performance from the list of contents.

Organization behaviour is at the leading edge in developing a more substantial understanding of performance. The structural contingency theory requires extensive revision. There are two major areas of revision. First, to account for the hidden impacts on performance of the national context of the firm. The hidden aspects include the roles of factor endowments (for example, raw materials), the institutions and the market characteristics (for example, size, homogeneity and speed of saturation). These hidden aspects impact on the performance of firms by creating an envelope of opportunity. Firms have to be aware of the envelope, yet can enrol elements in the context which reshape it. Second, it is important to be aware of the differences in approach between the practices of auditing performance within firms from the concepts and theories used in organization behaviour. Within firms of all kinds – public and private, commercial and custodial – there are extensive arrays of performance data covering very diverse aspects. The financial dimensions of the array are highly influential in constituting the recipe knowledge about strategic directions. The influence of accountancy on the everyday understanding of performance is significant, but should be closely scrutinized. The aim is to develop a theory which links organizational learning to the selective usage of performance measures, in particular, to explain the role of intangible assets. Undertaking these revisions is a major challenge.

*Peter Clark*

## Organizational populations

The study of organizational populations is inspired by evolutionary and ecological thinking. It considers the dynamic processes affecting the development of organizational populations over extended periods of time and, in contrast to the prevailing adaptive perspective, focuses on selection as the main mechanism of change. Organizational theory has long been preoccupied with the adaptation of single organizations to their environments. Early writers analysed the populations of organizations and suggested selection instead of adaptation to play a major role in shaping the development and composition of organizational communities. The role of structural inertia of organizations is stressed, that is, strong limitations on organizational flexibility and speed of response to changing opportunities and constraints in the environment are assumed. The driving force of global change is postulated to be selection – the excess of births over deaths of organizations that possess certain relatively fixed strategies. Selection in organizational ecology is mainly based on differential advantage among organizational forms in competition for scarce resources. In studying the dynamics of processes that influence vital rates of entries and exits, the full histories of populations of organizations are covered.

The observed diversity of organizational forms and populations is postulated to be the outcome of variation, selection and retention. These evolutionary and ecological processes involve analysis at several levels of complexity. The first level concerns the demography of organizations. It considers variations in vital rates and life cycle processes across individual organizations and tries to relate these variations to changes in environments. The second level deals with the population ecology of organizations. It analyses population growth and decline as the dynamic outcome of multiple, interacting populations occupying partially overlapping niches. The third level refers to the community ecology of organizations. A community of organizations, sometimes referred to as an organizational field, is a set of interacting populations, like an industrial setting composed of populations of firms, populations of labour unions and employers associations and populations of regulatory agencies. Studies at this level focus on the evolution of patterns of interaction among these populations and the emergence and disappearance of organizational forms. So far most attention has been devoted to demographic and ecological processes, while studies at the community level have been rare.

*Rolf Ziegler*

## Organizing, process of

The process of organizing can be considered either as an effect of organizations (organizing as what happens within organizations) or as a cause of organizations (organization as a result of organizing). The latter conception leads to a change in the approach to organizational analysis and in ways of understanding organizational life. Instead of searching for final and universal definitions, one looks for the definitions created and used by people engaged in organizing. Attention is focused not on structures but on processes.

The most clear and succinct formulation of the process view is undoubtedly that of the US organization theorist Weick. His work is closely related historically – both forwards and backwards in time – to a number of other approaches, despite his views on many matters differing from these. The earliest process approach to organization theory was that of Taylorism, which treated organizing as a kind of exercise in logistics, an exercise crucial to effective production. Quite a different position was taken by social constructionist approaches, both those regarding social construction as involving efforts directed outwardly – at creating and influencing the world by organizing it – and those emphasizing the fact that such efforts invariably mean organizing also being directed at acquiring both individual and organizational identity.

Empirical studies of how organizing occurs in actual practice reveal the emergence of patterns of organizing that seem indicative of the future: organizing in terms of networking. Networking is communicative activity, often on a large scale and symbolic in character, in which the establishing of connections is frequently facilitated by complex technological means.

*Barbara Czarniawska-Joerges*

# P

## Payment systems

A payment system can be defined as a method or means for determining employee wages or salary. As such, it represents a central mechanism for the regulation of the employment relationship. For management the importance of payment systems is reflected in what often appears to be an ongoing preoccupation with finding new and better ways of paying employees.

Given that pay is one of the defining characteristics of the employment relationship and consequently a powerful means for the exercise of managerial control, the pursuit of ever more 'efficient and effective' techniques for its allocation is hardly surprising. However, as a technique for the pursuit of managerial control, payment systems have been subject to countervailing workplace pressures exercised by employees, work groups and their representatives. Indeed, a well-established academic literature has developed which has sought to analyse the degeneration or decay of the payment systems in terms of competing managerial and employee interests as they relate to the operation of such systems.

It is clear, therefore, that payment systems cannot simply be perceived as structural artefacts captured through passive categorization or by simple typologies. Rather, a payment system is a process which raises questions about the exercise of choice, implementation, operation and impact.

It is important to distinguish between payment systems and other terms, such as pay structure and pay level. These terms are often closely associated with payment systems but are analytically distinct. A pay or grading structure is a rational ordering of jobs, often devised through the application of job evaluation and usually reflecting the different roles and the contributions they make to the organization. A pay level is the amount or rate received by an employee and is usually generated through the combined operation of payment systems and structures. While closely related to the development and operation of payment systems, the techniques associated with the establishment of pay structures or setting of pay levels are analytically separate and not dealt with here.

*Ian Kessler*

## Performance appraisal

Organizational productivity hinges upon controlling the interplay of at least three variables, namely capital, technology and human resources. Effective control systems require information on what is occurring and a means of correcting or adjusting inputs when sensors indicate that change is needed. Productivity gains due to capital are typically measured by sophisticated accounting systems (for example, profits and costs, pro-forma balance sheets and budgets). Gains due to technology are assessed through the control systems of similar operations (for example, comparisons of inputs and outputs, process time, equipment efficiency and effectiveness). The contribution of an organization's human resources to productivity is more difficult to measure but it can be assessed in terms of work outputs produced or work behaviours exhibited over a specified time period. Performance appraisal involves assigning a value to employee behaviours or work outputs in terms of a criterion of productivity effectiveness (quantity, quality, timeliness).

*Vandra L. Huber & Sally Riggs Fuller*

## Personnel management

Personnel management is the strategic approach to the human resourcing task which was thought to suit the mass producer best. Beginning as a support to the supervisory function, it developed in some countries (but not others) to the point where it made some claim to being influential over strategic thinking and decision making.

Personnel management has taken many diverse forms in different cultures. However, there are general tasks which all personnel managers must undertake, including the definition of work tasks, personnel selection, the definition, assessment and reward of performance, and the improvement of performance. The personnel function has contributed to increasing the validity and reliability of managerial judgements and has improved the ways in which organizations seek to control the behaviour of semi-skilled employees.

The underlying philosophy of the mass production organization is seen to be such as to encourage the personnel specialists to emphasize the value of, and to develop methods for, relying on a body of rules as a foundation for achieving stability in productive performance and relations. In some countries advocates of personnel management have become closely bound up with this strategy, possibly to the extent that they are seen to be incapable of switching to other strategies when the underlying market conditions change. However, personnel functionaries, however designated, are likely to continue to adapt their approaches to the strategies that emerge from current re-thinking of organizational objectives and strategies.

*George F. Thomason*

## Political risk

Political risk is a general term referring to a variety of political and quasi-political (economic and social) threats to the ownership or operation of a foreign investment. Different types of political risks are identified and discussed. Arbitrary governmental seizure of private assets, terrorist destruction of plant and equipment and politically induced labour strikes are examples of different types of political risk.

The levels of political risk vary by project, even within the same country during a single timeframe. Factors which can increase or decrease political risk include types of operation, lack of local employment, lack of local business participation and/or local borrowing, lack of overseas production inputs and lack of specialized overseas markets. Many types of political risk can be insured against, using a variety of schemes; the most ambitious of these is provided by the Multilateral Investment Guarantee Agency (MIGA), part of the World Bank Group. MIGA works closely with other governmental entities and offers insurance in all countries that are also members of the World Bank. There are also consulting and forecasting services that can help companies to better analyse the level of political risk they face, but this is an extremely complex and difficult task.

*Robert S. Frank*

## Power

In small organizations power operates principally through direct control premised on surveillance. The proprietor knows the work intimately. Others can be overseen easily by virtue of this knowledge. Power equates with command. The right to command is granted by ownership of the means of production and is typically vested in distinct proprietorial knowledge. This is not always the case however: there may be delegation from the principal to an agency.

Irrespective of the principal–agent relation as either personal or impersonal one may say that command is discursive. One does as one is told or shown. Hence, prototypically, when one wants a brief, rough and ready definition of power, it is usually offered in terms that stress strategies for achieving conformance with superordinate preferences. However, power may involve somewhat more than merely getting others to do what one wants them to, even against their will (the most usual definition). Such a definition stresses only the negative, not the positive, aspects of power.

Power in organizations necessarily concerns the hierarchical structure of offices and their relation to each other. The technical design of tasks and their interdependencies is closely related to the distribution of power. Some tasks will be more necessary to the functional interdependence of a system than others, and some of them may be the exclusive function of a specific party. It follows that these parties will have more power. In practice, as organizations evolve and change, the actual power structures rarely, if ever, conform to their depiction in the organizational chart.

Power can be used effectively, and does not have to be solely coercive in nature. The challenge for future power theory is to recognize, diagnose and respect the diversity of interests and seek to translate and enrol these within one's own course of action. Coercive power may still occasionally be necessary, but ideally it should be regarded as a last resort.

*Stewart R. Clegg*

## Pricing issues in marketing

Pricing is one of the most difficult areas of marketing decision making. Although price is an important element of the marketing mix, one which can send many signals to the customer about the quality and benefits of a particular good or service, final price decisions in many organizations are made by accounting and finance staff rather than marketing professionals.

When setting prices, it is particularly important for marketers to be aware of the market environment, including the prices set by competitors. Price sensitivity is a vital issue, as is an awareness of how prices need to change to reflect different stages of the product life cycle. Costs are an important element of price, but they need to be balanced by an awareness of issues such as sensitivity; good price-setting strategies can also be used to reduce costs, particularly in the area of transfer pricing. Marketers and accountants need to rethink the traditional relationship between price and cost.

In an international setting, pricing across borders poses further problems for the pricing decision maker, particularly as to whether to homogenize prices across a geographical area or to set local prices which reflect local market sensitivity. The value of a good or service as perceived by the customer is for most firms their major, if not their only, source of competitive advantage; and price is one of the most important components of that value. Prices must be set with a focus on the customer, not on costs.

*Michael J. Thomas*

## Privatization and regulation

A feature of the global economy through the 1980s and 1990s, which appears set to continue into the next century, is the sweep of privatization. From the UK to Latin America, from the previously centrally planned economies to the emerging post-apartheid South Africa, industries previously in state ownership have been and continue to be sold off in one form or another to the private sector.

The trend toward privatization has found its reflection inevitably in economic theory. The previous era, which witnessed significant degrees of nationalization and state ownership through most of the Organization for Economic Cooperation and Development (OECD) economies, was generally interpreted in mainstream economics in terms of various forms of 'market failure' requiring state intervention. The mainstream response to privatization has therefore been to interpret the changing industrial ownership structure in terms of 'government failure' or 'public failure', which in turn must have come to outweigh the original market failure. (The balance can also be interpreted as having shifted through reductions in the degree of market failure with, for example, technological developments reducing the degree to which certain industries displayed natural monopoly characteristics.)

The economic and political factors behind the various types of privatization which have been pursued, and continue to be pursued, vary hugely between the very different country settings. Furthermore, developments such as the globalization of financial and capital markets, the growing activities of multinational corporations and the switch to a more free market orientation by international institutions, including the World Bank, all need to be analysed not only as the economic, political and institutional backdrop to the swing to private ownership but also as being fuelled by the very process of privatization itself across the globe.

In the case of the World Bank, its report *The East Asian Miracle* interprets the economic success of the high-performing south-east Asian economies as being primarily due to market-friendly economic policies. This is in marked contrast to the success of South Korea, where an interventionist industrial policy, including the use of nationalization, is shown to have played a key role. Of course, the World Bank acknowledges that such policies were pursued, but makes a distinction between these, on the one hand, and market-friendly policies on the other, and chooses to recommend only the latter. However, to the extent that 'market-friendly' policies now embrace privatization, these have themselves become 'institutionally demanding' policies as new regulatory structures become required.

*Jonathan Michie*

## Problem solving

Problem solving is an important part of the managerial role. Few writers have written exclusively on this topic, but those who have agree broadly on the key stages of a systematic approach required to take effective decisions. First, there are different types of problems – mysteries, difficulties, assignments, opportunities, puzzles, dilemmas – each of which requires a different problem-solving approach. There are then different stages in the problem-solving process: analysing the problem, setting objectives and establishing criteria for success, information gathering, decision making, implementation and reviewing success.

There are a number of techniques that can be used to solve problem techniques more effectively. Problem identification techniques include situational appraisal and significance analysis. Brainstorming, the fishbone technique, Pareto charts and historograms are used for information gathering and analysis. Team-based problem solving has increased importance for a number of reasons; as organizational problems become more complex, more than one person is often involved in a particular problem, making a team approach more suitable.

Problem-solving processes are at the heart of total quality management, project management and continuous improvement programmes. Recent writers have also drawn attention to the need to create the right organization culture and climate for problems to be solved innovatively, particularly when the organization is undergoing dramatic change.

*Jane Cranwell-Ward*

## Product development

New products are the foundation of a company's future, underpinning its future character and wealth. One fundamental method of company valuation is based on the future returns from its product sales, discounted with time. From this viewpoint a significant proportion of shareholder value can be discerned by: examining the way that future new product ideas are formed; investigating how new products are advanced during their process of development; understanding the market's adoption and diffusion dynamics; and taking a snapshot of the embryonic new products throughout the company.

New products make up an increasing share of the total product mix in many markets because of the improving ability of technology to deliver a solution and because market needs are changing ever more rapidly. A product is more than manufactured hardware: the accessories, packaging and added services form much of its delivered value. A wide range of company skills is required for a successful new product introduction over and above the technical skills implied by 'research and development'.

The innovation content of these products need not be great. New products often meet customer needs by means of an intelligent rearrangement of known technologies. Innovation can be applied to both the content of the product itself and its manufacturing process, the relative emphasis depending on the maturity of the industry. Innovation can be applied to any element of the product delivery, including the development process itself. Reduction in development time-scales (reduced time to market) is one of the greatest pressures that leads to innovation in the development process.

The factors differentiating successful from unsuccessful new products are easily understandable but rarely achieved in full. The most important is the nature of the completed product. A product is most likely to be successful if it delivers unique benefits to its users. Many of the other success factors are linked to the quality of the process of development. Product development and introduction is more difficult to manage as a process than many business and manufacturing activities, since different developments are often quite dissimilar. Nevertheless there are considerable benefits from applying process thinking.

*Geoffrey S. Gardiner*

## Product policy concepts in marketing

The purchase and sale of physical products and services is the fundamental basis of all trade and commerce. Product policy issues have occupied the attention of selling organizations for a very considerable time, probably since the inception of trade itself.

Product theory has also always occupied a position of importance, if not actually centre stage, in various managerial disciplines. In economics, the development of market structure theories assumes the existence of products which are bought and sold in a market; because companies ultimately exist to sell these products, product policy has always been an implicit concern of strategic planning. Product policy issues have also been the subject of studies by the engineering, design and operations management disciplines, particularly as more sophisticated manufacturing technologies are now facilitating greater customization of goods and greater consumer responsiveness.

Despite this widespread interest in product issues, however, it is only the marketing discipline which has historically placed the product at the centre of its core paradigm, the marketing mix (the four elements of which are product, price, promotion and distribution). Interest by marketers in product issues dates back to the earliest marketing mix theories of the 1930s, and was subsequently developed in the period after the Second World War. Marketing interest is explained by the fact that, from the marketer's viewpoint, the product is the key medium through which customer satisfaction (or otherwise) is ultimately expressed. Many of the developments in modern product policy thinking (life cycle theory, product positioning, development and evaluation of new products, diffusion of innovation) can be credited to marketing, though other disciplines continue to provide conceptual and practical enrichment, leading to a substantial and well-documented field.

*Ronald McTavish & Chung Koo Kim*

## Productivity

Economists define productivity as the ratio of output to input, or the results achieved per unit of resource. This is a measure of how effectively the resources are utilized. Management has a very important role in maintaining and increasing the firm's productivity.

A comprehensive project to improve the firm's productivity requires a substantial commitment of resources. The first step should be strategic assessment of the firm's products' and services competitive position, its culture and the availability and quality of its resources.

A productivity plan's design and definition should be 'custom tailored' to the firm's needs and capabilities, but successful schemes do have some generic characteristics. First, a strategic integrated approach is required to link the plan to the firm's business needs; all major departments within the firm and key outside suppliers should be involved. Second, no comprehensive scheme can be successful without the chief executive's strong support and involvement. A successful scheme requires strategic input, a high priority, a commitment of resources and an integrated effort throughout the firm; only the chief executive can deliver all these and also provide the leadership needed to initiate and sustain the project.

Strategic productivity plans emphasize 'breakthrough' improvements, as compared with the incremental improvements sought by activities such as employee quality circles (though the two are not mutually exclusive). Technology is a key resource and an important factor in increasing productivity, as has been confirmed by a number of studies. Finally, a long-term view is essential if productivity improvement is to have a real impact on the firm's performance and profitability.

Barriers to success include limitations on management action, such as those imposed by restrictive work practices. In the 1990s globalization has increased awareness of the importance of productivity. Many of the economies of western Europe are experiencing no growth and historically high levels of unemployment; any solutions to these challenges must include substantial productivity improvement.

*Robert Conti*

## Profit sharing and employee shareholding schemes

Profit sharing and employee share ownership schemes have experienced a dramatic increase in popularity in Western industrialized countries since the 1970s, and numerous countries have introduced supportive legislation.

The prime motives for profit-sharing plans are to improve employee and company performance, to serve as a pension plan and to provide a more attractive benefits package, as well as for philosophical reasons. The importance of each motive varies across countries, largely depending on the legislative context. Research indicates that profit sharing is generally associated with improved company performance, but this varies with the nature of the plan and numerous other factors.

The prime motives for employee share ownership are improvement of employee and company performance, the provision of a tax supported employee benefit plan, the transferral of ownership from retiring owners of private corporations and the development of cooperative employee–management relations. As with profit sharing, these motives vary across countries depending on the legislative context. Evidence indicates that, when combined with employee participation in decision making, employee ownership is usually associated with a substantial improvement in company performance.

*Richard Long*

## Project management

Projects are carried out in every industry and profession and reflect not only the environment of rapid change which characterizes today's business world but also the move throughout industry and government towards defined, goal-orientated, divisions of work. In nearly every case the effort applied to the resultant projects is across the boundaries of the organization and the reason for the upsurge in popularity of the multi-functional project team approach to management is that it provides the flexibility necessary for organizations to adapt amid constant change.

Although on one level project management might be thought of as a practical application, comprising techniques aimed at the control of time and cost, it uses and enhances many of the common practices of management. Teamworking, cross-functional perspective, process orientation, logical progression and leadership are all important features of the project style of working and managing.

All projects comprise activities or tasks that must be completed to achieve the overall goal of completing the project on time, within budget and to technical specification. These activities require resources, including people, materials, equipment, materials and money, which contribute to the cost of the project. Project management includes six major issues: defining the project's goals and objectives, determining who will work on it, determining who will have responsibility for particular contributions, deciding how the work will be done, determining when the project will be completed and how much it will cost and assessing its progress over time. Work breakdown structures, project network techniques and charting techniques are all tools for tackling these issues.

The cycle of managing costs within the project starts with the estimating process and ends with historical cost reporting. Cost needs to be continually monitored. Project risk management also needs to be continuous. There are many areas of uncertainty in projects; risk management involves identifying those areas, assessing their likely impact and finally taking steps to remove or reduce risk. Although planning and control techniques are important, the role of leadership should not be underestimated; the project manager's or leader's role is vital to seeing projects through to their successful conclusion.

*Ralph J. Levene*

## Public relations

Public relations is an important business function which focuses on the management of an organization's reputation. Public relations has both a strategic role in seeking to build reputation over the long term and a tactical role, particularly in defending the organization against hostile or adverse publicity emanating from other sources.

As such, public relations is often linked to the marketing function within the organization, although its remit is typically wider than that of marketing. Marketing helps a company interact with its customers, but public relations assists interaction with a wide variety of other constituency groups including shareholders, employees and regulators. In general public relations is an increasingly sophisticated tool which can be used for a wide variety of purposes.

Public relations is being deployed ever more skilfully by a wide variety of companies and organizations. Public relations strategy is being recognized as having an importance beyond the mere tactical use of public relations techniques. Better, more skilled and seasoned practitioners are coming into the business both through educational or training schemes and from other allied disciplines. In the future practitioners will need to continue to develop their contributions to management including both the quality of their advice and the levels of their support, reinforcing not only the human resources and marketing functions but also the entire strategic management of the organization.

*Roger Haywood*

## Public sector management

Since the 1980s the public sector has been undergoing major changes throughout the Western industrialized world, the transitional economies of central and eastern Europe, Latin America and south and east Asia. The main thrust of these changes has been to bring public sector management practices closer to those of the private sector. This raises the question of how far public and private sector management are comparable and what are the potential benefits and problems that may emerge as a result of such changes.

The relationship between public and private sector management may be seen in terms of two fundamental issues. First, there is the issue of where the boundary between public and private sectors should be drawn. Second, there is the issue of how far public sector management may or may not be regarded as distinct in style and approach from that of the private sector. Classical public management theory emphasized the distinctions, and was primarily preoccupied with accountability. The 'new public management' on the other hand, has drawn closer to private sector styles as it adopts a new ethos emphasizing service quality.

Public organizations are obliged to present themselves as if they operated within the rational model of management. When they experiment with or adopt new approaches, there is a danger that the changes will be re-incorporated into a rational bureaucratic approach, a trend which can be seen in areas such as performance management. Public sector management has a greater need for legitimacy and accountability than the private sector.

*Adrian Campbell*

## Public sector organizations

Public sector organizations are enterprises committed to the provision of public goods and services. A variety of legal statuses and territorial areas have been set up by governments for this purpose. Publicness is characterized by public policy implementation, a mandate allocated by a principal, and close vicinity to the political arena.

As organizations, they show similarities and differences with business enterprises and voluntary associations in terms of bureaucratization, social stratification and cultural factors. Four main models of functioning can be identified: inward-orientated bureaucracies, environment sensitive organizations, outward-driven enterprises, informal inter-organizational systems. National cultures or styles can also be identified. Public management as an art and craft is closely linked to societal and governmental issues, such as defining a better fit between policy making and administrative behaviour or between efficiency and effectiveness, and a participative leadership style in politically sensitive contexts.

*Jean-Claude Thoenig*

## Purchasing

The role and importance of purchasing have gone through a significant change during the decades since 1970. Purchasing has traditionally been considered almost a clerical function, with the quite restricted short-term goal of buying specified products as cheaply as possible. Today, however, quite a number of companies regard purchasing as a function of major strategic importance. One of the main underlying reasons for this change is the increasing specialization characterizing the development of all industrial sectors. Manufacturing companies are successively concentrating on more and more limited parts of the production chain, which leads to a decrease in the degree of vertical integration. External suppliers become in this way more important, in economic terms as well as from a value-creation point of view. In order to capture the potential benefits, buying companies have to view efficiency and effectiveness in purchasing in a new way. The earlier perspective, based on obtaining low prices by using competitive pressure towards a number of suppliers, must be replaced. The focus of the new view is on obtaining low total costs, which include price as well as internal costs of the buying company. Furthermore, other benefits through working more closely with a reduced supplier base must be considered.

*Lars-Erik Gadde & Håkan Håkansson*

## Quantitative methods in marketing

At the heart of all forms of marketing is the need to analyse all available information and then make appropriate decisions. In practice, these two tasks are often extremely difficult. Many marketing problems require the analysis of very large amounts of information, and many cannot be solved by single simple decisions. Tools are needed which will reduce complexity and facilitate decision making, and quantitative methods are one important set of such tools.

Quantitative methods include any use of mathematical concepts or procedures in marketing practice or research. The two principal applications of quantitative methods in marketing are *descriptive methods*, which are used to observe or monitor marketing phenomena and then describe them in a way that represents the essence of those phenomena and reduces their complexity and uncertainty; and *decision support methods*, which are used to predict the outcome of marketing decisions. Central to this second application is the concept of the quantitative model, a series of numbers connected together with a structure containing functions, formulae or rules. Examples of such models include the product life cycle, market share models, promotions models and distribution models.

*Stephen K. Tagg*

## Queuing systems

Most of us encounter a myriad of queues every day, spending considerable time waiting for some type of service such as making a transaction at a bank, buying stamps at a post office, checking our shopping out at a supermarket, traversing an intersection at a traffic light or waiting for a bus to come by. Some of us in our professional life may encounter queues from a different perspective, namely, having to decide the level of service to provide (staffing levels for banks, post offices and supermarkets, the proper red/green timing cycle for traffic lights, the schedules for buses on various routes and so on). Providing the proper service level that balances customer waiting time against the cost of providing the service is the main goal of queueing theory. To do this, the system must be accurately modelled, generally through the use of mathematics, particularly probability and statistics, and often accompanied by extensive computer code.

*Donald Gross*

## Real estate management

All business activities, from industrial production to telesales, computer programming and beyond, occur within some kind of spatial environment. While the intensity of real estate use may vary, the need to provide a spatial work environment is common to all economic activities. Real estate management relates to the provision of the physical work environment. Its function is to control the use of physical corporate assets in accordance with the objectives of either investors or users of real estate. As such it impinges on the activities of firms of all sizes through a series of 'technical operations', ranging from items linked to facility management through to the service and use of legal notices. Although the explicit outcome of real estate management may not always be clearly articulated or defined in terms of the strategic management of an organization, they are important at the micro- and meso-tactical levels.

The link between the corporate strategy of an organization and its property requirements should not be underrated. When planning corporate activities, attention needs to be focused in the critical path analysis stage on the impact that property acquisition and disposal can have on the operation of the firm. Real estate has this effect due to its illiquid nature (real estate tends to take longer to sell or turn into cash than other assets such as equities or stock in hand) and 'lumpy nature' (property can be purchased in fixed amounts, it is not possible to buy £10 worth of property, lot sizes as determined in terms of cash tend to be fairly large). It is difficult to generalize about the exact contribution of real estate costs to total costs, but it has been estimated that for certain finance companies, rent might contribute to only 1 per cent of costs. The link between corporate real estate and management therefore has to be explicitly identified within the operational planning processes and the balance sheet.

Property use and occupation create both a potential asset and a series of liabilities that have to be carefully managed. Real estate should not be treated as a 'free good' within an organization: cost of provision and management have to be considered when calculating returns on capital, as well as the duration of the real estate asset being used. Accordingly, real estate management is of day-to-day importance to all companies in all sectors of the economy. This is emphasized even more by the fact that many organizations are not restricted to just one type of land use but may have demands for a diverse variety. A supermarket chain, for example, may require retail outlets of varying sizes both in and outside urban cores, with and without car parking, offices, warehousing and garaging facilities.

Interest in real estate management is not just restricted to those who specialize in the provision of real estate professional services and the property industry, a fact illustrated by the growth of in-house facilities-management units within companies and the growing involvement of chief executives in making real estate decisions.

*Tom Putt*

## Real estate resource management

Senior managers are realizing that the places from which they administer their organizations, manufacture their products and sell their services can have a direct impact on the ability of their organization to survive and succeed. The real estate resource, in the form of land and buildings occupied, has in the past been considered merely as something which was passed on from one management team to the next. It was static and often required little change during a typical planning cycle of less than five years.

During the 1980s, it was first recognized that real estate, compared to other key organizational resources such as people, finance and technology, was often undermanaged. Organizations possessed limited information on the real estate they occupied. The value and the cost of running the facilities was often not known, how effectively the buildings were being used was not considered, and whether the real estate was suitable for the current and future functions was not evaluated. A reactive approach to the management of the real estate resource was the norm.

Since then the fluctuating economic environment, the increasing pace of change and the shift in management style have resulted in greater scrutiny of the real estate resource. Work has been undertaken, mainly in the USA and the UK, to develop a new area of management related to improving the performance and contribution of the real estate resource. Real estate is now being incorporated into the strategic planning processes of major multinational organizations such as IBM and Rank Xerox and associated research is being undertaken to gain a better understanding of the relationship between real estate and other key resources. Real estate resource management is at an early stage of development in terms of management theory but emerging in the way that human resource management gained acceptance in the late 1970s and early 1980s.

*Virginia Gibson*

## Real options

Real options are options which arise in real investments, that is investments in real assets, in which there is flexibility to take decisions in the light of subsequent information. The flexibility may be the choice of either increasing the level of output of a production process now or waiting until later when more is known about the likely level of demand. Real option theory is primarily concerned with valuing this flexibility and determining the optimal timing of such investment decisions.

The freedom to wait before taking the complete investment decision makes it more difficult to value projects. In the absence of flexibility, the expected values of future cash flows from the investment are estimated and then valued in today's pounds or dollars, allowing a discount for the risk or uncertainty involved. The presence of flexibility makes the estimation of the future cash flows more problematic, and leads us to a different approach, in which we draw an analogy with options in the financial markets, where the investor has flexibility to choose over a period of time whether or not to invest in a certain financial security. Established methods for valuing such options help us value real investments with flexibility. It is clear that flexibility becomes more valuable as uncertainty about the future increases, other things being equal. This makes real options very different from investments without flexibility where uncertainty may reduce value.

A major feature of real option methods is that, not only do they put a value on flexibility, but they also tell us the optimal stage at which to exercise the flexibility. For example, as the market price of the output of a production process falls, it is possible to find the optimal point to stop producing. Of course, the presence of costs to interrupting production and uncertainty over the path of future prices may make it rational to continue producing goods even when costs exceed revenues. Likewise, it may be rational to wait before starting to produce until revenues considerably exceed costs. Such circumstances, in which it is economically sensible to produce even when costs exceed revenues or, in different cases, not to produce when revenues exceed costs, is a typical and important feature (called hysteresis) of many real option situations.

*C.G.C. Pitts*

## Recruitment and selection

Recruitment and selection make up the staffing function in organizations. The primary goal of staffing is to assure that companies get the qualified people they need in order for the company to operate as efficiently and effectively as possible. Prior to recruitment and selection, two steps must be taken. First, a company must scan and analyse the external environment and examine the company's internal situation to develop human resource plans and forecasts; these actions anchor the staffing effort. More broadly, these human resource plans form an integral part of an organization's strategic business plan. Ultimately, to be effective, the staffing function should be thoroughly integrated with the company's overall business strategies. The second precursor to beginning the recruitment and selection effort is job analysis. Although the human resource plans and forecasts identify general personnel needs, job analysis is used specifically to determine the types of individuals the company wishes to recruit and select. Each type of job is described in terms of its purpose, its major duties and activities, the conditions under which it is performed, and the necessary knowledge, skills, abilities and other requirements. This information guides recruitment and selection activities.

*Sally Riggs Fuller & Vandra L. Huber*

## Re-engineering

Re-engineering, or business process redesign, emerged in the early 1990s as a major new contribution to management thinking. It proposed that, by reorganizing themselves around processes rather than functions and exploiting the potential of information technology, companies could dramatically improve their performance. The commercial success of the concept gave rise to many imitators and to evidence of considerable differences of emphasis, and in some cases of interpretation, among its proponents.

Key features of re-engineering include the adoption of a process-oriented, rather than functional, perspective on the organization; a commitment to radical organizational change; and the integration of information technology into processes. The reasons for the widespread adoption of re-engineering are many and varied. In part, with its emphasis on radical change, re-engineering was perceived to be a break from the past, an opportunity to escape older, inefficient organizational forms. At the same time, the strong emphasis on IT can be seen as a continuity of older organizational initiatives, which had similarly urged the integration of IT but with less success. The persuasive advocacy of some of the early gurus of re-engineering may also have been a factor. Finally, in the USA at least there is a view that the time was right for the introduction of a new, home-grown business philosophy that offered American businesses the chance to become more competitive.

Re-engineering has attracted many criticisms. It has been dismissed as a fad; more seriously, it has been criticized for its overly mechanistic approach to organizations and the tensions created by the emphasis on top-down leadership of re-engineering initiatives on the one hand, and its advocacy of employee empowerment on the other. However, whether or not re-engineering is really as new or distinctive as its proponents make out, its promotion of systematic rethinking of established practices and the reassessment of the potential contribution of information technology to organizational change may be of value in many organizations.

*Matthew Jones*

## Relationship marketing

In the early 1990s interest in the concept of relationship marketing began to grow rapidly. Many organizations began to realize that success in highly competitive and mature markets is more likely to be achieved by devoting a greater part of their resources to retaining existing customers than to attracting new ones.

Relationship marketing involves an extension of traditional marketing. The key features of relationship marketing are a change in the nature of relationships with customers with a shift in emphasis from a transaction focus to a relationship focus, a broader view of the definition of a 'market', and a recognition that quality, customer service and marketing activities are closely related and need to be more closely integrated.

The basis of the relationship marketing philosophy is that the attraction of new customers is merely the first step in the marketing process; the important element is the retention of those customers. Relationship marketing is concerned with creating, developing and enhancing relationships with selected customer segments over time. This involves gaining a detailed understanding of the needs and behaviour of key customer segments and how they change over their life cycles.

*Adrian Payne*

## Relocation

Relocation, with both an operational and strategic role in international organizations, represents a major component in international human resource management (IHRM) research and practice. There are three phases in the relocation process. Each phase – pre-departure, expatriation and repatriation – has specific implications for the employees involved, human resource practitioners, and organizational strategy. Effective IHRM policies and practices throughout these phases in the relocation process will maximize the opportunities for successful outcomes for individuals and organizations.

*Helen de Cieri, Sara L. McGaughey & Peter J. Dowling*

## Retail management

Until recently, management within and for retailing was poorly developed as a professional and academic discipline. Even as late as the mid-1970s, retailing retained much of its 'barrow boy' or street trader image, dominated by managers who were relatively uneducated and largely self-made. Throughout the next two decades, however, in both western Europe and North America, there were profound changes within the sector. Retail outlets became significantly larger, many retail companies grew to immense size, investments were made in research, new product development and information technology, and the first MBA graduates appeared in retail firms. Moving into the 1990s, several retail companies are now among the most efficient and sophisticated companies in the world. And yet this remains an industry where individual flair and enterprise can still make their presence felt; there is a beguiling mixture of high productivity through strict conformity on the one hand and considerable risk-taking and creativity on the other.

Retail management education and development have also appeared since the mid-1980s, both as internal practices within companies and as external services provided by colleges, universities and consultancy organizations. There are numerous institutes of retail management in Western countries, and they are beginning to appear in the Far East as well. That the retail industry is studied and researched at the University of Oxford, the oldest English-speaking university in the world, in itself says something about how the industry has 'come of age'.

*Ross Davies*

## Retailing

Retailing is defined as the sale of goods and services to consumers for their own use. The term has been adopted by a wide range of service providers such as banks and other financial institutions, but the focus of this entry is on the sale of goods to consumers.

Retail outlets come in many forms, including shopping centres, retail parks, department stores, variety stores, superstores, hypermarkets, discounters and warehouse clubs. The main functions within the value chain of retailing include location, product selection, buying, retailer branding, pricing, advertising, in-store design, human resource management and logistics.

As large-scale retailers have grown in scale and in sophistication, they have gained considerable power over their suppliers. In some countries, the multiple chain is the dominant type of retail organization; independents, symbol groups, cooperatives and franchises do however play a significant role. A notable feature of retailing in the 1990s has been the rapid growth of internationalization.

*Peter J. McGoldrick*

# S

## Sales management

For the majority of firms, the success of their marketing efforts depends upon the ability of the sales force to contact customers and secure orders. However, the development of a stable, productive and motivated sales force does not happen automatically. Selling is not a single, homogeneous activity; one kind of sales work requires a radically different type of person from another, and salespeople must be trained, coached and managed in different ways if they are to be effective in helping the company meet its goals.

Salespeople are employed to persuade others to purchase, for themselves or on behalf of their organizations, the products, services or ideas which their own company sells. For most salespeople, this task is carried out in an unsupervised, socially lonely working environment, using carefully crafted sales techniques. These do not remain effective. Frequent customer refusals to buy erode both them and the salesperson's morale. Salespeople tend to associate their repeated but unsuccessful attempts to sell, using sales technique words and phrases, with customer refusals to buy; they reason that if they stop using these words or trying to sell, customers will then stop refusing them. Few salespeople are able to explain the complexities of their job or why they are successful; fewer still can on their own originate a sales plan and control its implementation from beginning to end without initial product and sales training, ongoing coaching, motivation and firm leadership. It is up to the sales manager to orchestrate these management techniques in order to multiply sales through the individual and combined efforts of the sales force.

The sales manager must translate corporate goals into sales goals, setting targets for both the sales force as a whole and individual members of the sales team. He or she must evaluate sales performance and ensure goals are met. Given that the sales force represents the forward edge of the company's market effort and provides the means by which customer needs are met and satisfaction is created, the role of the sales manager is a particularly pivotal one within the overall marketing effort.

*John Lidstone*

## Sales promotion

'Sales promotion' is a term often used to encompass all those elements of marketing communications which do not come under the headings of advertising, selling or public relations. Promotions seek to stimulate a direct response from customers, marketing intermediaries or the company's own sales staff, through the offer of benefits additional to those normally on offer. The most common forms of promotions are special offers such as coupons, discount prices or banded packs, which are targeted at consumers with the aim of generating increased sales. Such promotions are essentially temporary customizations of the standard marketing mix which change the product, its price or distribution arrangements so as to encourage consumers to switch brands, purchase early or stockpile products.

The 1980s witnessed widespread growth in the extent and variety of sales promotions used by companies. In an increasing number of markets and companies, promotions are accounting for a greater share of overall marketing communications budgets than classic 'brand sell' advertising. The appeal of promotions for marketing managers lies in their cost-effectiveness, flexibility, measurability and the speed with which they can be implemented; the benefits for consumers include increases in the value of the product offering, reduction of perceived purchase risk or simply the enjoyment of taking advantage of a promotional offer.

A common view of promotions is that they are short-term tactical marketing tools whose role is limited to temporarily boosting sales. This underestimation of their potential importance, combined with the fact that promotional campaigns are often put together under time pressure as a 'rapid response' to changes in the marketing environment, has caused many promotional campaigns to be less meticulously planned, implemented and monitored than campaigns based around advertising. This has led to some very high-profile promotional disasters involving major companies. Marketers are now learning to take a more strategic view of promotions and their potential to convert and capture competitors' customers, reinforce customer loyalty and fulfil a range of marketing objectives. This increasingly strategic role, often combined with a move towards a more integrated marketing communications strategy, has ensured that the creativity and impact of which promotions are capable is now being balanced by a more professional approach to planning and execution.

*Ken Peattie*

## Scheduling

Most companies operate on the basis of business planning methods that include forecasts of expected sales revenues or unit volumes of goods to be produced. The forecasting process enables the business to predict needs for goods to be produced, inventories, equipment, the size of the workforce and other related resources required to meet demand. Both manufacturing and non-manufacturing companies forecast demand for goods and services based upon market trends, economic conditions, competitor positions, consumer preferences and other external conditions. The forecasts are generally prepared through the marketing functions and reflect the estimated demand for product groups, promotional items, new products or items that are particularly sensitive to external factors.

Aggregate planning determines the organization's overall level of output and the resource inputs for achieving it for each of several future time periods. At this broad level of planning, some of the detailed decisions have not yet been made, nor have resources been allocated to specific production units. Detailed scheduling is the specification of when each job will run, where it will run and who will run it, as well as when and how much input is needed at each work station. It is most effectively based on required outputs, through a process of reverse scheduling or 'starting with the answer', which is the date the order is due to be delivered. Once the detailed schedule is completed, the work can be dispatched or delivered to the people who will actually complete the scheduled work. The entire process from aggregate planning through to the dispatch of the work to the work centres is the process referred to as scheduling.

Scheduling is the implementation phase of production planning. A schedule is in essence a timetable for carrying out the production plan, or in the case of service industries, a sequence of events that enables an organization to deliver the services it offers. Scheduling is the disaggregation of production plans into time-phased activities. Resources are allocated, facilities assigned and work activities sequenced for completion through the process of scheduling.

*Kathie S. Smith*

## Securities markets, international

Until the 1960s, there was no such thing as the international securities market. Securities markets were based in a single country and virtually all primary market new issues and secondary market transactions were undertaken by companies, investment institutions and individuals resident in that country. In consequence, securities firms (except those in London) dealt only in domestic securities and were unlikely to have overseas branches or subsidiaries.

Governments gave no special consideration to selling bonds to foreign investors since there was no reason to believe that this would reduce the cost of government funding. Indeed, it was more likely to raise it since enticing foreigners into a distant market where information was slow to reach them would require the payment of a premium return. For securities firms, there was little reason to consider overseas branches or subsidiaries since their customers undertook so little overseas business. To the extent that they did, this could be undertaken through commission sharing agreements with, for example, overseas stockbrokers.

The change during the 1970s and 1980s from a domestic perspective on the part of issuers, investors and securities houses, to a global cross-border perspective, arose for a number of reasons. Companies became more multinational in their operations, and consequently investors started to appreciate the advantages of global diversification. Telecommunications systems improved and costs fell; screen-based systems were developed to disseminate information globally. Computing power also fell in cost and allowed easy analysis of information. At the same time, rising government deficits (particularly in the USA) could only be financed at an acceptable cost by widening the investor base to include foreign investors, while the gradual worldwide abolition of exchange controls facilitated cross-border transactions.

By the beginning of the 1990s, there had developed an international financial mechanism comprising internationally oriented investors, global securities houses and market mechanisms facilitating cross-border securities transactions. By the year 2000, it is likely that this mechanism will be greatly refined and will be the major source of funding for international companies, governments and quasi-government bodies.

*Brian Scott-Quinn*

## Security and information systems

Without their information technologies, many organizations would fail within days. Even a few hours of partial loss is an extremely expensive possibility. Disruption of computer-based information systems costs business enterprises thousands of millions each year. Information systems security and computer security are largely synonymous concepts that regard the protection of information technologies from hazards. These terms are sometimes used naively to regard hazards intentionally posed by disgruntled workers, juvenile vandals or industrial spies. In practice, however, these terms regard both accidental and intentional hazards because the effects of various protective measures impact both types of hazard.

Information systems security shares some overlapping concepts with information systems design and software engineering. This is because well-designed and well-constructed information technologies are innately less vulnerable to certain hazards. For example, data input programs that carefully validate the incoming data will reduce the introduction of incorrect data into the system. This validation reduces the chance of either error or fraud. Similarly, information systems security shares some over-lapping concepts with EDP (electronic data processing) auditing, which seeks to verify the integrity of data repositories and processing.

Information systems security programs establish safeguards that protect the organization from information systems hazards. These safeguards range from people who follow operating procedures to machinery that performs encryption. The hazards may range from mice chewing through optical cables to hi-tech saboteurs placing time-bomb logic in sensitive process control programs. Organizations establish information systems risk management or security management functions that determine how safeguards should be integrated into information systems, and plan how the organization should react when major hazards arise.

*Richard Baskerville*

## Segmentation

Any company wishing to sell products or services in diverse consumer markets needs to understand the size and character of those markets in order to ensure success. Consumers vary widely in terms of their background, tastes and interests, and rarely will a single marketing approach satisfy or convince everyone to buy. Marketing professionals have therefore developed a range of techniques for dividing consumer populations in order to identify and define those sections of the population most likely to respond to a promotional campaign and buy a given product or service.

These techniques comprise what has become known as *market segmentation*. Market segmentation can be defined as the process of dividing a potential market into distinct subsets of consumers with common needs or characteristics, and then selecting one or more segments to target with a distinct marketing mix. The bases for market segmentation include both physical factors, including geographic, demographic and sociocultural factors, and behavioural or psychological attribute factors, including user behaviour, benefit factors and psychological classification. Ideally, a combination of all these factors is used to define a market segment.

*Barrie Gunter*

## Services, marketing of

Any discussion on marketing services should acknowledge why the subject needs to be treated separately from product or goods marketing. The major differences commonly cited are intangibility (a service cannot be seen, touched, tasted or displayed and, unlike a product, has no physical form), inseparability (services are produced and consumed simultaneously and are inseparable from their supplier) and heterogeneity (the consumer is involved in the service process, meaning that each service is a unique experience formed by the interaction of consumer and provider). These three factors serve to differentiate services from products, and ensure that services marketing requires a different approach from marketing tangible products.

However, there are also similarities, and some of the strategic issues involved in the marketing of services are similar to those in product marketing. Concepts such as the marketing mix and the product life cycle are still applicable, although they often need modification in order to reflect the unique nature of services mentioned above. Service quality too is an issue, but measuring the quality of an intangible service is again quite different from quality measurement with tangible products. Marketing strategies for services need to take all of these factors into account.

*Trevor Watkins*

## Short-termism

Short-term pressures (S-TPs) are defined as factors which tend to increase the rate of discount applied and/or which may foreshorten the time limit of revenue and capital investments. Accordingly, short-termism occurs where a firm, or some of its managers, applies an excessive discount rate or a foreshortened time horizon to investments. Revenue investments are particularly susceptible to S-TP because these expenses are charged to the profit and loss account of a period, having been incurred wholly or partly in order to enhance future profitability without affecting current trading. The effects of S-TPs on capital investment, such as investment in fixed assets and new equipment, are generally not as adverse as on revenue investment because the risks are relatively lower, payback period is shorter and the amount spent is often capitalized and therefore does not affect the current period's profit. This definition of short-termism also allows S-TP to include factors like high interest rates and low profitability, which increase the opportunity cost of capital. The effect of these pressures would be to reduce capital investment, in particular revenue investments in research and development and in other intangible assets – such as training or education – with their attendant uncertainty and long-term nature, and to increase the bias towards projects with short-term payback periods.

Short-termism within management can distort decision making and add difficulties in international competition. The counter-argument is that such pressures, to the extent that they are felt at all, are useful because they help to eliminate corporate slack, to the long-term benefit of the businesses. Supporters of industry argue that the financial markets pay more attention to the short term and managers are therefore acting under pressure from the City of London. There is some evidence to support such an argument: the contested takeovers in the UK and suggestions that the financial markets do not understand or that they ignore the technological information given out by companies. Others, who are in favour of the City, claim that the stock market's short-termism is not proven, and argue that the real culprits are the managers who favour short-term decisions quite independently of any spur from the financial markets. Accordingly, the debate on the causes of S-TP focuses on how far they arise from external and internal factors.

*External factors* are found outside the organization and include: general economic environment; institutional shareholders (owners of firms) and their objectives; performance evaluation of fund managers acting on behalf of the owners; type of investment and treatment of revenue investments within generally accepted accounting practices and standards; efficiency of financial markets including the quality of information given by the management of companies to their owners; and managers' perception of the financial markets.

*Internal factors* are generated within the management itself and include: organization structures and management control styles; performance evaluation measures; and remuneration of top managers.

*Istemi S. Demirag*

## Simulation modelling

Socrates argued that virtue is knowledge. Contemporary systems thinkers such as Ackoff concur. Engaging in simulation modelling for learning helps firms compete by creating new knowledge about the system structure lurking behind managerial decision situations in business and government. Creating new knowledge often requires capturing unknown and unknowable aspects of system structure that may be neither easy to observe nor easy to measure.

Combined with the pre-scientific state of modelling human systems, the elusive nature of system structure may account for the frequently observed gaps between model assumptions and computed simulation scenarios. These gaps often required a quantum leap in logic and thereby undermined confidence in simulation modelling. New computational and diagramming tools have been developed, however, which can now ease the transition from problem framing to full-scale simulation modelling.

The evolution of computer simulation and mathematical modelling has turned simulation modelling into a prelude to institutional learning. Modellers can still choose the organizational issues they tackle as well as the content of simulation. Yet simulation modelling of managerial decision situations has witnessed a shift in emphasis since the 1960s, focusing more on the ill-structured problems of business and corporate strategy than merely on the well-structured problems of tactics and production.

*Nicholas C. Georgantzas*

## Small business finance

Small businesses dominate enterprise numbers in the economy and make significant contributions to employment and income. They are not just scaled-down versions of larger businesses and their financing has unique features. These include a primary reliance on bank debt as a source of funding, higher failure rates with associated higher lending margins, and the potential for internal and external constraints on funding in both the debt and equity markets. Such funding 'gaps' are due to informational asymmetries, scale economies in the provision of funds and the greater market power of large businesses over small. Government small firm policies have been largely directed at rectifying these perceived market failures, in particular to obviating funding gaps. However, the empirical evidence suggests that market failures are less widespread than is commonly thought.

*Robert Cressy & Marc Cowling*

## Small business marketing

Since the 1970s small firms have been the subject of much interest from governments throughout the world, keen to stimulate both the cultural endowments of entrepreneurship and the job creating potential of small firms. During the same period, there has been a substantial growth in the small firms sector of many countries, both numerically and in employment share.

Small firms tend to survive in the face of competition by large firms by adopting a combination of cost-based and specialization strategies. Small firms are adept at exploiting niche markets and at forming their own unique cost-cutting strategies in order to survive. The use of networks has proved beneficial for many firms. However, owner-managers of small firms tend to perceive marketing as at best peripheral to the management function.

Small firms often grow without any formal marketing effort, and owner-managers often feel it is unnecessary to switch to formal marketing planning; those that do often use marketing in a wasteful and inappropriate way. The solution to the problem is likely to lie in an adaptation of formal marketing techniques to suit the situation of small businesses, whereby owner-managers can benefit from the integrity of the marketing process but remain unburdened by the rigours of the technique. Small firm marketing also needs to be matched to the evolutionary process of small firms, and be appropriate to the business at each stage of its growth.

*Sara Carter*

## Small business strategy

Approaches to business strategy are well developed for large businesses and organizations, but until recently these contributions to business strategy appeared unsuited to small businesses. Some recent thinking suggests a convergence in thinking, although this has not been taken very far.

Two approaches to small business strategy have emerged. First, there are extraneous models, which define a pattern that it is alleged small firms must follow if successful growth is to be achieved. The processes involved are seen as mainly externally dictated, with the owner-manager constrained by these external forces. Owner-managers can undermine the process through poor decision making; success occurs where their behaviour and decisions fit the demands of external forces.

The second approach consists of entrepreneurial models, in which the owner-manager/entrepreneur's vision is central. All decisions revolve around the entrepreneur with little reliance on formal planning techniques, except where these are harnessed to the entrepreneur's vision. Owner-manager decisions can be swift, opportunistic, instinctive and bold, and are rarely committed to paper.

One practical difficulty which remains in this field is the perceived reluctance of small business owner-managers to take professional advice, or to engage in formal planning of any kind. There is evidence that few generate plans unless pressed to do so by their bank manager or accountant. Clearly there is a strong barrier to formal strategy and planning in this sector.

*James Curran*

## Statutory audit

A statutory audit refers to the verification by a professional public accountant of information in financial statements prepared by the management of an organization or enterprise. The purpose of an audit is to detect material misstatements in the information, thereby making the information more credible or believable in the eyes of financial statement users, such as shareholders and creditors. While audits are sometimes mandated by law (hence the term 'statutory audit'), an economic demand for auditing can arise whenever one party (for example, management) assumes stewardship over resources owned by another party (for example, shareholders).

The audit process begins with a set of financial statements, which can be viewed as containing numerous management assertions about transactions that took place during the reporting period, and their effects on the assets, liabilities, and shareholders' equity of an entity. Specifically, management asserts that transactions and their effects are valid (they actually exist) and complete (all are included in the financial statements).

In addition, legal rights and obligations (for example, asset ownership) are properly recognized. Finally, valuation, along with presentation and disclosure, are in accordance with generally accepted accounting principles.

The auditor's objective is to collect the type and quantity of evidence, at an appropriate time, to support a reasonable degree of belief or assurance that the assertions in the financial statements are true, in all material respects. The concept of reasonable assurance recognizes that there is only a probability (not certainty) that assertions are true, while the concept of materiality recognizes that there is an acceptable degree of imprecision in assertions. For example, the valuation of transactions need not be exactly correct.

After completing an examination, the auditor communicates his or her beliefs to financial statement users in a formal report which contains an expression of opinion. The auditor's opinion will usually be unqualified, but may be modified to reflect a lack of sufficient appropriate evidence or because the financial statements contain an uncorrected material misstatement.

*Dan A. Simunic*

## Strategic choice

The 'strategic choice' perspective was originally advanced as a corrective to the view that the way in which organizations are designed and structured has to be determined largely by their operational contingencies. This view overlooked the ways in which the leaders of organizations, whether private or public, were in practice able to influence organizational forms to suit their own preferences. Strategic choice drew attention to the active role of leading groups who had the power to influence the structures of their organizations through an essentially *political* process. It led to a substantial re-orientation of organizational analysis and stimulated debate on three key issues: the role of agency and choice in organizational analysis; the nature of organizational environment; and the relationship between organizational agents and the environment.

Since the intention was to redress an imbalance in organization theory, the exposition of strategic choice at the time contributed to the diversity of perspectives on the subject, along with other emerging approaches such as radical organization theory. Over twenty years later, the situation has changed considerably, in that the field is now extremely diversified with a wide range of competing perspectives.

While different theoretical perspectives or paradigms may be irreconcilable in their own philosophical terms, when applied to the study of organizational phenomena they are not necessarily 'incommensurable'. It does not follow from the attachment of different meanings to the same concept that reference is being made to wholly different phenomena. Without an attempt to draw upon, and even to reconcile, the insights offered by its various perspectives, organization studies will run a serious risk of becoming little more than an arena of 'clashing cymbals' (or indeed symbols), making little real theoretical advance and having nothing useful to say for practice either.

A major contribution of strategic choice analysis today derives from its potential to integrate some of these different perspectives. This integrative potential derives from the fact that strategic choice articulates a political process, which brings agency and structure into a dynamic tension and locates them within a significant context. In so doing, it not only bridges a number of competing perspectives but also adopts a dynamic, non-deterministic position. Strategic choice analysis has been from its inception critical of determinism within organizational analysis, which derives from the adoption of an essentially mechanistic paradigm. The model of strategic choice points to the possibility of a continuing adaptive learning cycle, but within a theoretical framework that locates 'organizational learning' within the context of organizations as sociopolitical systems. Strategic choice is thus consistent with a more *evolutionary* model of organizations, in which organizational learning and adaptation proceed towards not wholly predictable outcomes within the shifting forces of organizational politics. This model finds a parallel in the new evolutionary political economy that bids to revitalize microeconomics.

*John Child*

## Strategic competence

Firms compete in product markets on the basis of resources that they have either acquired externally or built up by themselves. The first kind of resources, even if not necessarily tangible, can be specified and hence bought and sold. The second kind is much more difficult to specify. It represents a slow accumulation of know-how and competences that are tacit, organization-wide, and for that reason, specific to a firm. Such competences become strategic or 'core' when they confer distinct benefits on a firm's customers and provide the firm with competitive advantages that are hard to discern and imitate.

Not all firms possess core competences, and those that do find it difficult to identify and nurture them. Their effective exploitation requires a corporate level perspective which does not always sit comfortably with the more extreme forms of decentralization to strategic business units that is sometimes associated with profit centre management. There are also problems concerning the longevity of competences; there may be points beyond which core competences become a trap for the firm. To put it another way, firms may need periodically to divest themselves of old competences to develop new ones.

Despite such problems, senior managers have found the strategic competence perspective to be of value. It provides a useful corrective to the natural tendencies shown by executives to focus unduly on the day-to-day competitive dynamics of current products in existing markets. It places a firm's future competitiveness firmly on the strategic agenda, and does so with a degree of clarity and persuasiveness that few other management concepts have been able to match.

*Max H. Boisot*

## Strategic marketing planning

Planning consists of looking ahead and making decisions about what to do in the future. For companies, the planning process is a systematic approach to these questions: Where is the company now and how did it get there? What is the future? Where does the company want to go? How can it get there? How much will this process cost? How can progress be measured?

There is considerable debate as to how strategic marketing planning should be conceptualized. Some writers focus on developing a sequence of steps which will define strategic planning as a logical procedure; others claim there is a need to understand decision-making processes in order to deal with the problems of biased thinking, and to recognize the political nature of the strategic planning process. Finally, there are those who point out that following logical procedures and processes is not enough, commenting that doing so is analogous to focusing on the computer program and neglecting the data itself; the focus, it is argued, should be on strategy content.

*John O'Shaughnessy*

## Strategic turnaround

Corporate turnaround has been variously defined, from recoveries from sustained losses which threaten the company's existence, decreasing revenues resulting in negative earnings and depletion of cash reserves, declining return on investment (ROI) or loss in industry position, declines in sales or market share, to relative declines in returns in relation to corporate growth rates.

Effective turnaround measures depend on the severity and nature of the decline. Crisis measures – those actions taken to ensure solvency in the short term – must be addressed quickly, while operational measures – cost-cutting and sales-increasing efforts – can be engaged in to strengthen a company with cash flow or net income problems. Companies with less obvious financial problems must look towards those strategic moves –

acquisitions or expansion of potential growth businesses and divestiture or redirection of failing businesses – that can position the company for long-term success.

Most of the recommended interventions in turnaround situations can be categorized as operational cost-cutting (efficiency-increasing) or debt-reduction measures, operational revenue-increasing (pricing and advertising) measures, strategic asset redeployment (retrenchment or expansion), or strategic repositioning (changes in product offerings or market scope).

*Joan Winn*

## Strategies, east Asian business

In recent decades, many countries in east Asia have experienced some of the world's highest economic growth rates. Business opportunities in this region will continue to abound into the twenty-first century. In order to take advantage of these developments, and to cooperate and compete effectively with east Asians, it is imperative to understand the mind-set which lies behind their business dealings. This mind-set influences both approaches to competition and cooperation, and the formulation and execution of business strategies.

In general, business people from Japan, South Korea, China, Hong Kong and Taiwan tend to draw their inspiration in the formulation and execution of business strategies from several ancient works, widely disseminated and read in east Asia but little known in the West. These works include Sun Tzu's *The Art of War* and Miyamoto Musashi's *The Book of Five Rings*, which are known to some extent in the West, and the lesser-known *The Three Kingdoms* and *The Thirty-Six Stratagems*. The important themes which underlie these works affect east Asia's overall approach to business cooperation and the formulation, reformulation and implementation of general business strategies.

*Rosalie L. Tung*

## Strategy, concept of

The concept of strategy applied to business and management is of relatively recent origin. Modern research in the area largely stems from Chandler's study of strategy and structure. Two approaches have typically been adopted to the concept of strategy. The first involves a consideration of the components or dimensions of strategy. The second involves the development of typologies of strategies or what are often called generic strategies.

Much of the writing in the area of strategy is overly rational and has a strong tendency to be prescriptive. It is also disproportionally dependent upon case studies rather than comparative research. There has been a lack of overarching or integrating theoretical perspectives, with theoretical ideas being borrowed from a variety of different subject areas. Strategy typically involves a determination of strategic objectives which often have only a limited relationship to official organizational goals and missions. The making of strategy is normally a senior management function, but many others may have an involvement depending on the nature of the company or organization in question.

The main components of strategy relate to strategic objectives, the definition of scope or domain, competitive advantage, synergy, resource deployment and organizational structure. A variety of typologies have been developed by writers in the strategy area. The best known of these stems from the work of Porter, who suggested just three generic strategies, namely a cost leadership strategy, a differentiation strategy and a focus strategy.

*Roger Mansfield*

## Strategy, implementation of

Traditional approaches to strategy implementation contribute to a damaging dichotomy between strategy formulation and interpretation. In turn, that dichotomy has many implications for managerial motivation, the effectiveness of the strategy formulation process and subsequent implementation problems in organizations.

Strategic gap analysis can help to identify implementation barriers. These can range from organizational inertia and organizational myopia to active resistance to change, designed error in organizations and problems relating to information flows, measurement systems and time horizons. Strategy implementation approaches in turn fall into three categories: unilateral, which rely on the use of power by the implementor; manipulative, in which implementation is viewed as a game or 'unfreeze-refreeze' process; or delegative, which aim to co-opt those involved in change by involving them in some way in the change process. Other relevant process issues include participation, developing strategic understanding in the organization, identifying champions and leaders, shaping the strategy process, moving towards the 'learning organization', the use of liaison units and the development of career paths and the design of management development programmes to enhance implementation capabilities. Ultimately, the key is to remove or overcome the formulation-implementation dichotomy.

*Frank V. Cespedes & Nigel Piercy*

## Strategy and buyer–supplier relationships

The importance of strategy in the area of buyer–supplier relationships is demonstrated by its use by state of the art companies such as Toyota, as well as in the fact that the average company spends more on bought-in resources than on those employed within its four walls.

It is only since the 1970s that purchasing has been recognized as having a place in strategy. However, there are many early examples where suppliers have yielded competitive advantage to their customers. More recent modelling and research has begun to emphasize the strategic role of the buyer–supplier relationship, although the majority of this work suffers from the fact that the causality relationships were not discussed, with the implication that a close or partnership relationship is possible simply by improving one or other feature of the relationship such as trust, length, number of suppliers or asset specificity.

A review of the state of the art situation, including a summary of the position taken by Toyota and their suppliers, shows that the creation of very close relations is a far more complex matter. Further analysis reveals that there are two primary features which are seen to cause the type of relationships demonstrated by Toyota, namely supplier coordination and supplier development. The other features of network sourcing are partly or mainly effects of supplier coordination and development.

Outside Japan, a Western version of the *kyoryoku kai* or supplier association has been developed. This successful early work has led to a number of important policy implications for British companies, professional institutes and government agencies alike. The future direction of work in this area is likely to centre around broader and deeper application of the *kyoryoku kai* as well as the search for other appropriate tools.

*Peter Hines*

## Strategy and information technology

It is widely recognized that one of the most important business questions today is the way in which one's organizational strategy impacts on the kind of information technology (IT) which is acquired and adopted in the company; and, conversely, the impact of IT systems on organizational strategy. This represents a considerable development since the early days of IT, when its main function was perceived to be the performance of number-based functions. Today, however, thanks to the rapid growth of global communications networks, IT is no longer a humble servant or even an ally of capital; instead, it is catalysing the possibility of a genuinely integrated world economy, raising large questions for politics, economics and even society as a whole. The challenge for companies is to employ people at top levels who understand the possibilities created by IT across the boundaries of traditional businesses, and who have the aspiration and the competences to bring these possibilities about.

*Prabhu S. Guptara*

## Strategy and internal marketing

The history of the development of the internal marketing concept is relatively short, but there have already been a wide variety of conceptual developments and influences. At least five major streams of thought can be seen as having an influence on its development, including services marketing, human resource management, quality management, organization theory and planning and strategy considerations.

From this background, a number of propositions may be said to describe the 'state of the art' in internal marketing. First, it is recognized that internal markets exist within organizations, and that these and the organization's external markets are often interdependent. Second, many external marketing approaches may be modified and adapted for use in internal marketing. Different levels of internal marketing can be identified, including strategic and operational levels. Internal marketplaces should be an important focus of attention in strategy formulation, and are critical to achieving effective strategy implementation. Finally, internal marketing has associated costs; explicit internal marketing activity can add significantly to the time and resources consumed in the planning activity.

As noted above, internal marketing can be vital to effective strategy implementation on a broader basis, helping to overcome internal resistance to change. Accordingly, managerial interest in internal marketing is great and growing. It is entirely possible that the greatest contribution of the internal marketing framework lies in the area of strategy formulation and has largely yet to be realized.

*Neil A. Morgan*

## Strategy, Japanese business

The Japanese enterprise system is based on three forms of industrial organization: factory, firm and inter-firm network. In the late nineteenth century, the introduction of the corporation into Japan revolutionized the Japanese business system, but Japan remained characterized by strong relationships both between firms and between firms and the government. Technical and economic change have thus resulted in an environment which has some of the properties of both a capitalist development state and a free market economy. The business strategies which have evolved in this environment have led to the establishment both of a group of robust institutions and of a dynamic which activates and interrelates them, the Japanese business system.

One of the results has been a transformation of industrial work. During the past twenty-five years, fundamentally new forms of manufacturing organization and strategy have matured in Japan. One example is 'knowledge works'. Knowledge works are categorically different from mass production factories, with a distinctive strategy and structure. Their aim is to maximize product and process innovations through organizational renewal while at the same time minimizing the time and cost of bringing products to market through organizational integration. Knowledge works are an example of the kind of business strategy that will take Japanese business into the twenty-first century.

*W. Mark Fruin*

## Strategy making, politics of

The politics of strategy making is one of the core areas of management theory and practice. This centrality derives from the way the subject has emerged from among the specialist research on strategy, decision making and corporate politics. Consequently, an understanding of the politics of strategy formation leads to an appreciation of the more general develop-ment of the strategy and organization fields.

Political analysts of strategy have drawn attention to the varieties of power exercised from within and outside the organization and their impact on decision making. They have uncovered an array of sources of power and, in particular, the problems of those decision makers who endure 'powerlessness'. The subject has produced some potent frameworks for understanding the politics of strategy, especially in the case of unobtrusive power and the management of meaning.

The strength of the literature lies in the way scholars have taken seriously the processual dimension of strategy. Leading exponents have been responsible for major advances in comprehending the more subjec-tive or interpretative aspects of strategic activity. In so doing, they have forged strong links with other theories of management. The limitations of the field arise from its qualities; it is questionable, for example, how far the hidden political features of strategy are recognized. Equally, the practical relevance of academic work on power and strategy still has not been fully demonstrated to practitioners.

*Richard Whipp*

## Strategy and rationality

Rationality and strategy are both very active areas of research, so any account of their inter-relationship must remain open to subsequent revi-sion or extension. The general theory of rationality incorporates many diverse but distinctive forms of rationality, together with their meta-ra-tional relationships. 'Rationality', thus conceived, is not a single idea but an elaborate and interwoven fabric of principles and prescriptions for cognition and behaviour; but so too is strategy. However, one important distinction between strategy and rationality pertains to the diverse nature of strategic entities versus the nature of rational agents, although it has been argued that this difference has been overplayed.

In strategic management (strategy) the term 'rational model' is normally associated with the use of formal strategic plans. Each form of rationality corresponds closely in meaning with some well-documented concept within the field of strategy. The general theory of rationality involves meta-rational relations and criteria that lend a complex structure to the set of rationalities. This theory also illuminates the interface relationships between corresponding strategy concepts. In addition, there are many new types of strategic entity and rational agent made possible by technological change.

*Alan E. Singer*

## Strategy and technological development

Technological change is both an outcome and an important driver of competition. As technological developments lead to shorter life cycles and as the degree of national and international competition increases the ability to develop, introduce and commercialize new products and services quickly, as well as the capacity to rationalize, administrative and production processes become a prominent prerequisite of economic success. Thus, the anticipation of and participation in technological changes are crucial elements in the process of establishing and securing competitive advantages.

Technology can be defined as the entire set of capabilities, the theoretical knowledge, practical know-how and equipment, that is used to develop, produce and deliver products and services. Since tangible or intangible technological assets are incorporated in virtually everything which is done by firms, technological change can influence industry structures as well as corporate competitiveness through its impact upon almost any activity. Therefore, technological change is not merely a question which only concerns the management of research and development (R&D). Rather, the competition-induced compulsion to renew technology bases and add to them is an issue calling for overall strategic guidance and cross-functional collaboration.

*Klaus Macharzina & Dietmar Brodel*

## Stress

The term 'stress' is used in a variety of ways, often synonymously with pressure. Understanding of stress has developed from both medical and psychological research. Originally it was viewed from an engineering perspective and seen as an external force on the person giving rise to strain and finally permanent damage. It is now widely viewed as the physiological or psychological reaction which occurs when individuals meet a threat or challenge and the individuals perceive, consciously or subconsciously, that it is beyond their immediate capacity. Long-term, unacceptably high levels of threat lead to chronic conditions which we know as stress. Physical, mental, emotional and behavioural reactions can result.

In recent years organizations have become much more aware of the need to help employees manage stress. Help has taken a number of different forms, ranging from counselling to cope with post-traumatic stress to stress prevention by creating a healthy environment, staff development and organizational development. However, attention is likely to be focused on these issues still more strongly given the recent trend towards litigation by employees against employers in connection with work-related illnesses, especially in the USA. Stress is likely to remain a critical issue from an individual, team and organizational perspective.

*Jane Cranwell-Ward*

## Sun Tzu

Predating Carl von Clausewitz's *On War* by some twenty-two centuries, *Sun Tzu Ping Fa* – often called *Sun Tzu's Art of War* in English – is the oldest extant systematic military treatise in the world, yet its fundamental ideas on strategy have been described as ageless. Overall, the book demonstrates the Chinese emphasis on the concrete and specific, awareness of complex multiplicity and interrelationships, the eschewal of the abstract and absolute, and esteem for both hierarchy and nature. Many of the principles expounded in the text are considered to apply outside purely military spheres, in particular in diplomacy, interpersonal relationships and business strategy. Although direct transference of Sun Tzu's principles of strategy to business is not without problems, never the less his work can serve as a source of information for contemporary strategists.

*Yao-Su Hu & Pierre Berthon*

## Supply chain

Supply chain management (SCM) consists of a number of linked managerial approaches which are deliberately considered from the viewpoint that a given organization is but one constituent member in an interconnected, interacting and interdependent chain or network of other enterprises. The essence of the approach is that all groups, individuals and organizations act as both customers of and suppliers to other enterprises in at least part of their total range of activities.

From this viewpoint the critical managerial issues relate to how best to organize such a network of potentially disparate interests so that both individually and collectively the constituent organizations are more effective compared to competitor groupings. The process is further complicated by the reality that organizations at early stages in a particular chain will also be part of other chains, that is, they are nodes in an extended network.

In competitive terms SCM is partly about improving basic capability at all points in one's chosen chain and partly about emphasizing and developing those aspects of supply chain performance which positively differentiate the chosen chain from competitor ones. Organizations at nodal points in a network of chains must satisfy the minimum requirements of their immediate customers but may be influenced to contribute more effectively to the chain which is managed more pro-actively to support mutual supply chain objectives.

The subject draws on a number of managerial processes: customer service is the major driving force; time is a major competitive lever; communications across organizational boundaries must be free flowing; other flows of materials, investment and technology (for example) must also take place; wastes, however, are frequently observable and can be tackled, often through the use of control systems. Different managerial structures are possible while the principles of dealing with the other supply chain organizations as partners and not adversaries opens up new opportunities. Aspects of physical distribution along the chain must also be catered for.

SCM is important because it brings together aspects of competitive business structures and behaviour through an understanding of the importance of the customer and the improvement potential of a full understanding of the role of quality in all aspects of life. It has the potential to provide new frameworks and understanding about working effectively in complex organizational environments. Seen from this network point of view its importance has only been recognized in the West since the late 1980s although some of the best practice models come from excellent Japanese organizational practice for twenty-five years prior to that.

*Douglas K. Macbeth*

## Supply-side economics

In one sense, supply-side economics is the oldest economics there is. The 'supply side' is nothing other than the capacity of the economy to produce under normal conditions, that is when no shocks are unsettling it; a concept similar to that of a 'normal year' in agriculture. It may never occur, but it is a useful benchmark.

The early economists' concern with demand was simply that it should generate stable prices, be suitable for the normal needs of trade and not destabilize an economy inevitably subject to the business cycle. The main focus of economic studies by early writers such as Smith and Mill was on conditions that would favour prosperity in the sense of maximum capacity to produce under normal circumstances for the supply side. However, following the Great Depression and the work of Keynes, attention switched to the demand side, with an emphasis on producing full employment.

More recently, interest in the supply side has begun to revive. This revival is due both to the perceived failure of demand management in the 1960s and 1970s, and to the intellectual development of monetarism and especially to the new classical economics with its rational expectations assumption that people are as capable in their use of information as in their other decision making. Failures such as weak growth and high unemployment now had to be explained in terms of poor supply side policies. Theory and evidence now tends to suggest that poor policies can explain both poor static or allocative efficiency and poor dynamic performance. These developments have restored the long-term issues of an appropriate environment for successful modern capitalism – that is, supply-side economics – to the centre of public debate.

*A.P.L. Minford*

## Systems

The word 'system' is always taken to refer to a set of elements joined together to make a complex whole. The word may be used to refer to an abstract whole (the principles constituting a system of justice, say,) or a physical whole (a railway engine); but in both cases the justification for using the word is the same: the whole is seen as having properties which make it 'more than the sum of its parts'. This is the everyday-language expression of the idea of so-called 'emergent properties', that is to say properties which have no meaning in terms of the parts which make up the whole. Thus, a heap consisting of the individual parts of a bicycle does not have vehicular potential. However, when the parts are linked together in a particular structure to make the bicycle as a whole, which does have the potential to get someone with the ability to ride from A to B, that is an emergent property of the bicycle as a whole.

The idea of emergent properties is the single most fundamental systems idea and to use this (and other) systems ideas in a conscious organized way is to do some 'systems thinking'. To use systems thinking to tackle some perceived problem is to take 'a systems approach' to it. Since the field of management deals with complex matters, and systems thinking has been developed to cope with complexity, it is not surprising to find systems thinking closely associated with the field. Indeed, many systems ideas and several versions of both systems thinking and a systems approach have all been developed in work on management problems.

*Peter Checkland*

## Systems analysis and design

Systems analysis and design is a systematic approach to the improvement of business through the help of computer-based information systems. The people who accomplish these tasks are known as systems analysts. The systems development life cycle approach to systems development took hold in the 1960s and it remained highly popular throughout the 1980s. Recently, CASE (computer-aided software engineering) tools have been adopted by many systems analysts. CASE tools automate many traditionally labour-intensive tasks, while also adding new capabilities to the systems analyst's work.

To analyse, design and document a system, a systems analyst might draw entity-relationship diagrams, create data flow diagrams, build a data dictionary and data repository, provide detail on process specifications and logic, and draw structure charts. In addition an analyst needs to design the output, input and user interface.

New, alternative approaches to the structured development methodology are also being tried. These methods include prototyping, project champions, ETHICS, Soft Systems Methodology, Multiview and using metaphorical analysis. Object-oriented systems analysis and design is becoming increasingly important.

*Julie E. Kendall & Kenneth E. Kendall*

# T

## Taxation, corporate

Almost every country in the world levies some kind of tax on company profits. Yet companies are, in a sense, no more than the sum of their employees and shareholders, linked together with customers and suppliers by a web of contracts. Since most of these people will be paying tax themselves, the role of a separate tax on companies is not straightforward. The strongest justification for a separate corporate tax is as a withholding tax on investment income, in the absence of an adequate capital gains tax. Other possible arguments for a separate tax, based on the benefits of limited liability or on the value of public services to the company, are less persuasive.

The key features of any given corporate tax system are the base on which tax is levied, the rate, and the relationship with other parts of the tax system. The immediate effect of the corporate tax is to transfer funds from company to government. But the structure of the tax system can alter real decisions on how much, in what and in which country to invest. It can also alter financial decisions on how to fund investment, and on what proportion of profits to pay out as dividends, as companies try to minimize their tax liability. The actual impact on financial decisions will depend on the level of integration between corporate and personal taxes, and on the relative personal tax burdens on dividends, interest and capital gains. That said, tax is only one of many factors involved. Investment is driven mainly by the likely returns, and managers will always trade-off the benefits of a low-tax financial structure against the non-tax costs. Empirical studies indicate that non-tax factors dominate most important corporate decisions.

The growth of international capital and product markets puts new strains on domestic corporate tax systems: on the one hand, companies have more opportunity to arrange their affairs to reduce their overall tax burden but, on the other, they face new obstacles to seeking out the most profitable investments, as more than one government seeks to share in their profits. Fundamental questions are raised about whether corporate taxes are sustainable in a world capital market and how governments can best cooperate to raise revenue without limiting new investment opportunities.

*Lucy Chennells*

## Teams in manufacturing

The terms 'team' and 'teamwork' have been applied in a wide variety of ways within manufacturing industry. Sometime they refer to fairly vague notions of improving cross-departmental cooperation and cultivating more constructive interpersonal and inter-group relations within a manufacturing plant, without any implications for the way jobs are defined or work organized. In other circumstances, they refer to comprehensively innovative forms of manufacturing organization, based around multi-skilled operations teams, usually consisting of between ten and twenty workers. Authorized to make decisions with considerable autonomy, each team carries out most aspects of the manufacture of a product, family of products or portion of a larger manufacturing process. To achieve this, individual team members need to exercise considerable discretion and flexibility in their duties. This contrasts with the highly prescribed, routinized and rigid shop floor jobs characteristic of earlier forms of work organization based on scientific management or Taylorism.

*Richard Holti*

## Technology and organizations

In the study of organizations, 'technology' is often defined as an operational tool, the design of which is dictated by the demands of efficiency within given market conditions. In the past technology has been treated as an independent or exogenous causal factor shaping organizational design. It is evidently the case that machines designed to transform materials, information or people (through means such as medicine or transport) can incorporate design principles that are not readily understood outside an engineering discipline and are therefore not easily challenged. However, organizational theorists have questioned the immutability of engineering design along a number of dimensions.

Taken more broadly, technology can be interpreted as all the means used by humans to control their environment, including bureaucracy or organization itself. Thus, like organizational structure, technological configurations can be regarded as modes of control or of means of reducing uncertainty in the exercise of managerial power. As such, they can provide more or less ability to monitor and meter their performance by central management. Communications and information technology (CIT) can be seen to be rapidly taking the place of bureaucratic modes of operational metering and monitoring within contemporary society.

As well as contributing to the value-adding functions of the organization, technology has always been incorporated into the service provided by many consumer products. Competitions or contests between rival corporations are now increasingly based on product innovation rather than price; hence the study of the management of innovation and of means of creating conditions conducive to creativity among organizational members has recently experienced an enormous revival. Nevertheless it remains true that the speed of technological innovation is presently accompanied by enormous social costs. Without adjustment in national and international infrastructures designed to cope with technological change, long-term effects on wider society may ultimately be described as destabilizing.

*Ray Loveridge*

## Technology strategy, international

Technological change as a response to outside environmental forces has in the past to a large degree determined the fate of individuals, organizations and nation states. Today more than ever before, the key to survival hinges on the ability to capitalize on the opportunities of technological change and implementation. The present is a very exciting time for both the understanding and the practice of management and technology; there is a growing awareness that the success of organizations is directly dependent on the effective management of technology in order to create competitive advantage.

The management of technology has as its goal the improvement of the products and the productive capability of an organization. There are a number of models of technology management, but none are considered to be universally applicable. There are different international perspectives on the management of technology; within the Triad (Europe, with Germany at the core, Asia, with Japan at the core and North America, with the USA at the core), there are different approaches to the value of management or technology activities. One important cause of these differences is differing emphases on technology in higher education within the various regions; for example, more than 25 per cent of all US university students take some type of business degree, while over 50 per cent of students in Japan and Germany take technical degrees. This fact alone may result in different approaches to the management of technology.

There are also different concepts of the role of technology within the organization. Technology is not the sole domain of the research and development personnel of an organization. Successful business use of technology requires strategic decisions concerning factors such as innovation, knowledge, time, value-added costs, strategic alliances as well as other functional areas such as marketing, production and finance. Understanding the relative contributions of several different models of technology, and how these models relate to one another, can lead to a greater appreciation of the importance of the management of technology.

*Pat Joynt*

## Telecommunications

Telecommunications technology has improved the way we communicate with and understand each other, and has altered the way we do business throughout the world. The telecommunications infrastructures have been undergoing revolutionary changes worldwide since the 1970s.

The rapid and dynamic changes that have taken place and those still to come pose a challenge to both researchers and practitioners. Research has a great potential in assisting the effective use of telecommunication systems to gain competitive advantages. Topics of interest to researchers of telecommunication systems include, but are not limited to: interconnection of local area networks; personal wireless communications; global network interconnection; distributed computing and distributed databases; rural telecommunications and performance management of telecommunication systems.

Clearly, telecommunication is the technology that will provide the lifeline of our civilization in the next century. With the increasing globalization of national economies and growing interdependence among the nations of the world, the need for communications cannot be overemphasized. Rapidly evolving communications technologies certainly have the capacity to integrate the world. The challenge is to provide universal access to all citizens of the world, irrespective of their geographical and national boundaries.

*Sufi Nazem, Yong Shi & Heeseok Lee*

## Teleworking

The basic concept behind teleworking is that workers can work 'at a distance' from the office site, at their own times, by using advanced computing and telecommunications technologies then electronically transferring the results to the office or to another location. Teleworking constitutes an additional step taken by organizations in their search for increased flexibility in response to the rapidly changing business and human resources environment. The growing need for flexible work patterns may be regarded as stemming from social, economic and technological developments. As employers reorganize their businesses, focusing on optimizing productivity and reducing costs, they are also trying to respond to many of the challenges facing the modern employee – work and family obligations, career development and stressful lifestyles. The rapid and far-reaching advances of telecommunication devices during the last decade has afforded employers the option of employing salaried workers remotely from their office, in more supportive environments for performing tasks requiring long hours of uninterrupted concentration. The employment of remote workers without constant continuous presence at the workplace makes it possible to work from home or from distributed work centres. One form of telework, the home-based employment, was quite common historically, and a conventional form of work before the Industrial Revolution led to the currently dominant work pattern – working in offices according to a fixed time schedule. An attempt to quantify the overall losses or gains from teleworking to the individual worker, the employer and society would be problematic due to the multiplex concept.

*Judith Richter*

## Term structure of interest rates

Financial securities that promise one or more fixed cash payments in the future are known as fixed interest securities. Examples include central government bills and bonds, local government (municipal) bonds, corporate bonds and mortgages. The rates of return offered on these various securities differ for a number of reasons, including the risk of default and the tax treatment of the promised payments. The term structure of interest rates describes the relationship between fixed interest securities that differ only in their time to maturity, that is, the length of time until the principal amount of the loan is repaid. The differences between interest rates for payments at different maturities reflect expectations about future interest rates and the preferences of investors.

Pure discount (zero coupon) bonds make a single cash payment at a fixed future date. The rates of return on pure discount bonds are the interest rates that make up the term structure. In many practical situations, the pure discount bond market does not cover the full maturity spectrum of all fixed interest securities, and sophisticated mathematical techniques are required to estimate the term structure. In addition, models have been developed to describe the behaviour of the term structure over time. Knowledge of the term structure is important for the accurate comparison of fixed interest securities, particularly newly issued securities against existing securities, and for understanding the future direction of general interest rate movements.

*James M. Steeley*

## Third party intervention

Any process of bargaining between parties with different interests in its outcomes creates some risk that they will not be able to agree and, accordingly, that they will break off negotiations. Where the parties are able to select other bargaining partners with whom they can reach agreement, failure to agree presents no problem. Where, as in the case of bargaining between employers and workers, this option either is not open or open only at considerable cost to both parties, it is generally considered that some alternative course of action which avoids breakoff or breakdown needs to be available to the parties. This mechanism may take one of three forms, which differ in the amount of discretion assigned to the third party.

*Conciliation* is a method of resolving differences by involving an impartial third party in the actual negotiating process, the objective being to assist the parties in exploring other methods of resolving their differences and to arrive at an agreement which accords with their values and interests. Of the three methods, this allows the parties the most discretion to decide the issue for themselves on their own terms.

*Mediation* is a method of achieving the same result but where an independent third party is either required by law or requested by the parties to make one or more recommendations on the way in which the difference might be resolved, leaving the parties some discretion to decide the form that any resolution should take.

*Arbitration* is a method of resolving differences or disputes between two (or more) parties over the establishment, interpretation or application of the terms and conditions of a contract. It involves an independent third party who is either required by law or requested by the parties to make an award on the disputed issue(s) after considering the parties' evidence and arguments.

These mechanisms are often seen to provide an alternative method of resolving disputes to those found in the courts of law, where similar processes are often followed. Mediation and arbitration, for example, are being adopted increasingly either to settle disputes which do not lend themselves to resolution in terms of right and wrong (in which area the courts are well-equipped) or to take advantage of their greater informality and lower cost. All three mechanisms offer distinct advantages for cases where disputes are concerned with the interests of the contending parties and where the constraining framework of law is at best replaced by a framework of convention developed largely by the parties themselves.

*George F. Thomason*


## Time management

Time is perhaps the most valuable resource in any organization or personal endeavour. Even though time is an endless commodity, it is the one resource that is constantly depleted, cannot be reproduced, and once lost can never be recovered. Time management is the art and science of using time effectively.

Time management is a key element of effective management. Organizations and people who manage time well are better equipped to face both the personal and professional challenges of the business world. Time has become not only a tool for organizational study, but also a means to gain competitive advantage in the marketplace. Time-based management, cycle-time reduction and value-added time have become key features of competitive strategy. The same factors apply to the management of time in business management as in personal management. Goal setting, objective setting, priority setting and understanding of the critical factors that rob an organization of this resource are critical to effective time management. Actions designed to prevent lost time and to use time as a competitive advantage in getting goods and services to market more quickly are a large-scale application of personal and organizational time management. While it is critical to set realistic goals and objectives, it is essential that tasks once scheduled are periodically reviewed to ensure completion in a timely manner. In addition, goals must be set so as to make the most effective use of the time available.

*Kathie S. Smith*

## Total quality management

Total quality management (TQM) means different things to different people. An operations management person may associate it with a modern management approach adapted to cope with the recent and acute worldwide quality management problem; a quality management person may emphasize the quality origins of TQM and describe it as the climax of the stepwise evolution of quality-oriented schemes and techniques; and a production person may see it as yet another manifestation of improved productivity. In fact, the reality is that TQM partakes of all these cases.

In the USA, the quality movement developed through three stages, inspection, statistical quality control and quality assurance, the latter leading ultimately to the zero defects movement. Meanwhile in Japan, organizations using the early theories of Deming and Juran began developing the quality organization. At the core of this new philosophy was the concept of continuous improvement (known as *kaizen* in Japan). This implies not only a set of techniques but also a cultural change within the company; the phrase 'total quality management' implies total commitment on the part of the firm. In particular this requires participation by the human resource function to motivate and train employees, and the information function, to ensure that relevant information is quickly disseminated.

Dissemination of the TQM concept has been very rapid, reaching industry, research, education and healthcare. Managers seeking solutions to organizational problems often adopted TQM as a cure-all or panacea. There have been many successes for organizations using TQM, but there have also been many failures.

*Miryam Barad*

## Tourism management

Few industries have evolved as rapidly, broadly and prosperously as tourism in the relatively short span of recent decades. Despite its age-old origins, its phenomenal expansion followed the Second World War when, prompted by its envisioned economic prospects, both developed and developing countries rediscovered tourism and seriously committed themselves to, and heavily invested in, its development and promotion locally, nationally and internationally.

As this unprecedented worldwide popularity continued to spread at a steady rate, tourism quickly evolved into a vigorous industry, an internationally competitive business and a global trade, ranked just below the oil industry, then on a par with it, then above it and now as the largest industry in the world, according to the published data and estimates of the inter-governmental World Tourism Organization (WTO) and the industry-driven World Travel and Tourism Council (WTTC). Notwithstanding this already impressive and well-established magnitude, tourism is now believed to be in its infancy, about to soar to untold heights in the millennium ahead.

This recent burgeoning of global tourism has not been limited to its business and operational aspects only. Its pronounced economic towering has inspired the planting of its seeds on the fertile grounds of university campuses. Today, tourism occupies an impressive spread of academic footholds worldwide, with perhaps over a thousand institutions of higher education committed to offering training and education programmes in tourism and to developing knowledge in this new field of study, some up to doctoral level.

*Jafar Jafari & Abraham Pizam*

## Trade unions

Trade unions are associations established for the purpose of maintaining or improving the conditions of the working lives of wage earners. Although some contemporary unions may trace their origins to the medieval guilds, the present day form of trade unions primarily is the result of the Industrial Revolution and the large wage-earning class which it created. Unions exist in almost every contemporary nation-state, where they are typically considered to be a principal representative of the interests of employees.

There are different varieties of union, but most can be categorized as falling into one of two types: social democratic unions, which have a strong political function and are often associated with a labour or socialist political party, and business unions, which are purely unions of workers without strong political interest. One of the most important tasks of the union is collective bargaining for workplace conditions and terms of employment on behalf of union members. The right to strike remains the primary basis of union power.

The contemporary era has been difficult for trade unions, with declining membership and harsher legislation in at least some developed countries. However, they continue to be an important feature of most nations, and are generally considered to be a fundamental pillar of democracy. They are likely to continue to play a significant role in society.

*Roy Adams*

## Training

Training is any systematic process used by organizations to develop employees' knowledge, skills, behaviours, or attitudes in order to contribute to the achievement of organizational goals. It is also referred to as human resource development. Training is used to improve the performance of employees in their present positions; to prepare workers for positions to which they are likely to be promoted in the future; and to respond to changes in the workplace, such as new technology and systems, internationalization, global competitiveness and the need for greater service orientation. In addition, training is provided by governments and organizations to improve the future employability of the hard-core unemployed, under-employed minority groups and workers whose present skills are becoming obsolete. Training is directed toward employees at all levels of the organization, from workers on the shop floor through to executives, and covers applications from specific technical skills to complex social and cognitive skills.

Most organizations dedicate substantial resources to training and see it as an integral function of achieving their goals. In the USA alone training expenditures have been estimated to be as high as $100 billion per year and training professionals have estimated that organizations' commitment to training is likely to grow.

Despite its pervasiveness in industry, however, training must be viewed as only one of several human resource interventions used to improve the match between the knowledge, skills, behaviours or attitudes possessed by employees and those required in particular jobs. Alternatives to training include changing the way in which personnel are selected; changing job requirements through job redesign or technological change; and changing the way in which performance is managed (for example, introducing goal setting, feedback or reward systems). All of these alternatives can be used in place of, or in conjunction with, training initiatives.

The development of training programmes involves three phases: (1) training needs analysis; (2) training design and delivery; and (3) training evaluation. In the first phase, specific training needs which address organizational objectives are identified. Within the training design and delivery phase, training objectives are set, specific training content is identified and principles that will maximize learning and transfer of skills are applied. In training evaluation, criteria are established and a method of evaluation is developed: (1) to ensure that training has met its objectives; and (2) to make necessary changes to improve the programme's effectiveness.

*Paul Taylor*

## Training, economics of

The economics of work-based training comprises two overlapping theories: human capital and institutionalism. Human capital theory, assuming rational individualism and competitive markets, analyses the incentives to employers and trainees to develop skills. Its view of the training outputs of an unregulated market system is broadly optimistic. Its extension to include recruitment costs, informational attributes and wage rigidities results in a more institutionally-orientated and less optimistic account. Further institutional influences evident in national training patterns include industrial relations, labour market structure, collective organization, system-wide interdependences and historical path dependence.

Economic interest in training is generated by several attributes. Vocational learning, of which it is part, contributes strongly to the economic performance of companies, regions and countries. Increased knowledge and skill are associated with higher pay; unequal skill is an important cause of economic inequality. Public unemployment policies today emphasize training rather than job creation and income maintenance. Training is central to theories of internal labour markets, efficiency, wages and labour market segmentation. Finally, market failure is endemic to training, creating a potential case for public intervention.

*Paul Ryan*

## Transaction cost economics

The origins of transaction cost economics (TCE) can be traced back to a classic article on the theory of the firm by Coase. In it, he tried to explain the existence of multiple person hierarchies (firms) in terms of market failures, which he thought were due to the high costs of exchanging (transacting) in markets. Coase later extended his analysis to attribute the existence of law and the State to market transaction costs.

After a long gestation period, these ideas have been taken up, elaborated, extended and criticized by numerous economists. The emergent new perspective has found applications not only in explanations of economic phenomena, such as the market, the firm, the transnational and the State, but also in sociology, economic history, organization studies and strategic management. It would appear that TCE has the potential to transform not only economics and social science, but also, perhaps, to provide the elements of a unified social sciences research programme. It comes as no surprise therefore that Coase was awarded the 1991 Nobel Prize for economics. Moreover, the 1993 Prize went to a disciple of this approach, North. In his work, North has attempted to explain the whole of economic history by pursuing a brand of TCE theorizing that goes beyond conventional economic thinking. This school of economic analysis is also currently finding applications in macroeconomics and is rapidly influencing both government policy on industry and competition, and the competitive and corporate strategies of firms.

Despite its widespread influence, TCE has been the focus of widespread criticism from various vantage points, such as economics, sociology and management studies, and a number of alternative perspectives have been proposed. Nevertheless, the TCE perspective has substantial implications for both public strategy on industrial competition and for the competitive and corporate strategies of firms. The policy implication of conventional industrial economics and organization has traditionally been that oligopoly and monopoly are forms of market failure. TCE raises doubts about this prescription. If large firms result from transaction costs-reducing conduct, efficiency will be the result. TCE also provides firms with an account of the conditions under which they should make or buy, integrate or disintegrate, or export or undertake foreign direct investment. It suggests the most appropriate form of market and hierarchy.

*Christos Pitelis*

## Transfer pricing

Many intra-firm transactions are non-market transactions and therefore lack a market determined price. A transfer price is the price assigned to such non-market intra-firm transfers. Transfer prices are especially important for multinational corporations, since a parent company typically has subsidiaries or branches in other countries, and transfers are often made between the component parts of the multinational.

As the world has become more internationally dependent, these transactions and the associated transfer prices have come under increased scrutiny. The fear often expressed by governments is that a multinational corporation may manipulate transfer prices in order to transfer profits from one country to another, and thereby affect various government policies. Most notably, transfer prices can affect the tax revenues of both the home and host country.

A general international consensus is that the appropriate transfer price is the 'arm's length' price. This is the price that would be charged by two unrelated parties. However, it is often difficult to find such a comparable transaction.

*Timothy J. Goodspeed*

## Transportation models

Transportation models are mathematical aids that are used to facilitate decision-making processes concerning transportation projects. To fulfil its role a model must meet four requirements: (1) describe the perform-ance of a transportation system; (2) analyse and forecast transportation demand; (3) set guidelines for supplying transportation services; and (4) match supply, demand and performance of transportation systems. Thus, four types of model exist, one for each need: performance models, demand models, supply models, and equilibrium and evaluation models, respec-tively. Although non-discrete mathematics can be present in the four, they generally utilize discrete mathematics. Statistical techniques are also used in many of the models.

The need for using models in transportation decision making has paralleled an increasing perception of the complexity of most transporta-tion systems. Such systems are entities designed to serve multiple, con-flicting goals and usually consume considerable amounts of resources. As such, it seems natural to make use of the universal language of mathemat-ics in order to aid transportation managers.

One of the first uses of a transportation model took place in Germany around 100 years ago. However, in practice transportation planning and decision making, the use of transportation models, did not become a well-established science until about ten years after the end of the Second World War. Although transportation models have evolved a great deal since then, today nobody in the transportation profession would consider conducting a transportation project at the strategic, tactical or operational level without using any sort of mathematical model. Thus, all profession-als dealing with quantitative aspects of transportation systems must have some training in transportation modelling.

*Luiz F. Autran M. Gomes*

# U–Z

## Venture capital

The impact of venture capital on Western industrial economies, in recent years, has been immense. It has backed new industrial enterprises that could not have taken shape in any other way. Venture capital transactions have facilitated large-scale restructuring by making possible the division of large industrial organizations into smaller, more efficient units. Other transactions have enabled small industrial units to grow. From the point of view of managers of industrial enterprises, venture capital backing has often been regarded as more satisfactory than going to the stock market, with the unpredictable consequences of ownership by large numbers of shareholders.

There is no universally accepted definition of venture capital, but for the purposes of this entry it refers to capital that meets four criteria. First, venture capital is provided by institutional investors or by funds, rather than individuals, put together for investment in certain types of transaction. Second, it is invested in companies that are not listed on a stock market. Third, investment opportunities are identified by the managers of the institution or fund as being likely to yield a rate of return commensurate with the risk. Fourth, the essential core of venture capital is equity, which provides the investor with the potential of substantial capital growth. However, equity is commonly geared up with debt, and a range of other financial instruments may be involved.

*Charles R. Richardson*

## Whistleblowing

Ethical conflict in organizations has increased as the complexity of working practices has increased. Most employees will experience situations in which they could blow the whistle, or see others doing so. A working definition of whistleblowing is the unauthorized disclosure of information that an employee reasonably believes evidences the contravention of any law, rule or regulation, code of practice, or professional statement, or that involves mismanagement, corruption, abuse of authority, or danger to public or worker health and safety.

A comparison of US and UK law suggests that whistleblowing is devoid of significant protection in the UK, but public sector whistleblowers in the USA are better provided for. Most whistleblowers suffer harm, however justified their cause. Research on whistleblowing shows that the average whistleblower could be regarded as a model employee. A suitable code of practice can assist in harnessing the energies of whistleblowers.

*Gerald Vinten*

## Wholesaling

Wholesaling is a business function which can be best described as playing an intermediary role between the manufacturer and the retailer. As a consequence, wholesalers do not have a high level of visibility in the eyes of the final consumer. However, they do provide a broad range of services which are indispensable to both retailers and manufacturers, and which ultimately lead to a more effective system of distribution for products. The functions provided for the manufacturer include market coverage, selling, stockholding, order processing, market research and customer support, while benefits to retailers include availability, assortment, the breaking of bulk supplies into smaller units, credit, service and advice. In line with changes in the role of manufacturers and retailers in most countries, the wholesale function has also undergone some shifts in emphasis, affecting both the importance of wholesalers and the roles they play.

*Sean Ennis*

## Women in management and business

International Women's Day is held in March of each year, providing an annual opportunity to review opportunities available to the world's women. Each year's findings are similar: while the world's women are making progress, much more progress is possible. According to a 1993 United Nations report, women remain an under-utilized human resource worldwide.

In many countries, differential treatment for women includes poor access to basic safety, security, nutrition or health care resources; in other countries, differential treatment frequently is related to educational opportunities; and in other parts of the world – particularly industrialized nations – differential treatment often is reflected in unequal pay for women and men. For example, the International Labour Organization (ILO) reported that Japanese women earned about 57 per cent of men's earnings for comparable work, while in Norway women typically earned 85–93 per cent of what men were paid in the mid-1990s. Available data also show that women in business worldwide frequently have limited access to professional and managerial jobs.

Just as women in different countries face a range of challenges, women in the same country also might experience distinctive obstacles in becoming part of the paid workforce. Women are by no means a monolithic group either within or across nations.

Furthermore, national cultures differ in how they view women's actual or potential contribution to the paid workforce and, as a result, different theories have emerged to explain women's contributions to this area. Cultural differences also may account for the barriers that women face in becoming managers, and cultural stereotypes about women can play a large role in shaping the educational, legal and organizational opportunities offered to women. Just as women in different nations are not likely to face the same challenges to paid workforce participation, neither are they likely to share the same aspirations, hopes or dreams.

*Barbara Parker & Ellen A. Fagenson*

## Women in management in Japan

The distinctive features of the Japanese management system discriminate severely against women. The practices of long-term employment, internal promotion and wage increases on the basis of age and years of service (*nenko*), and in-company training, governing the internal labour markets of large Japanese firms, apply exclusively to the core, predominantly male workers. Women constitute a high proportion of the flexible periphery workers excluded from the core jobs. Their exclusion is reinforced by many discriminatory personnel practices and justified by a strong familial ideology. Increasing economic and social pressures for change in recent years have prompted Japanese firms to introduce new personnel strategies to utilize the abilities of women, yet without disrupting the existing work norms and the stability of the male career hierarchy.

*Alice Lam*

## Work ethic

The work ethic is an important concept, since working is an essential activity in every economy. A considerable amount of cross-national research evidence is available and some findings have practical policy relevance. The original historically derived concept of a 'Protestant work ethic' is no longer appropriate, since particularly high work ethic (centrality of work) scores exist in Japan, Israel and Slovenia. However, almost everywhere one or more of four values are thought to characterize working; it can be seen as a burden, a constraint, a responsibility, or a social contribution. Another useful distinction shows that people distinguish between work as an obligation or an entitlement. The USA, for instance, has very low entitlement expectations while several European countries have high scores on entitlement and Japan is in a middle position.

It should also be noticed that the term 'work' in the work ethic concept should include many important but usually unpaid activities, like rearing children, looking after a household, and doing voluntary jobs for local as well as international societies and charities.

The most policy-relevant practical findings from the available literature suggests that work ethic values everywhere are high with people who have interesting, varied jobs which enjoy a fair amount of autonomy or self-regulation. This would suggest that investment in education and job design are appropriate policies for strengthening the work ethic.

*Frank Heller & S. Antonio Ruiz-Quintanilla*

## Work and leisure

Human action can be loosely differentiated into work (creation) and leisure (recreation) activities. 'Work' can be defined as economically purposeful activity requiring substantial human coordination of task and action, while 'leisure' and leisure activities are motivated by non-economic and non-exchange purposes such as relaxation and pleasure. Although the two categories have never been mutually exclusive, both work and leisure have traditionally taken identifiable forms, such as 'the job', 'holidays' and so on.

Today human work and leisure are being radically redefined. The key words are empowerment, self-reliance, autonomy and self-service, replacing the more traditional notions of division of labour, specialization, manual work and the physically remote workplace of the mass production, mass assembly and mass consumption era. Most human activities – work, labour, jobs, leisure, recreation and the overall ways and quality of life – have changed and are going to change even more by 2000.

*Milan Zeleny*

## Work systems

People combine their skills and knowledge in an effort to produce and distribute goods and services. It becomes necessary to combine the various inputs in the work process: labour and capital (including raw materials and energy) in the context of the available technologies, such as equipment and buildings, then produce an output of goods or services. Work organization, or work systems, are the manner in which these variables are arranged.

Work organization determines the way that employees undertake their specific tasks. This usually involves the formation of a hierarchy which shapes the relationship between members of an enterprise, an arrangement for the division of labour and a set of explicit or implied work rules. Through these arrangements, certain individuals may be subordinate to and controlled by others. Types of work system include craft production, bureaucratic work organization, Taylorism/Fordism, human relations systems, sociotechnical systems and lean management.

*David E. Simmons & Greg J. Bamber*

## Zaibatsu (Keiretsu)

The Japanese management system has developed in the twentieth century based on three pillars – state-led growth, industry-finance links, and industry structure. The last of these three pillars, industry structure, developed around large conglomerate forms of business organization, known as *zaibatsu*. Since 1945 they have become better known as *keiretsu*.

The *keiretsu* member companies act as mutual support groups, providing markets and financial support for one another. They have been of interest to Western practitioners as an alternative form of business organization to that prevalent in Anglo-Saxon capitalism. Recently, they have become central to a political debate on the nature of free trade and competition. There has also been speculation as to the future of these forms of business organization as the Japanese economy matures and internationalizes.

*Jonathan Morris*